A Facsimile Edition
of the
Dead Sea Scrolls

VOLUME I

A Facsimile Edition of the Dead Sea Scrolls

Prepared with
an Introduction
and Index
by
Robert H. Eisenman
and
James M. Robinson

VOLUME I

BIBLICAL ARCHAEOLOGY SOCIETY
Washington, DC
1991

Library of Congress Number 91-058627
ISBN 1-880317-01-X (Volume I)
ISBN 1-880317-00-1 (Set)
©1991
Biblical Archaeology Society
3000 Connecticut Avenue, NW
Washington, DC 20008

The Biblical Archaeology Society
is grateful to the
Irving I. Moskowitz Foundation
for its generous funding
of this publication.

Table of Contents

Introduction

THE DEAD SEA SCROLLS, DISCOVERED IN 1947 AND THE YEARS IMMEDIATELY THEREAFTER, comprise one of the most important manuscript discoveries in the field of biblical and early Jewish and Christian studies to have been made in our century. The comparable Chester Beatty Biblical Papyri and Bodmer Papyri were published promptly after their discovery, and even the Nag Hammadi Codices, after an initial period of delay due to scholarly self-interest and Near Eastern politics, have now become fully available, whereas much of the more fragmentary parts of the Dead Sea Scrolls have remained inaccessible. Hence arrangements that initially seemed reasonable need, a generation or so later, to be supplemented by some mechanism by means of which scholars who were beginning their careers when the discoveries were made (not to speak of scholars then not yet born) can gain full access to them before their careers have been completed. It is under this higher claim of the academic community and society at large that the present edition has been initiated.

A Facsimile Edition of the Dead Sea Scrolls makes use of a photographic archive of largely unpublished fragments collected in what is now the Rockefeller Museum in Jerusalem. Since the bulk of the photographs go back to the early years, they neither reflect the joins and placements, nor the deterioration and loss, which may have taken place subsequent to photography. The painstaking work involved in such preparation of the fragments as had taken place up to that time is often quite indiscernible, since the original state in which the fragments were discovered is not documented for comparison. Given the absence of any accompanying notes, identifications can only be fully appreciated once the texts are edited and it has been ascertained to what extent fragments have been placed side by side in the photographs because they actually belong together, and to what extent their position is more random. The work had not been completed at the time the photographs were made, and indeed has no doubt in many cases still not been completed, in that the critical edition itself has not been completed. Users of this *Facsimile Edition* should hence understand that the photographs do not represent the definitive work of those who have had access to them over the years but have not felt ready for various reasons themselves to publish them, nor do they in any way represent our own work.

This *Facsimile Edition* publishes the photographs as they are, since verification by the originals is not possible. New research seeking to effect further identifications and placements on the basis of the photographs alone would have been very difficult and would have delayed considerably the appearance of this edition. Attempts to join one fragment with another are best left to the work of the academic community as a whole, beginning here with the raw data on which such work can go forward.

Included in this *Facsimile Edition* are photographs of manuscript material from caves in the Khirbet Qumran region, especially Cave IV, as well as material discovered at other locations, including Wadi Murabba'at, Wadi Daliyeh and Naḥal Ḥever. These materials are all included in this photographic archive and are generally associated by the public with the Dead Sea Scrolls among the manuscript discoveries of the Judaean Desert.

An Index is appended to this Introduction, supplying for each of the plates the numeration on the photographs themselves. An unpublished and restricted "Catalog of the Dead Sea Scrolls" prepared in Israel a decade ago, listing many of these photographs by their numbers and even identifying some so listed, is out of date, inexact and incomplete, though it is circulating informally. In practice it is of limited usefulness, especially since the fragments themselves are often no longer located where they are shown on these photographs. Yet, given the paucity of available information, even such a tool should at least be mentioned. However, a new and improved Inventory has already begun to appear, though beginning with the already-published materials. There the contents of each photograph, listed by its number, are itemized, and publication information is provided. Once the fascicles containing the unpublished material become available, this Inventory can be correlated with the Index so as to identify, to the extent known from previous scholarship, the contents of each plate of this *Facsimile Edition*.

This edition is intended to bring into the public domain an archive that consists especially (but not exclusively) of unpublished materials. Duplicates of plates photographed more than once, and sometimes at different times with different contents or arrangements, have been included, though photographs of material other than manuscripts are omitted. Skipped numerals in the sequence of the photographs do not necessarily indicate lacunae in the archive. Because the Catalog itself bypasses many numbers, the existence of photographs corresponding to such numbers is from case to case an open question. On the other hand, a large quantity of numbered photographs whose numbers were skipped in the original Catalog are included here.

The availability of this *Facsimile Edition* should of course not be used as a still further reason for delay in making the originals in the Rockefeller Museum fully available under appropriate conservation procedures to the scholarly community. For critical editions prepared on the basis of this *Facsimile Edition* will at best be provisional publications (as indeed are all *editiones principes*). They will be subject to subsequent verification and the improvement of obscure readings on the basis of the originals, when the current situation with its restrictions is overcome.

Robert H. Eisenman, one of the principal voices calling for the immediate publication of a facsimile edition of unpublished Dead Sea Scrolls and the exponent of a theory of his own of Qumran origins, and James M. Robinson, known for leadership in the publication of *The Facsimile Edition of the Nag Hammadi Codices*, were engaged not only to help prepare this edition, but also to provide an Introduction and Index. We ourselves make no claim to credit for the preliminary scholarly work reflected by the photographs in the archive, such as the selection of which fragments should be on a given plate or how they would be arranged on the plate, nor for the actual photography itself. We were merely enlisted in and have cooperated with the effort to implement the right of the academic community to obtain access to this important material without further delay.

In view of our relations to California State University, Long Beach, and to the Institute for Antiquity and Christianity of Claremont Graduate School, and our proximity to a sister institution in Claremont, the Ancient Biblical Manuscript Center, it should be explicitly stated that though we are not privy to the source of these photographs, we are satisfied that they do not come from the University or the Institute, since they have no such photographs, nor from the Center, since the restrictions under which it does have such photographs have not permitted their use for this purpose.[1]

5 JUNE 1991

ROBERT H. EISENMAN
CHAIR, RELIGIOUS STUDIES DEPARTMENT
CALIFORNIA STATE UNIVERSITY, LONG BEACH
LONG BEACH, CALIFORNIA

JAMES M. ROBINSON
CHAIR, RELIGION FACULTY
CLAREMONT GRADUATE SCHOOL
CLAREMONT, CALIFORNIA

---

[1] There should now [8 October 1991] be added: . . . nor from the Huntington Library, which in the best tradition of academic freedom made its microfilms of the Dead Sea Scrolls available on 22 September 1991, after this edition had already gone to press.

Publisher's Foreword

It is with sadness, not with triumph, that we present these volumes to the public.

Anyone perusing these plates, however briefly, cannot help but be struck by the difficulty of making any sense of them. The best are mere fragments. Many are simply unintelligible scraps. What were they hiding? one may well ask.

Yet in the end, these tatters will tell us where we came from. Surely we must admire the dedicated people who have devoted their professional lives to arranging and deciphering these seemingly impenetrable pieces of our common past.

For the most part, the people who do this are not only dedicated but brilliant—experts in what they are doing, conscientious and sensitive to the nuances of their work. For this, all honor to them.

But for their pride and greed—their unbending determination to keep exclusive control of these treasures for themselves, their heirs and their students—they must bear the shame. Even in the face of worldwide condemnation, they refused to acknowledge the claims of the rest of the world. One is reminded of the words of Oliver Cromwell, "I beseech you, in the bowels of Christ, think it possible you may be mistaken."

On September 25, 1991, General Amir Drori, the director of the Israel Antiquities Authority, and Professor Emanuel Tov, the new editor in chief of the official scroll editing team, issued a grudging press release (Figure 1), obviously forced on them by waves of condemnation even they could not resist, in which they "agree[d] in principle to facilitate free access to photographs of the Scrolls." They announced that a meeting "of all concerned parties" would be held in December 1991 to consider how this might be done. The press release also expressed a reservation—Drori and Tov still want to assure "that the work of scholars who in recent years have taken upon themselves to publish texts should not be harmed by any new arrangements." In light of the fact that the Huntington Library in San Marino, California, had already announced its intention to make its microfilm available to all scholars, this last statement can only be understood as a final, vain grasp at control, a vestige of the 40-year possessive mentality that the official team editors have grown so comfortable with.

But the fact is that the Huntington's release of its negatives of the unpublished scrolls will "harm" no one. The team scholars are free—and encouraged—to work just as they have been. When they publish their work, it will doubtless be exemplary. If it is better than what a free market has theretofore produced, it will quickly replace the earlier inferior product. Without question, there will be inferior products that need replacing. But that is also true of the work of the official team editors: Some of their work has been exceedingly good; some of it has been mediocre; and some of it has been very bad. Even they would not deny this.

In his wrath and fury at the Huntington's decision to release the negatives, General Drori announced that making the texts available to anyone would put the possibility of a "definitive interpretation" at risk. This is pernicious doctrine. It is, in a word, unscholarly. Scholarship can thrive only in a free marketplace of ideas. A "definitive interpretation" is the antithesis of intellectual freedom.

In short, we see no "harm" to the scholars who are presently working on these texts. If anything, they have a 40-year advantage over any newcomer. Let them continue their work.

Moreover, making these texts available to all has created an enormous interest in Dead Sea Scroll scholarship. Indeed, we foresee a burgeoning of this scholarship, to the benefit of all.

And so, all hail to the Huntington! Only its power and prestige, accompanied by a massive media condemnation of the monopolists, was able to break the back of the cartel.

Even after the Huntington Library announced on September 22, 1991, that it would release its negatives, the cartel did not immediately surrender. Nevertheless, the action of the Huntington must be regarded as the turning point. Until then, the monopolists remained the bully, ready to take on all comers.

It is worthwhile to recount the cartel's earlier tooth-and-nail efforts to maintain the secrecy of the unpublished texts. These efforts were accompanied by a remarkable disdain for anyone who dared question the wisdom of the cartel.

This disdain is reflected in a letter I received from the Israel Antiquities Authority (then the Department of Antiquities) regarding a publication timetable. Under pressure, the Antiquities Authority had promised a timetable for the completion of work on the unpublished scrolls. As I had requested, a copy of the timetable was sent to me (Figure 2). However, it was an unsigned document and was labeled only "*Suggested* Timetable" (italics ours) (Figure 3). As editor of *Biblical Archaeology Review*, I had been complaining for years about the publication delays and the accompanying secrecy. When I received the "Suggested Timetable," I wrote to the Antiquities

Authority asking who suggested the timetable, who had agreed to it and what would happen if the staggered deadlines in the timetable were not met. The Antiquities Authority's answer, in effect, told BAR that it was none of our business, or—in the slightly more polite language of the letter from Mrs. Ayala Sussman of the Antiquities Authority—the "Suggested Timetable" was what "we wish to bring to the attention of the public" (Figure 4). In short, the Antiquities Authority declined to answer our questions.

A similar attitude is reflected in the remark by then-chief editor John Strugnell on ABC television after criticism by some of the world's leading scholars, such as Geza Vermes of Oxford and Morton Smith of Columbia. Said Strugnell: "It seems we've acquired a bunch of fleas who are in the business of annoying us."

Another kind of disdain is reflected in some of the arguments made by cartel members not only against releasing the texts, but even against speeding up the official editing team's work. For example, Magen Broshi, a member of Israel's scroll advisory committee and curator of the Shrine of the Book, stated on nationwide television, "There's no urgency; it's not like we were dealing with cancer."

Eugene Ulrich of Notre Dame, who became a member of the official editing team by inheritance and who is now one of the chief editors, went even further. According to an interview in the *Jerusalem Post*, Ulrich maintained that the pace of publication had been too fast, not too slow: "The editing of the scrolls has in fact suffered not from foot-dragging but from undue haste." We should not succumb, he said, to the demands of our "fast-food society" looking for speedy gratification.

Ulrich then added, even "average university professors. . . are barely able to judge competently [our work]." He did not deny the hauteur reflected in this remark. "I'm sorry if this sounds arrogant, but it's true," he said.

That only the official team editors (and their students) were competent to do this work became an oft-repeated theme. When asked why no scholars from Tel Aviv University were included on his team of editors, Strugnell replied, "We are looking for quality in Qumran studies, and you don't get it there."

In an interview in *Scientific American*, Strugnell asserted that Oxford don Geza Vermes was not "competent" to examine an unpublished scroll because Vermes had not done serious work. Vermes is the author of several highly acclaimed books on the Dead Sea Scrolls, including the widely used Penguin edition, *The Dead Sea Scrolls in English*, now in its third edition. The *Scientific American* interviewer was incredulous: "A full professor at Oxford, incompetent?" So were we all.

Broshi justified continued secrecy on the ground that if all scholars had access, "It would flood the market and swamp the area. . . with third- and fourth- and fifth-rate productions." So much for intellectual freedom and the marketplace of ideas.

Disdain was reflected in action as well as in speech. In early 1990, a major American philanthropic foundation expressed to me its willingness to make a $100,000 grant to publish a book of photographs of the unpublished texts—much like the book you are now holding—so that all scholars could study them. It even suggested that, once the book of photographs was published, it might be willing to fund additional research. On April 2, 1990, I transmitted this offer to the then-editors of the official team—chief scroll editor Strugnell, Harvard professor Frank M. Cross, J. T. Milik and Emile Puech of the Ecole Biblique in Jerusalem (Figure 5). Not a single one extended to me even the courtesy of a reply.

In the face of this rebuff, I persuaded the foundation to make the offer in writing to the government of Israel (Figure 6). By this time a colloquium of Qumran scholars from the United States, England, Israel, Germany, France, Australia, Poland, Russia and other countries meeting in Mogilany, Poland, had unanimously passed a resolution calling for the publication of just such a facsimile edition. The Israeli embassy in Washington passed the foundation's letter on to Jerusalem, where it eventually made its way to the Antiquities Authority for reply (Figure 7). The answer was no. A facsimile edition "would seriously infringe [the team editors'] rights, while taking advantage of their scholarship," the Antiquities Authority reply stated.

On November 7, 1989, a British journalist, Michael Baigent, interviewed Mrs. Ayala Sussman of the Israel Antiquities Authority with respect to a facsimile edition such as the present volumes. Here is a partial account of the interview from a book* Baigent and another journalist wrote:

"[Mrs. Sussman (the same Mrs. Sussman who had written me, in response to my questions, that the 'Suggested Timetable' was what 'we wish to bring to the attention of the public')] clearly. . . regarded [the interview] as an unwelcome intrusion on her already busy schedule. While being scrupulously polite, she was also therefore impatient, dismissive and vague, vouchsafing few details, endeavoring to get the conversation over with as soon as possible. . . What about BAR's suggestion, Baigent asked, and the resolution adopted by the convention at Mogilany two months before— of making facsimiles or photographs available to all interested scholars? Mrs. Sussman's gesture was that of a woman dropping an irrelevant letter into a wastepaper basket. 'No one discussed it seriously,' she said."

Eventually the cartel descended to what can only be described as bullying.

The effort to prevent disclosure of the important text known as MMT (*miqsat ma'aseh ha-torah*) is illustrative. The text was assigned to John Strugnell for publica-

---

* Michael Baigent and Richard Leigh, *The Dead Sea Scrolls Deception* (London: Jonathan Cape, 1991).

tion nearly 40 years ago. However, he did not even disclose its existence until 1984. Then, with a colleague, Strugnell proceeded to write a 500-page commentary on this 120-line text. The commentary is still not published and no one knows when it will be. But Strugnell won't release the 120-line text until the commentary is published. He has, however, given copies of his transcription to friends and colleagues. Many of them teach classes on it. Several have written important articles on it (as of this writing, over 30 articles about MMT have appeared; that is how we know of its importance). It will, we are told, revolutionize Qumran studies. But no one outside the charmed circle can see it.

In mid-1990 a Polish scholar named Zdzislaw J. Kapera received an anonymous copy of Strugnell's transcription of MMT (Figure 8). Kapera is editor of a journal called *The Qumran Chronicle*; he decided to print the transcription in his journal. BAR announced that scholars could obtain a copy of MMT by subscribing to *The Qumran Chronicle*. Kapera was swamped with orders. But before he could fulfill them, he was cornered by the cartel at a scholarly conference in Madrid; one outside scholar (Philip R. Davies of Sheffield University, England) has described what ensued in Madrid as a 20th-century version of the Spanish Inquisition. Antiquities director General Amir Drori then wrote Kapera a letter (Figure 9), pointedly sending a copy to the president of the Polish Academy of Sciences (Cracow Section). In the letter Drori accused Kapera of "a violation of all legal, moral and ethical conventions and an infringement on the rights and efforts of your colleagues. I am very dismayed. . . . We are awaiting your immediate reply prior to further action." Kapera promptly decided to discontinue distributing MMT and to destroy all copies. Outsiders must still await publication of the commentary if they want to see the text (unless they look at Figure 8). Kapera wrote his would-be subscribers that "unfortunately, after the Madrid congress I am no longer able to supply people with a copy. I am very sorry because of that." He described his publication of MMT as "a desperate act" for which he apologized.

Nor did BAR escape the bullies.

When I'm in Israel, I talk to archaeologists and often commission articles for BAR. I do that once or twice a year, most recently in April 1991. One of the people I called during my last trip was Yitzhak (Itzik) Magen. We were planning two articles in *Bible Review* (BAR's sister magazine) about the Samaritans.* Magen had directed the most recent excavations of the Samaritan's holy mountain, Mt. Gerizim. I thought it would be a good idea to publish an article about his excavations with the other two articles about the Samaritans. He said he would be delighted to write the article. He

---

* They appeared in the October 1991 issue: Alan D. Crown, "The Abisha Scroll—3,000 Years Old?" and Reinhard Pummer, "The Samaritans—A Jewish Offshoot or a Pagan Cult?"

was ready to sit down and do it. He had the material ready and sounded excited about it. There was only one problem: Itzik Magen works for the Antiquities Authority; his boss, Amir Drori, had told him not to write for BAR.

I immediately called Professor Benjamin Mazar, the doyen of Israeli archaeologists who is known to be Drori's chief sponsor within the archaeological community in Israel. "Impossible," Mazar said. "It's illogical. It makes no sense. Drori would never say that. There must be some misunderstanding."

That afternoon I saw Drori at an archaeological congress. He confirmed what Magen had told me. The "committee" had turned down Magen's request to write for BAR. I would later hear more about this "committee."

When I returned to the States, I wrote Mazar asking him if he could use his good offices to change Drori's mind (Figure 10). He tried but was unsuccessful, he reported to me by telephone; for Drori it seemed to be something "psychological." Mazar suggested that perhaps I could stop writing about the Dead Sea Scrolls for a while. I wrote to Jerusalem mayor Teddy Kollek to see if he could help. He replied that if Mazar couldn't change Drori's mind, he, Kollek, wouldn't be able (Figure 11); perhaps the best thing to do would be to let time pass. But I knew that letting time pass wouldn't help if I continued my criticism of the handling of the Dead Sea Scrolls.

On that same trip to Israel I had commissioned two other articles—and our managing editor Suzanne Singer had commissioned a third—by employees of the Antiquities Authority, which, as is our usual practice, we confirmed in writing (Figures 12 and 13). We soon received a letter from Ronny Reich, who was to be the author of one and the co-author of another (with Zvi Greenhut) and another letter from Ehud Galili (Figures 14 and 15). The letters were short and to the same effect. Antiquities Authority employees must now obtain permission from a "committee" to write articles about excavations undertaken by the Authority; "unfortunately," the committee had denied permission to write the articles for BAR. "I understand there is some trouble between you and Drori," Ronny told me by telephone. "Maybe this is the result." These were the only cases in which permission was denied. "We don't have full academic freedom," Ronny added sadly.

I knew, although the world did not, that we were planning to publish computer-reconstructed transcripts of still-secret texts that were being regenerated from a concordance by Hebrew Union College professor Ben Zion Wacholder and his doctoral student Martin G. Abegg. Wacholder is 67 years old, white-haired and nearly blind. He knew that at the rate the official team of editors was publishing the texts he would never see them in his lifetime. With the help of computer-buff Abegg and what Wacholder calls "Rabbi Computer," they did an end-run around the official editing team's obsessive secrecy. By the late 1950s the official team had made transcripts of the non-biblical fragments. They then retained four young scholars to make a concordance of these transcripts. The concordance, a kind of index of words arranged alphabetically, gave the document, column, line and adjacent words for each word in the transcripts. The existence of both the transcripts and the concordance remained secret, however. Then in 1988 the scroll team printed 30 copies of the concordance. From this Wacholder and Abegg reconstructed the transcripts. On September 4, 1991, the Biblical Archaeology Society published the first fascicle of these computer-reconstructed transcripts. The next day the *New York Times* and the *Washington Post* covered the publication of the transcripts in front-page stories.

Both papers also printed approving editorials (Figures 16 and 17). The *New York Times* editorial was particularly powerful:

"The team of scholars charged with publishing the Dead Sea Scrolls has sown bitterness the world over with the way it has managed the 2,000-year-old scrolls. . .

Clannish and slow, the team dribbled out its findings, rebuffing inquiries from scholars who feared they would finish their careers without seeing the most important biblical discovery of their lifetime. . . Amazingly however, two scholars at Hebrew Union College in Cincinnati have now broken the scroll cartel. . . The first volume of the reconstructed text has just been published by the Biblical Archaeology Society of Washington, D.C. . . . These developments also bring fresh grounds for skepticism about the scroll committee's motives. . . [and] suggests that the members of the team are more interested in their own control than in prompt dissemination of their findings. . . Some on the committee might be tempted to charge the Cincinnati scholars with piracy. On the contrary, Mr. Wacholder and Mr. Abegg are to be applauded for their work. . . The committee with its obsessive secrecy and cloak and dagger scholarship, long ago exhausted its credibility with scholars and laymen alike. The two Cincinnatians seem to know what the scroll committee forgot: that the scrolls and what they say about the common roots of Christianity and Rabbinic Judaism belong to civilization, not to a few sequestered professors."

The *Economist* of London [Sept 14, 1991] put the matter pungently: "The wall of academic secrecy has now been breached, and the hoarders flushed blinking into the light."

The *New York Times'* prediction that we would be accused of piracy was accurate. Former chief scroll editor Strugnell accused us of "stealing." I took occasion to answer in an op-ed piece in the *New York Times* (Figure 18). I argued that these men were given the scrolls to publish as fiduciaries, as trustees for all mankind. When they produced these transcripts they were working for us. "By keeping them secret for more than a generation they have breached this trust and violated their obligation. It is they who are the lawbreakers. It is they who are stealing from all of us, not we from them."

Neither the worldwide condemnation of the hoarders nor the applause for our publication of the transcripts affected the monopolists in the least. Emile Puech, a member of the team by inheritance, accused us of "a violation of international law" and threatened to sue. Jonas Greenfield, a member of Israel's scroll advisory committee, charged us with "intellectual thievery." Magen Broshi wrote me a letter quoting from the Talmud: "For what purpose does the starling follow the raven?" (Babylonian Talmud, *Bava Kamma* 92b). The discussion in the Talmud is about things that are unkosher (*treif*). The raven is clearly *treif*—and so is the starling in following it. The reference is as insulting to Wacholder as it is to me.

At the same time we were being vilified by the scroll insiders,we were planning to publish these volumes of photographs of the still-secret texts. All involved were fearful.

Then came the Huntington's announcement—a breath of fresh air. But this is getting a little ahead of the story.

Feeling the increasing pressure and afraid that there might be some leaks (which of course there were), the official scroll editors decided to make certain that the Huntington negatives did not become the source of any leaks. (I doubt that they suspected that the Huntington itself would actually release its photographs.) Ironically, the official team's effort to assure that the Huntington negatives were not the source of leaks led to Huntington's decision to release all of its negatives.

To assure the security of the Huntington negatives, Eugene Ulrich, on behalf of the team, wrote an oleaginous letter to the Huntington, extolling the library for caring for the scroll negatives all these years, profusely expressing the profound gratitude of all for what the Huntington had done—and of course asking the Huntington to now relieve itself of this burden by turning the pictures over to another depository, which was under a contractual obligation (from the Israel Antiquities Authority) not to release them(Figure 19). "It is important to us that no copies of them be retained hereafter in your care," the letter carefully admonished.

This letter produced exactly the opposite reaction from what was intended. Instead of transferring the negatives as requested, the Huntington decided to release them. Once we published the computer-reconstructed transcripts, the Huntington moved up its date of release.

When the Huntington made its announcement, we were delighted. In effect, the Huntington was going to run interference for us—and it was in a much better position to withstand the onslaught than we were. There was even the possibility that the cartel would realize from the outset that it could not push around an institution like the Huntington Library and would simply throw in the towel. If the cartel had any sense, it would know that even if it were successful in threatening the Huntington to the point that it changed its mind, the cartel would still bring down on its collective head the condemnation of the rest of the world. But this had never stopped the cartel before, and it did not stop it now.

The initial reaction to the Huntington's announcement was quick and furious. Antiquities Director Drori and chief scroll editor Emanuel Tov faxed the Huntington in their customary tone (Figure 20). They accused the Huntington of "a breach of agreement"; what the Huntington was doing was neither "legal" nor "moral"; by reversing itself, the Huntington would "save us the trouble of taking legal steps."

Simultaneously, the cartel began bombarding the Huntington with expletives. "This is not ethical, and they shouldn't do it," Drori told the press. Magen Broshi said that legal action was being considered. According to the *New York Times*, "Some of the controlling editors charged that photographs in the [Huntington] library's hands were stolen property." Drori told the press: "They are not permitted to publish them or show them to the public without permission." The Huntington was doing this, Drori charged, as "a mere publicity stunt."

The Huntington was not to be cowed, however. "When you free the scrolls, you free the scholars," said Dr. William A. Moffett, the director of the library. He replied promptly, politely, but firmly, to the fax from Drori and Tov accusing the library of not acting morally and threatening a lawsuit:

"You, I am confident, respect and understand the principle of intellectual freedom we are committed to uphold. . . . It is my sincere hope that the Authority will not permit itself to be maneuvered into taking steps that have as their aim the blocking of access to information in the public domain. Surely now is the time for statesmanship to prevail, and for the Authority to lay claim to the gratitude and approval of the world."

Unfortunately, the Antiquities Authority did not follow the path so clearly demarcated in Moffett's reply. As described by a Jewish Telegraphic Agency report, the Huntington's action "was bitterly attacked by the Israel Antiquities Authority in Jerusalem as tantamount to trafficking in stolen property and as a flagrant violation of a longstanding agreement."

But within days the Antiquities Authority did a grudging and humiliating *volte-face* under an avalanche of condemnation by the media, reflecting widespread public outrage. An editorial in the *Washington Post* called the Antiquities Authority "ridiculous" (Figure 21). Perhaps the most biting criticism came from the acid pen of columnist William Safire (Figure 22). He called the Antiquities Authority "insular jerks. . . long captive of the cartel." Safire's advice: "Prime Minister Shamir should shut them up."

The cartel began crumbling. It withdrew its threat of a lawsuit. Then the Antiquities Authority issued its carefully worded press release. It agreed "in principle to facilitate free access" ("facilitating" is quite different from simply giving free access to all). It also wanted to assure "that the work of scholars who in recent years have taken upon themselves to publish texts should not be harmed by any new arrangements"— words that reflected ominous backtracking. But we have been assured by the Huntington that it will not retract from its own principles.

Meanwhile, Drori took one last parting shot by suggesting that the source of the pressure to release the scrolls was anti-Semitic: "It seems," he said, "to have something to do with the fact that Israel and Jews are in control." The fact is that Geza Vermes of Oxford, Norman Golb of Chicago, Theodor Gaster of Columbia, Robert Eisenman of California State, Ben Zion Wacholder of Hebrew Union College and Hershel Shanks of *Biblical Archaeology Review*—all leaders in the fight to free the scrolls—are themselves Jewish. That is not to say that there were not also many Christian scholars who vociferously opposed the cartel. But it was definitely a multireligious effort. There was certainly no justification for Drori's impulsive reaction that anti-Semitism was involved.

Perhaps exaggerating the extent to which the cartel was giving up, an exultant Moffett proclaimed on behalf of the Huntington, "The Antiquities Authority has caved in. This is the big break." Whether or not this is an accurate description, it is undoubtedly true that the Huntington's initial announcement to release its microfilm and its subsequent commitment to it paved the way for the present publication of the photographs. Since the Huntington would now provide access to its microfilm, it seemed sensible to make available photographs of the unpublished texts in as convenient a format as possible. That is the true meaning of access and that is what we have done.

The 1,787 plates in these volumes purport to be the unpublished Dead Sea Scroll texts. We have printed these photographs just as they came into our hands. We printed all of them, even though in many cases what was to be seen seemed worthless.

Many of the photographs have been enhanced by infrared photography, so the texts in these cases are more readable than the original. In other cases, the original fragments have deteriorated after these pictures were taken, so that in this case too the photograph is better than the original. In other cases, we have photographs of documents that have been lost or stolen. (When the full story is out, we will learn more details of the abysmal management of this project by nearly all authorities involved; they were—and are—brilliant scholars, but terrible managers.)

On the other hand, later photographs—and photographs still to be taken—may well yield better results than are presented here. In such cases we hope they will be available soon.

And of course it must be recognized that we may not have photographs of all the unpublished texts.

What we have here is basically raw material—the source for scholarly work to proceed. We don't even have identifications of the documents, except by the so-called PAM number—that is, the number of the photograph in the secret catalogue of the Palestine Archaeological Museum, as the Rockefeller Museum in Jerusalem was known before 1967. When Stephen Reed's catalogue (produced for the Ancient Biblical Manuscript Center in cooperation with the Israel Antiquities Authority) is completed and made available, we should be able to correlate the PAM number with other information about the plates.

Of course it would be better if we could say more about these photographs, but we cannot. At this time, it seemed best to make available to the scholarly world what we have—and then to begin the laborious effort to make sense of it.

We invite all scholars to work on the plates in these volumes. Please let us know of your work. We will then circulate the information. (It will be of special interest to scholars that these unpublished photographs include not only texts from the caves in the Wadi Qumran, but also texts from nearby sites along the Dead Sea and north near the Jordan River.)

If any scholar undertakes to transcribe any of the texts or to translate them, please send us copies of your work. We hope to provide a secretariat to exchange this material with other scholars (giving due credit to all). For consistency, please use the symbols in the "Key to Symbols" in the fascicle of computer-reconstructed transcripts published earlier this year by the Biblical Archaeology Society (Ben Zion Wacholder and Martin G. Abegg, *A Preliminary Edition of the Unpublished Dead Sea Scrolls— The Hebrew and Aramaic Texts from Cave Four*).

Our address, incidentally, is Dead Sea Scroll Project, c/o Biblical Archaeology Society, 3000 Connecticut Ave., NW, Washington DC 20008.

HERSHEL SHANKS
PRESIDENT
BIBLICAL ARCHAEOLOGY SOCIETY

Figures

Figure 1

ISRAEL ANTIQUITIES AUTHORITY

HERE IS THE ISRAELI ANTIQUITIES AUTHORITY RELEASE   Israel
Antiquities Authority

Jerusalem,25/9/91

International Meeting on Access to the Dead Sea Scrolls Amir Drori,
Director of the Israel Antiquities Authority in conjunction with
Professor Emanuel Tov, Editor in Chief of the International Dead Sea
Scrolls Project plan to convene in December 1991 a meeting of all
concerned parties wih regard to the issue of free access to the
unpublished fragments of the Dead Sea Scrolls.

The Israel Antiquities Authority agrees in principle to facilitate
free access to photographs of the Scrolls and suggests at the planned
meeting to discuss issues relevant to the preservation and
publication. To this meeting will be invited the editors of the
international team who are engaged in the publication of the Dead Sea
Scrolls as well as representatives of the institutions which over the
years received negatives of the manuscripts for safekeeping. The
following institutions are involved: The Ancient Biblical Manuscript
Center, Claremont CA, and through it The Huntington Library in
Pasadena, CA; the Hebrew Union College, Cincinnati; The Oxford Qumran
Centre of the Oxford Centre for Post-graduate Hebrew Studies,
England. It is hoped that a frank and open discussion will bring
about a consensus on procedures to be followed to the benefit of all
those interested in these documents that pertain to the history of
the Jewish people and its cultural heritage in the Second Temple
Period and their relevance for early Christianity. The Scrolls
discovered in and around Qumran near the Dead Sea between 1947 _and
1956 are considered the cultural heritage of all mankind, and since
1967 they are preserved, maintained and administered by the Israel
Antiquities Authority. As in the past an international committee is
responsible for the official publication of the fragments of an
estimated 800 complete documents. This committee is presently
directed by Professor E. Tov of the Hebrew University, and its
activities are supervised by an academic committee, appointed two
years ago by the IAA. Over the years much criticism has been voiced
against the delay in the publication of the Dead Sea Scrolls, some
20% of which have still not yet been released. These unpublished
texts, at times very fragmentary, are often very difficult to read
and many of them contain hitherto unknown compositions, so that their
reconstruction is very difficult. In all fairness, the criticisms
pertaining to the delay in publication relate to the situation which
obtained until some three years ago after which time many fragments
have been released for publication and others reassigned with an
increase of the number of editors. While the initial group of editors
consisted of only 7 members, at present some 40 scholars are involved
in preparing editions of the fragments. Many of these scholars belong
to a younger generation of Quaran specialists and several of them are
Jews from Israel and other countries who until recently have been
excluded from work on the Scrolls. To date eight volumes of
fragments have been published by the Oxford University Press in the
series "Discoveries in the Judaean Desert" and two additional volumes
are presently with the press. Several other volumes have been
published elsewhere. A time-table has been devised for the
publication of all the remaining fragments to be published until
1997. A catalogue of all fragments is about to be completed. While
all parties involved are in favour of free access to the photographs
of the Dead Sea Scrolls, it is also felt that the work of scholars
who in recent years have taken upon themselves to publish texts
should not be harmed by any new arrangements. This concern receives
the utmost attention of the Israel Antiquities Authority and the
Editor in Chief in their discussion of the matter of access to the
negatives with those institutions which presently hold them for
preservation purposes. This and related questions will be discussed
in the December meeting for which invitations are being sent today.

Main Office: P.O.B 586, Jerusalem 91004, Tel. 02-392607, 02-292827, Fax 02-292828

Amir Drori
Director, Israel
Antiquities Authority

E. Tov
Emanuel Tov
Editor-in-Chief
The International
Dead Sea Scrolls
Project

Figure 6

THE RALPH M. PARSONS FOUNDATION
1055 Wilshire Blvd. · Suite 1701 · Los Angeles, California 90017 · (213) 482-3185

April 16, 1990

Consul General Moshe Aumann
Embassy of Israel
3514 International Drive, N.W.
Washington, D C. 20008

Dear Sir:

We were very pleased that through the good offices of Mr. Hershel Shanks we were able to visit with you at the Embassy of Israel concerning the publication issue surrounding the Dead Sea Scrolls research. The Parsons Foundation is a friend of scholarship. However, it studiously avoids controversy.

Hershel Shanks occupies what appears to us to be a position remarkably free of any interest other than scholarship in this matter. It is his opinion, expressed to us, that the scholars of the world have too long been denied access to the original Scroll material and that those who are privy to such material have taken an unconscionably long time to make it available in its totality to other scholars. It would appear that there are many reasons advanced why this is reasonable. The longer the delay (now forty years) the less well grounded those reasons appear to be.

The Ralph M. Parsons Foundation has timorously inquired of Mr. Shanks if there is any way we can be of assistance. He has suggested that under the control of the Israeli Government is a photographic stash which encompasses all of the Scroll pieces. It is his opinion that reproducing this photographic material in a finely published book would be a boon to the science surrounding these Scrolls. Mr. Shanks believes that the Israeli Government can cut the Gordian knot which may have dismayed other scholars up until now.

The Parsons Foundation suggested to me that a budget of $100,000 would be assigned for the actual job of making this publication.

Our questions probably are these:

Are there reasons of substance which should prompt The Ralph M. Parsons Foundation to withdraw from this inquiry and to attend to our other matters?

If you should encourage us to look further into this matter, is the Israeli Government a willing participant in cutting through the underbrush of "gentlemen's agreements" which supposedly have hampered this project?

Page two
April 16, 1990
Consul General Moshe Aumann

Mr. Shanks suggests to us that there are three complete sets of high-resolution photographs distributed at various places throughout the world which completely inventory all pieces of the Scrolls. He says one such set is under the control of Claremont University here in California. You expressed some surprise at that, but if you find it to be true, perhaps we could work with Claremont as we have excellent relations with them.

We reiterate, The Parsons Foundation has only the interests of scholarship at heart. We are pushing nothing. We are merely inquiring if there is a vacuum which we can render a service by helping to fill.

Respectfully,

Joseph G. Hurley

JGH:kmr

Figure 7

ISRAEL ANTIQUITIES AUTHORITY

September 5, 1990

Mr. J.G. Hurley
Ralph M. Parsons Foundation
1055 Wilshire Blvd.
Suite 1701
Los Angeles CA 90017

Dear Mr. Hurley,

Your letter to Mr. Aumann of our Embassy in Washington - regarding
the unpublished Dead Sea Scrolls - was recently referred to us.
We do hope we can be of help in explaining some of the points you
made.

We were pleased to hear of your interest in this project and your
offer to support it generously. However, several basic matters of
substance should be clarified.

As the Scroll material is really not <u>Scrolls</u>, but was largely
acquired in fragmentary condition, scholars devoted years in
arranging the bits and pieces in plates, each plate now presenting
a coherent entity.

We have taken significant steps towards the acceleration of the
work involved in the preparation of the edition of the Scrolls.
The appointment of the editor and chief was ratified, subject to a
timetable which limits the scholars engaged in this study to
complete their work by 1997. A significant number of scholars has
recently been assigned material subject to a tight schedule. A
project which is now being advanced is that of a complete,
detailed inventory of the Scrolls. We are of opinion that a rushed
publication, precluding the participation and intervention of the
scholars who meticulously pieced together these manuscripts, would
seriously infringe their rights, while taking advantage of their
scholarship.

Moreover, a publication lacking a minimal commentary would be a
venture which, although satisfying the appetites of many
justifiably curious scholars, would be misleading in many other
respects.

Main Office: P.O.B 586, Jerusalem 91004, Tel.

Department _____

We regard this as an unjust approach, both towards the scholars
involved as well as the scholarly world at large. We are
therefore striving at a fair compromise.

We hope that all the measures taken will indeed .   accelerate
the pace of scholars in preparing material for publication in
accordance with the timetable.

However, we have now resolved to examine a group of three hundred
fragments which seemed unidentifiable to the original team engaged
in the project. If we reach the conclusion that these fragments
can be dealt with and presented, would it interest you to take
part in this venture or in any other closely related Scroll
project.

Thank you again for your interest.

Sincerely,

Amir Drori
Director

cc: Mr. Aumann, Israeli Embassy, Washington DC
     Prof. Y. Greenfield
     Prof. S. Talmon
     M. Broshi
     A. Sussman
     Prof. J. Strugnell

Figure 8

1 A [ושמונה בן] שבת שלו אחר ת[ו]שבת האחד והשני יום שלישי]
2 [נוסף ושלמה השנה שלוש מאת וששים וארבעה]
3 יום
1 B אלה מקצת דברינו [כתורה אל שהם מקצת דברי]
2 [המעשים שא אנ]חנו חושבים וכול]ם על]
3 ומהרת [הר]   ועל תרומת דג]ן תגרים שה מ.ים]
4 ופגיעים בה את   דם ומטמאים ואן לאכול]
5 מדגן [הגוים ואין] לבוא למקדש]   ועל זבח]
6 שהם מבשלים [אותה] בכלי [נחושת ומ.ים בה את]
7 בשר זבחהם ומ.   ם בעזרה ומ.ים אותה
8 במרק זבחם ועל זבח הגוים [אנחנו אומרים שהם זובחים]
9 אל הן   שא ה[אה] [ו]שבת אליו [ואף על תודת זבח]
10 השלמים] שמניחים אותה מיום ליום אנ]חנו חושבים
11 שהמנ]וחה נאכלת] על החלבים והבשר ביום זובחם כי לבני]
12 הכוהנים ראוי להזהר בדבר הזה בשל שלוא יהיו בני אהרן]
13 מסא]ים את העם עוון ואף על מהרת פרת החטאת
14 השוחט אותה והשורף אותה והאוסף [א]א. אפרה והמזה את [מי
15 החטאת לכול אלה להערב]ות השמש להיות מהורים
16 בשל שא יהיה המהר מזה על הממה כי לבני
17 [אהרן] ראוא'[להיות מ]
18 [ועל עורות הבקר והצאן שהם מ.ים שדם מ.ים   [מן
19 [עורותי]הם כלים   [אין]
20 להביא]ם למקדש   [.]
21 [ה ואף על עורות ועצמות הבהמה הטמאה אין ל [ ]
22 שהמה עושים [מן עצמותמה] ומן עו[רותמ]ה עשים ידות כלים ואף עור נבלת]
23 [הבהמה] המהורה [הנושא אותה נבלתה ולוא יגש למהרת הקודש]
24 [ואף על הט[ ]ת שהמ]ה מ.ים [ ]

25 כי לבני [ ]
26 הכהנ]ים ראוא' ו]להשמר בכול הדברים האלה בשל שלוא יהיו
27 משיא]ים את העם עוון ועל שא כתוב [וא]יש כי ישחט במחנה ומן
28 [שוצטם] מחוץ למחנה שור [וכשב ועז כי מקום השחמה בצפן המחנה]
29 ואנחנו חושבים שהמקדש [משכן אהל מועד הא ורו]שלים]
30 מחנה היא וחת[ץ] למחנה [הא חוצה לירושלים] הא מחנה
31 עריהם חוץ מהמחנה [אל ת החטאת ומוציאים את דשא
32 [ה]מזבח ושורפים שם את החטאת כי ירושלים] היא המקום אשר
33 [בחר בו מ]כול שבטי ישראל

34 [ ]
35 אי]ם שוחטים במקד]ש [ ]
36 [ועל העברות אנחנו חושבים שען לזבוח א[ת] האם ואת הולד
37 ביום אחד [ ] ועל האוכל אנחנו חושבים שאיאכל את הולד
38 [שבמ]ע אמו לאחר שחמתו ואתם יודעים שהוא כן והדבר כתוב עברה
39 ועל העמוני והמואבי והממזר ופצוע הדכה וכרות השפכה שהם באים
40 [בקהל   [ונשים]ל[ו]וקחם עצם
41 [ואת ובאים למקדס   [ ]
42 במאות ואף חוש]בים אנחנו
43 [שאן] ואין לבוא עליהם
44 [ואין להת]ח]תם]ולעשותם
45 [עצם אחת ואין להביא]ם
46 [למקדש] ואתם יודעים שמקצת] העם
47 [וה.. מ.ים.] מתע]רבים
48 [כי לבני ישראל ראוי להזהר מכול ת]ועבת [הגבר
49 ולהיות יראים מהמקדש ואף על הסומ]ים
50 [שאינם רואים להזהר מכול תערובת] ותערובת
51 [א]שם אינם רואים
52 [ואף על החרשים שלוא שמעו חוק [ומ]שפמ] נמהרה ולא
53 [שמ]עו משפמ]י ישראל כי שלוא ראה ולא שמע לוא
54 [ידע לעשות והמה באים] [למהרת] המקדם
55 [ואף על המוצקת] אנחנו אומרים] שהם שאן בהם
56 [מהרה ואף המוצקות אינם מבדילות בין הטמא
57 [ל]טהור כי לחת המוצקת והמקבל מהמה כהם
58 לחה אחת ואין להביא למחני ה[קוד]ש [כל]בים כלבים שהם
59 אוכלים מקצת עצמות המקדש   והבשר עליהם כי ·

60 ירושלים היאה מחנה הקדש היא המקום
61 שבתר בו מכל שבטי ישראל כי ירושלים היא ראש
62 ומחנ]ות ישראל ואף [ועל מצטעת עצי המאכל הנטע
63 בארץ ישראל כראשית הוא[ ]לכוהנים ומעשר הבקר
64 [ה]צון לכוהנים הוא ואף על הצרועים אנ]חנו
65 אומרים שלוא יבואו עם מהרת הקוד]ש כי בדד
66 [יהיו מחוץ למחנות ואף כתוב שמעת שיגלח וכבס ו]ישב מחו]ץ
67 לאהולו שבעת ימ]ם והזרועים בהיות טמאתם עמהם
68 הצרועים באים עם מהרת הקודש לבית ואתם יודעים
69 [ונעלה ממנו להביאה]
70 [ה]טמא ועל העושה ביד רמה כתו]ב שהואה בוזה ומגדף
71 [ואף בהיות להמה טמאת נגע] אין להאכיל מהקוד]שים
72 עד בוא השמש ביום השמיני ועל [ממאת נפש]
73 האדם אנחנו אומרים שכול עצם שהיא חסרה]
74 ושלמה כמשפט המת או החלל הוא]
75 ועל הזונות הנעסה בתוך העם והמה בני [זרע תמים]
76 קדש משכתוב קודש ישראל ועל בהמתו המהורה]
77 כתוב שלוא לרבעה כלאים ועל לבושו כתוב שלוא]
78 יהיה שעטנז ושלוא לזרוע שדו וכרמו כלאים]
79 [ב]גלל שהמה קדושים ובני אהרן קדושי קדושתם]
80 [ואתם יודעים שמקצת הכהנים תהם מתערבים]
81 [והם] מתכבים ומטמאים] את זרע [הקודש ואף]
82 [את [זרעם עם הזונות כי לבני אהרן]

1 C [ ]
2 [ועותו]   [שלבו]
3 ומ' ישׂנ   [יהיה מרו]
4 ועל הנשים   [החמ]ס והמעל [ ]
5 כי באלה [בגלל] החמס והזנות אבדו מקצת]
6 מקמות [ואף כתוב בספר מושה שלוא תביא תועבה אל
   ביתכה כי]
7 התועבה שנואה הלאה [ואתם יודעים ש]פרשנו מרוב העם
   ונמגענו]
8 מהתערב בדברים האלה ומלבוא עמם לגב אלה ואתם יודעים
   שלוא]
9 י[מ]צא ביתו מעל ושקר ורעה כי על אלה א]נחנו נותנים
   את   ואף]
10 [כתבנו אליכה שתבן בספר מושה] ובדברי הנגביאים ובדויד
    ובדבר]
11 [וימ כול] דור ודור ובספר כתוב [ום על] שלוא [ ]
12 [שה ואף כתוב שתסור] מהדרך וקרת אותכה הרעה
    ובתוב]
13 [ך וקי]בנו ת [ ]
14 וכתוב והא בי
15 [יבוא עליך [כול הדברים] האלה באחרית הימם הברכה
16 [והקללא] והשיבות]ה אל ל]בבך ת]שבנתה אלי בכל לבבך
17 [וב]כול[נפשך באהרי]ת [העת] חייות]
18 כתוב בספר מושה ובדברי הנגביאים שיבואו עליך ברכות
    וכללה שלן]
19 [הברכות שבאו בכ]ימ[י] ור]ובעם בן נבט ואף כ]ל
20 [שבאו ב] מימי ירובעם בן נבט ועד גלו]ת ירושלם וצדקה
    מלך יהודה]
21 [שיב]יאם בו [ ] ואנחנו מכירים שבאו מקצת הברכות
    והקללות
22 שלכתוב בספר מו]שה וזה הוא אחרית הימם שישובו בישראל
23 לתמד [ ] ולוא ישובו אחור [הרשעים ירשיעו] ואם
24 חת [זכור] את מלכי ישראל והתבנן במצו]תמה שכל מי שהיה
25 שהיא ירא [את התורה היה מצול מצרותהם לבקש]ת תורה
27 [ונסלחו] עונות זכור [את] דוד שהיא איש חסדים [ואף
28 הוא נ[צל מצרות רבות ונסלוח לו ואף אנחנו כתבנו אליך
29 מקצת מעשי התורה שחשבנו למוב לך ולעמך שרעינו]
30 עמך ערמה ומדע תורה הבן בכל אלה ובקש מלפניו שתקן
31 את עצתך והרחק ממך מחשבת רעה ועצת בליעל
32 בשל שתשמח באחרית העת במצאך מקצת דברינו כן
33 ונחשבה לך לצדקה בעשותך הישר והמוב לפניו למוב לך
34 ולישראל

xxxi

Figure 9

ISRAEL ANTIQUITIES AUTHORITY

March 12, 1991

Dr. Z.J. Kapera
Ul. Borsucza 3/58,
30-408 Cracow, Poland

Dear Dr. Kapera,

We were astonished to see the pamphlet entitled "An Anonymously Received Pre-Publication of 4QMMT", which you printed. As you are well-aware, Prof. J. Strugnell of Harvard University and Prof. E. Qimron of Beersheva University have, for a number of years, been engaged in the decipherment and study of the manuscript known as Miqsat Ma'aseh Torah, one of our Judaean Desert Documents, assigned to them. Profs. Strugnell and Qimron have devoted much energy and erudition to this recently completed task and have produced a scholarly edition which is now being presented to the Oxford University Press for the DJD series.

We were therefore extremely distressed to learn that you, a representative of a scholarly institution, seemed to be threatening your learned colleagues with the distribution of an unauthorized pamphlet. Let me stress that this would clearly be a violation of all legal, moral and ethical conventions and an infringement on the rights and efforts of your colleagues. I am very dismayed that you did not apply to the Israel Antiquities Authority before distributing the pamphlet amongst your friends, as we have been informed.

Thus, we wish to approach your good judgement to cancel your plans to distribute this unacceptable pamphlet.

We are awaiting your immediate reply prior to further action.

Sincerely,

Amir Drori,
Director

cc: President, Polish Academy of Sciences, Cracow Section
     Members of Scrolls Advisory Committee of the Israel
     Archaeological Council of the State of Israel: Prof.
        S. Talmon, Prof. J. Greenfield, Mr. M. Broshi, Ms. A.
        Sussmann
     Editors: Prof. J. Strugnell, Prof. E. Qimron
        Dr. J. Milik, Prof. F.M. Cross, Prof. E. Tov
     Ms. H. Feldman, OUP
     President, Israel Academy of Sciences and Humanities

Figure 10

BIBLICAL ARCHAEOLOGY SOCIETY

Publisher of BIBLE REVIEW and BIBLICAL ARCHAEOLOGY REVIEW

HERSHEL SHANKS
Editor & Publisher

April 29, 1991

Prof. Benjamin Mazar
9 Abarbanel
Jerusalem, Israel

Dear Prof. Mazar:

As always, it was wonderful seeing you in Jerusalem.

Even before you told me about the great things the Antiquities Authority was doing, I had written to Amir Drori on December 28, 1990, suggesting he write an article for us on all the things that were happening at the Authority (copy enclosed). He replied on January 29, 1991 (copy enclosed) that the matter would best be handled in an interview.

Then you told me about the new computers at the Authority, the tripling of the budget, the excavation of Ein Hozerah, the plans for Modi'in, the new generation of archaeologists that was at work, the increase in employees, etc. I was looking forward to talking to Drori.

Then before I saw him, I talked to Itzik Magen about writing an article on his excavations at Mt. Gerizim. (We already have an article by Alan Crown on the Abisha scroll and another by Reinhard Pummer on Samaritan history.) As you know, Itzik has already published an article on his excavations in Qadmoniot, and we had been talking to him about a popular article for BAR. When I called Itzik on this trip, he said "I would be happy to do it." He said he had plans and pictures. He also had especially exciting inscriptions that included the names Pinchas and Yahweh. "I'm ready to sit down and do it," he told me, "but Amir Drori has told me not to write for BAR."

I was, of course, shocked to hear this. I immediately called you. As you will recall, your reaction was: "Impossible. It's illogical. It makes no sense. Drori would never say that. There must be some misunderstanding."

That afternoon I saw Drori at the archaeological

5208 38TH STREET N.W. WASHINGTON. DC 20015 (202) 966-9888

2

congress. It turned out there was no misunderstanding. Itzik had understood correctly. It is, as you said, illogical and it makes no sense, but that is what happened. Moreover, Drori certainly did not seem to be inclined to give me any information about what is happening at the Authority that I could write up concerning its accomplishments.

I cannot imagine that the Authority would want to deprive BAR's half-million readers of the results of the excavations at Mt. Gerizim. The only thing I can think of is that the Authority wishes to punish BAR for its stand on the Dead Sea Scrolls.

I wonder if there isn't a better way to resolve this. Could you possibly use your good offices with Amir Drori to permit Itzik to write the article for us and to insure that no retaliatory measures will be taken against us because of our stand on the Dead Sea Scrolls? Indeed, Drori could crown his achievements here as well, by supporting the prompt release of all the photos. This would hurt no one. Any publication of the texts would soon be superseded by the editio princeps whenever it comes out; in the meantime, other scholars would have something to work with.

Please let me know as quickly as possible whether you can reverse the decision prohibiting Itzik from writing for BAR.

With warm good wishes and great respect.

Sincerely,

Hershel Shanks

Hs/cac

Enclosure: copy of HS letter of 12/28/90 to Amir Drori and Drori's reply of 1/29/91.

xxxiii

Figure 11

ראש העיריה
رئيس البلديــة
MAYOR OF JERUSALEM

June 3, 1991

Mr. Hershel Shanks, Editor & Publisher
Biblical Archaeology Society
5208 38th Street NW
Washington, D.C. 20015

Dear Hershel:

As you can well imagine, I was sorry to learn of the situation which
you describe in your letter to me and in the copy of your letter to
Professor Mazar. I am only afraid that there is no way for me to be
helpful in this connection, particularly if Professor Mazar was
unsuccessful.

Perhaps the best advice is to let time pass since it does have a way
of healing all wounds.

I trust this finds you well and send you all good wishes.

Yours,

Teddy Kollek

TK/sn

Figure 12

BIBLICAL ARCHAEOLOGY SOCIETY

Publisher of BIBLE REVIEW *and*
BIBLICAL ARCHAEOLOGY REVIEW

HERSHEL SHANKS
Editor & Publisher

April 26, 1991

Ronnie Reich
Shimoni 54
Jerusalem 29630, Israel

Dear Ronnie:

It was good talking with you in Jerusalem. This
will confirm that by July 1, 1991 you will send us
manuscripts for two articles:

1. The first you will write with Zvi Greenhut. He
   will write the part about the tomb with full
   background and finds and you will write the part
   about the Caiphus inscription.

2. The second you will write as the sole author. It
   will be on the Mamillah tombs.

Best regards.

Sincerely,

Hershel Shanks

HS/cac

cc: Zvi Greenhut.

5208 38TH STREET N.W., WASHINGTON, DC 20015 (202) 966-9888

Figure 13

March 18, 1991

Ehud Galili
Abber Street 4
Haifa
ISRAEL

Dear Ehud Galili:

As we discussed on the telephone, you will write a short article ontthe "rock of ants" that emerged from the Kinneret near Migdol.

Describe what happened this year. Tell the background of what we know about Migdol. Discribe the grooved surface, the basalt columns. Explain why you think they stood on the rock. If they did, what is the significance of that fact? How is the possible structure dated?

Assuming that the very low water level is rare, why would the ancient residents have built a structure on a low rock in the lake. And if they did, why would it be a migdol if the rock was largely submerged?

When you send your writeup include pictures--preferable slidesj-with detailed descriptions of them. Also include a photo of yourself that shows your face close up witnout dark shadows and a c.v.

Sincerely,

Suzanne F. Singer
Managing Editor

SFS/crwm

Figure 14

ISRAEL ANTIQUITIES AUTHORITY

June 21, 1991

Hershel Shanks
BIBLICAL ARCHAEOLOGY SOCIETY
5208 38th Street NW
Washington DC 20015

Dear Hershel,

In response to your letter dated April 26 requesting that I write
articles for BAR, it is required that permission be granted by the
IAA publication committee for articles on excavations conducted on
behalf of the IAA. Unfortunately, my request was not approved and
I will not be able to submit my articles.

Sincerely,

Ronny Reich

Figure 15

To
Suzanne F.Singer
Managing Editor
Biblical Archaeology Society
3000 Connecticut Ave,
Washington, D.C 20008

Ehud galili
Israel Antiquity -
Authority
Jerusalem 91004
P.O.Box 586

7.7.91

Dear Editor,

Attached ↓

Thank you for your letter from March 18, 1991.
As you know, every publication written by staff —
members of the Israel Antiquity Authority
requires permission from the publication's committee
of the authority.

    Unfortunately I didn't get permission for the
publication we discussed about the rock of
ants - Ancient Magdala, Sea of Galilee, Therefore
I will not be able for the time-being to
submit the manuscript,

                Sincerely yours
                Ehud galili
                Head of Marine Branch,

Copies: Publication- Committee , Israel
        Antiquities- Authority

Figure 16

The New York Times

NEW YORK, SATURDAY, SEPTEMBER 7, 1991

Breaking the Scroll Cartel

The team of scholars charged with publishing the Dead Sea Scrolls has sown bitterness the world over with the way it has managed the 2,000-year-old scrolls, which it took control of in the early 1950's, not long after the first of them were discovered in caves along the Dead Sea's western shore.

Clannish and slow, the team dribbled out its findings, rebuffing inquiries from scholars who feared they would finish their careers without seeing the most important biblical discovery of their lifetime — and what it might reveal about the origins of Christianity and Rabbinic Judaism.

Amazingly, however, two scholars at Hebrew Union College in Cincinnati have now broken the scroll cartel. The two, Ben-Zion Wacholder, a professor of Talmudic studies, and his research associate Martin Abegg, created a computer program that reconstructs what the scrolls say from a concordance — a dictionary-like listing that includes all the words appearing in the scrolls, along with details about where the word appears and the context in which it is used.

The first volume of the reconstructed text has just been published by the Biblical Archeology Society of Washington D.C. More will be forthcoming as the researchers press on with their work.

These developments also bring fresh grounds for skepticism about the scroll committee's motives. The concordance came to light in 1988, but was actually compiled almost 30 years earlier. This delay helps explain why nearly half the scrolls still languish unpublished in a Jerusalem museum. It also suggests that the members of the team are more interested in their own control than in prompt dissemination of their findings.

Some on the committee might be tempted to charge the Cincinnati scholars with piracy. On the contrary, Mr. Wacholder and Mr. Abegg are to be applauded for their work — and for sifting through layer upon layer of obfuscation. The committee, with its obsessive secrecy and cloak and dagger scholarship, long ago exhausted its credibility with scholars and laymen alike.

The two Cincinnatians seem to know what the scroll committee forgot: that the scrolls and what they say about the common roots of Christianity and Rabbinic Judaism belong to civilization, not to a few sequestered professors.

Figure 17

The Washington Post

SATURDAY, SEPTEMBER 7, 1991

The Dead Sea Printouts

FOR SOME years now, Biblical scholars have been arguing among themselves over the pace at which the Dead Sea Scrolls were being assembled and published. The scrolls, a lode of precious documents dating back some 2,000 years, were found in the late 1940s and early 1950s in caves along the Dead Sea. A stunningly valuable source of information on the development of both Judaism and Christianity, they were turned over to a small group of scholars, and many of the relatively intact documents were then published in fairly good time.

But much of the remaining material consisted of mere bits and pieces—thousands of fragments that had to be pieced together. The work on them went much more slowly. Some of the authorized scholars aged and died, passing on to associates their parts of the scrolls—pictures of the parts actually, for that is mostly what the scholars are working with. For 20 years, from 1967 to 1987, little was published. Others in the field waited and chafed at the proprietary treatment of the material.

More recently the authorized scholars have moved to speed things up, often "sub-assigning" material to their graduate students. But as Hershel Shanks, editor of Biblical Archeology Review, noted in an article in The Post last year, this procedure has also "raised a number of scholarly hackles. If you're a graduate student at Harvard, you can publish a Dead Sea Scroll for your dissertation. But not if you go to Yale or Princeton or Columbia." And the whole thing was still taking too long, he argued, one reason being that the scholars who had access to the scrolls often printed lengthy interpre-

tations along with their excerpts. He cited a case in which 121 lines of the text were accompanied by "a commentary of nearly 500 pages."

The authorized scholars have argued that exclusivity is needed to prevent the materials' being misinterpreted or inaccurately presented. Mr. Shanks and others on his side of the issue believe the scrolls will be best understood if they are treated like any other such source material—that is, made as freely available as possible to all who wish to study, interpret and debate them.

Now, advocates of this point of view have taken things a step farther, and possibly made the debate pretty much academic (as if it weren't already). Using a concordance to the scrolls and a desktop computer, two Biblical scholars this week brought forth their own version of some of the unpublished scrolls and promised to produce more. The computer was programmed to follow clues in the concordance—which is an alphabetical listing of all the important words in the scrolls and a bit of their context—to arrange the material in a coherent whole.

Judging their effort by the material that is known, they believe they've been remarkably successful, and they intend to do more. Some of the authorized scholars are irked; they doubt the accuracy of the effort and question its propriety. Some even talk of lawsuits. They'd do much better to accept the fact that things are inevitably going to move a lot faster now with regard to the scrolls, and to proceed in a spirit of cooperation and, where they think it's helpful or needed, correction.

xl

Figure 18

Scholars, Scrolls, Secrets and 'Crimes'

By Hershel Shanks

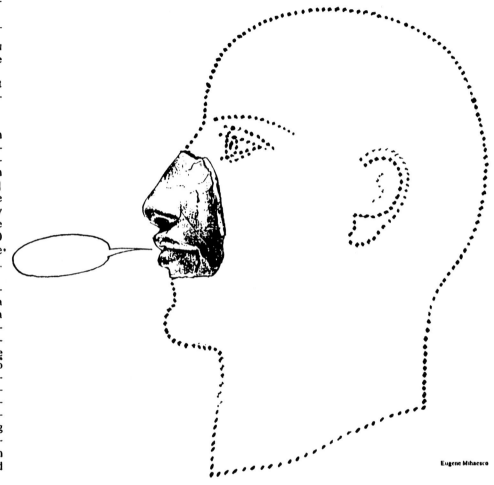

Eugene Mihaesco

WASHINGTON

"What else would you call it but stealing?" asked John Strugnell, the former editor in chief of the Dead Sea Scroll publication team who was fired for describing Judaism as "a horrible religion ... a Christian heresy ... [that] should have disappeared." What he claims was stolen (by me and my associates) were transcripts of the Dead Sea Scrolls made more than 30 years ago by his team of editors. We are stealing them, according to Mr. Strugnell, by publishing them.

The first step in researching ancient documents like the Dead Sea Scrolls is to make a transcript — a copy of the letters (in this case, Hebrew letters) that appear on the documents. This is necessary because many letters are unclear, hard to read, partially cut off, erased or written over. Once the letters are transcribed, they can be read easily — although not necessarily easily translated or understood. In the ensuing translation and interpretation, missing parts are reconstructed, errors in the transcripts are corrected and sometimes changes are made.

By the late 1950's, the Dead Sea Scroll editorial team had transcribed all the texts. But it kept secret not only the transcripts, but the very fact that they existed. After nearly 40 years, it has released only about 20 percent of the texts it was assigned to publish.

In the late 1950's the editorial team hired four young scholars to make a secret concordance of these transcripts. A concordance is an alphabetical list of each word in the texts with a notation as to where each word appears and the words adjacent to it. In 1986, having heard rumors of a Dead Sea Scroll concordance, I asked the director of the Israeli Antiquities Department about it. He denied any knowledge.

In 1988 a very small edition of the concordance was printed. From this concordance, with the help of a computer, Prof. Ben-Zion Wacholder of Hebrew Union College in Cincinnati, and a graduate student, Martin G. Abegg, reconstructed the transcripts.

Hershel Shanks is editor of Biblical Archaeology Review and president of the Biblical Archaeology Society.

The Biblical Archaeology Society is now publishing this reconstruction; it is what we are accused of stealing.

But we are taking only what is rightfully ours. The men who were entrusted with these documents were not given title to them, although they act as if they own them. In fact, several of them have died and bequeathed their "publication rights" to faithful colleagues. They have even given some of the treasure to their graduate students to research — a prestigious assignment, indeed — while denying senior scholars access.

I believe that under international law these editors are trustees, fiduciaries. The real beneficiaries of this trust are all people whose heritage is illuminated by these precious texts — not an elite group of scholars or even a single country, culture or religion. In making these transcripts they were furthering their fiduciary as-

'It is they who are stealing from all of us, not we from them.'

signment; they were working for us. By keeping them secret for more than a generation they have breached this trust and violated their obligation.

It is they who are the lawbreakers. It is they who are stealing from all of us, not we from them.

They have an easy means of exculpating themselves — by simply making available photographs of the unpublished texts to anyone who is willing to pay for a copy.

As it happens, the editors recently turned down $100,000 from a major American philanthropic foundation to publish a volume of the photographs.

The question remains: Why do the team editors insist on this secrecy?□

Figure 19

DEPARTMENT OF THEOLOGY
UNIVERSITY OF NOTRE DAME
NOTRE DAME • INDIANA • 46556
AREA CODE 219-239-7811

23 July 1991

Daniel H. Woodward, Librarian
The Huntington Library
1151 Oxford Road
San Morino, California 91108

Dear Mr. Woodward,

I am writing concerning the photographic collection of Dead Sea Scrolls and related materials which you hold as placed in your care through the interests and generosity of Elizabeth Hay Bechtel in 1981. I think you may know that the responsibilities of Professor John Strugnell of Harvard, formerly editor-in-chief of the International Team of Dead Sea Scrolls Editors, have since last fall passed to a committee composed of Professor Emanuel Tov of Hebrew University, le R.-P. Émile Puech of the École Biblique in Jerusalem, and myself. I am writing on behalf of the committee.

Our committee wishes to express gratitude to you and to the Huntington Library for the care with which we are confident you have stored and preserved, for the past decade, the films entrusted to you by the late Mrs. Bechtel. Your contribution in this regard to the field of Dead Sea Scrolls scholarship has been much appreciated by ourselves and our predecessors.

We now respectfully request, however, that the entire collection left in your care by Mrs. Bechtel be transferred and entrusted to the Ancient Biblical Manuscript Center for Preservation and Research in Claremont, California. The Manuscript Center in Claremont is the institution officially designated in 1980 by the International Team, and by the Israel Antiquities Authority (formerly the Department of Antiquities) of the State of Israel, as a safe repository for Dead Sea Scrolls films and photographic images. The Center in Claremont, under the presidency of Professor James Sanders, is the responsible institution with which we work in executing our own responsibilities regarding these films.

The current acting director, and continuing trustee, of the Manuscript Center is Professor Bruce Zuckerman, photographer of ancient manuscripts and inscriptions with whom we are currently working in numerous ways. The cataloguer of the Manuscript Center, Dr. Stephen Reed, is currently compiling a catalogue and index to all the Dead Sea Scrolls and is in need of various items in the collection you currently hold in order to complete his work.

We would greatly appreciate your working with Professors Sanders and Zuckerman, and with Dr. Reed, in effecting safe transfer of all that you hold in this regard to the Manuscript Center in Claremont. It is important to us that no copies of them be retained hereafter in your care but that the Manuscript Center in Claremont henceforth take responsibility for all of the DSS films currently in California.

Thank you again for the care until now you have given the treasures in your trust. We shall always be grateful. Would you please let me know if this request is agreeable? If you agree in principle, you may work out the practical details with Professor Sanders. Many thanks for your consideration.

Sincerely yours,

Eugene Ulrich
Chief Editor, Biblical Scrolls from Qumran Cave 4

cc Professor J. A. Sanders
    Professor E. Tov
    Professor E. Puech

Figure 20

ISRAEL ANTIQUITIES AUTHORITY

September 22, 1991

William A. Moffett
Director
The Huntington
1151 Oxford Road
San Marino, CA 91108
Fax: 818-405-0225

Dear Mr. Moffett:

From the news releases we heard that the Huntington Library intends to release access to the Dead Sea Scrolls negatives which were deposited by Mrs. Bechtel in your library for retention and safekeeping some ten years ago.

If this information is correct, we consider these actions a breach of agreement between us and the party which was given permission to prepare the negatives. It is your legal and moral obligation to comply with the stipulations of the agreement which clearly forbids such actions. We expect you to honor the terms of the agreement and save us the trouble of taking legal steps.

We expect your immediate reply. Our fax number is: 972-2-292-628 and the telephone number of Prof. E. Tov is: 972-2-815-714 (H), and 972-2-883-514 (O).

Amir Drori
Director
Israel Antiquities Authority

Prof. E. Tov
Editor in Chief
Qumran Project for the
Publication of the DSS

Figure 21

The Washington Post

The Dead Sea Photographs

"WHEN YOU free the scrolls, you free the scholars." And with that the director of a private library in California opened to the public a collection of photographs of the tightly guarded Dead Sea Scrolls. The Huntington Library in San Marino will now honor reasonable requests of historians and others who wish to view one of the few copies of the 800 or so Hebrew and Aramaic manuscripts that are an ancient sourcebook on Judaism and early Christianity.

More than 40 years have passed since the first decaying scraps of the precious texts were discovered in caves near the Dead Sea. Since then most of the coveted material has been in the custody of a handful of graying Western scholars or their appointed associates and research assistants. They have managed over the decades to complete about a quarter of their assignment—that is, to publish the scrolls in their possession. Meanwhile, others with an interest—scholarly and otherwise—have become increasingly impatient to learn the mysteries of the other fragments. Why was a small academic coterie taking so long to release the contents of some of the most important archeological documents ever found, as painstaking and arduous as the task certainly is? People began to question the repeated rationale for keeping the scrolls under close wraps—to minimize the risk of inferior editions and flaky interpretation.

The academic iron curtain, for that is what it was, began to fall earlier this month when the Biblical Archaeology Review published a version of some of the scrolls based on a computer analysis of the words said to be found in them. Now Huntington Library director William Moffett has liberated a set of photographic negatives made of the original scrolls. More quietly, other scholars have also agreed to share their copies.

The cries are now coming from the weakened professors and others who imagine their precious goods subject to intellectual besmirchment and distributed to the masses. So far, however, no raucous lines have formed outside the Huntington Library, though there have been inquiries. There have also been threats of lawsuits and impassioned protests—the most ridiculous coming from the Israeli Antiquities Authority, which supervises the work of the few who've had access to the scrolls in Jerusalem. If these ancient artifacts found by shepherds in a Biblical land are ever entangled in arguments over "intellectual property" and copyright law, it will be just another strange and disappointing chapter in the modern history of the scrolls. We hope that fresh scholars get to the Dead Sea copies before the lawyers and that the interpretations and publications issue forth before the depositions and the briefs.

xliv

Figure 22

The New York Times

SEPTEMBER 26, 1991   A27

Essay

WILLIAM SAFIRE

Breaking the Cartel

. PASADENA, Calif.

A little band of willful academics, representing no interest but their own arrogant selfishness, have for 40 years kept clutched to their scholastic bosoms a substantial portion of the Dead Sea Scrolls.

These treasures are the ancient documents found in a West Bank cave that cast light on the religious politics roiling the world between 200 B.C. and a century after the birth of Christ.

The Kingdom of Jordan first made a deal with a tight coterie of scholars to decipher and publish the precious texts; after the 1967 war, the Government of Israel went along with this cozy arrangement, which meant that the non-biblical portions of the scrolls would be dribbled out by the favored academics over a period of decades.

Now the cartel has been broken. The Huntington Library in San Mari-

---

The scroll in the hole.

---

no, Calif., refusing to be pushed around by scholastic monopolists at Harvard, Notre Dame and Hebrew University, has this week made available to all other libraries microfilm of the complete set of scrolls — all 3,000 negatives. Freedom of information now extends clear back to the era that made possible the emergence of Jesus.

Of course, the Judases to academic freedom who are now subject to scholarly competition are furious. Harvard's · John Strugnell, cartel boss until he was kicked out last year for what was reported to be anti-Semitism or incompetence, sees an assault on "the intellectual investment of the individual scholars who are preparing these editions." Their private preserve has been invaded by Philistines: they claim that this may lead to hurried publication and shoddy, non-establishment research.

Here in the Huntington Library near Pasadena, William Moffett, the library's director, punctures that pompous balloon: "I've never known a real scholar to be intimidated by

the possibility of somebody else's shoddy research." He showed me the negatives, some of which may cast light on the psychology of Masada, where Jews committed suicide rather than surrender. "We could not go along with protecting the position of anachronistic privilege."

Here's what happened. A farsighted and irascible philanthropist named Betty Bechtel built an ancient manuscripts center in Claremont, Calif., and persuaded Israeli officials to deposit a microfilm of the scrolls there in case of new war in the Middle East. But she was a pest; the trustees she appointed ultimately kicked her off the board, keeping the microfilm in their center's vault.

They did not reckon on the fury of a philanthropist scorned. She kept her own separate copy on two small spools, which museum officials refer to informally as her "scroll in the hole." In 1980, she slipped them to the Huntington, with a hundred G's to build an air-conditioned vault. When that indomitable old lady died in 1987, title to her private set passed to the library.

The cartel got wind of the extra set's existence and imperiously sought its return to monopoly control. Mr. Moffett, an Oberlin history professor who became library director last year, bridled at this intimidation and his board backed him up: as a result, the negatives are available to all scholars through inter-library services. We shall know the truth and the truth shall make us free.

The original scrolls found in the West Bank, first claimed by Jordan, are now owned by Israel; if Mr. Bush establishes a P.L.O. state, Yasir Arafat is sure to claim ownership. However, the intellectual property — the thinking and writing of the ascetic sect called the Essenes, infinitely more valuable than the crumbling scrolls — is the common heritage of civilization, even including independent scholars.

One minor irritation: some insular jerks in Jerusalem's antiquities bureaucracy, long the captive of the cartel, have been quoted making threats of legal action against the Huntington for setting the information free. I am privately assured, it will not happen, but Prime Minister Shamir should shut them up: he should publicly welcome the dissemination of the scrolls' contents, symbol of the winds of freedom that must one day rock the cradle of civilization. □

Index

Plate No.	PAM*No.	Plate No.	PAM No.	Plate No.	PAM No.	Plate No.	PAM No.	Plate No.	PAM No.
1	40.068	58	40.595	115	40.965	172	41.164	230	41.289
2A–B	40.074	59	40.596	116	40.966	173	41.165		
3	40.077	60	40.597	117	40.967	174	41.166	231	41.290
4A–B	40.132			118	40.968	175	41.167	232	41.291
5	40.171	61	40.598	119	40.969	176	41.168	233	41.292
6	40.217	62	40.599			177	41.170	234	41.293
7	40.218	63	40.600	120	40.970	178	41.171	235	41.294
8	40.219	64	40.601	121	40.971	179	41.172	236	41.295
9	40.220	65	40.602	122	40.972	180	41.173	237	41.296
10	40.221	66	40.604	123	40.973			238	41.297
		67	40.605	124	40.974	181	41.174	239	41.298
11	40.222	68	40.606	125	40.975	182	41.175	240	41.299
12	40.223	69	40.607	126	40.976	183	41.176		
13	40.239	70	40.609	127	40.977	184	41.177	241	41.300
14	40.240			128	40.978	185	41.178	242	41.301
15	40.282	71	40.610	129	40.979	186	41.179	243	41.302
16	40.284	72	40.611	130	40.980	187	41.181	244	41.303
17	40.289	73	40.612			188	41.182	245	41.306
18	40.290	74	40.613	131	40.981	189	41.183	246	41.310
19A	40.292	75	40.614	132	40.982	190	41.184	247	41.311
19B	40.338	76	40.615	133	40.983			248	41.312
		77	40.617	134	40.984	191	41.185	249	41.313
20	40.341	78	40.618	135	40.985	192	41.186	250	41.314
21	40.342	79	40.619	136	40.986	193	41.187		
22	40.559	80	40.620	137	40.987	194	41.188	251	41.317
23	40.560			138	40.988	195	41.189	252	41.321
24	40.561	81	40.621	139	40.989	196	41.190	253	41.324
25	40.562	82	40.622			197	41.191	254	41.346
26	40.563	83	40.624	140	40.990	198	41.192	255	41.347
27	40.564	84	40.625	141	40.991	199	41.193	256	41.348
28	40.565	85	40.626	142	40.993	200	41.194	257	41.349
29	40.566	86	40.627	143	40.994			258	41.350
30	40.567	87	40.628	144	40.995	201	41.195	259	41.351
		88	40.629	145	40.996	202	41.196	260	41.352
31	40.568	89	40.630	146	41.138	203	41.197		
32	40.569	90	40.631	147	41.139	204	41.198	261	41.353
33	40.570			148	41.140	205	41.199	262	41.363
34	40.571	91	40.632	149	41.141	206	41.200	263	41.366
35	40.572	92	40.633	150	41.142	207	41.201	264	41.367
36	40.573	93	40.634			208	41.202	265	41.368
37	40.574	94	40.635	151	41.143	209	41.203	266	41.371
38	40.575	95	40.636	152	41.144	210	41.204	267	41.372
39	40.576	96	40.637	153	41.145			268	41.373
40	40.577	97	40.638	154	41.146	211	41.205	269	41.374
		98	40.642	155	41.147	212	41.207	270	41.375
41	40.578	99	40.643	156	41.148	213	41.208		
42	40.579	100	40.644	157	41.149	214	41.209	271	41.386
43	40.580			158	41.150	215	41.210	272	41.387
44	40.581	101	40.645	159	41.151	216	41.211	273	41.388
45	40.582	102	40.646	160	41.152	217	41.213	274	41.389
46	40.583	103	40.647			218	41.276	275	41.390
47	40.584	104	40.648	161	41.153	219	41.277	276	41.391
48	40.585	105	40.649	162	41.154	220	41.278	277	41.400
49	40.586	106	40.659	163	41.155			278	41.401
50	40.587	107	40.660	164	41.156	221	41.279	279	41.402
		108	40.661	165	41.157	222	41.280	280	41.403
51	40.588	109	40.662	166	41.158	223	41.281		
52	40.589	110	40.663	167	41.159	224	41.282	281	41.404
53	40.590			168	41.160	225	41.283	282	41.405
54	40.591	111	40.666	169	41.161	226	41.284	283	41.407
55	40.592	112	40.962	170	41.162	227	41.286	284	41.408
56	40.593	113	40.963			228	41.287	285	41.409
57	40.594	114	40.964	171	41.163	229	41.288	286	41.411

*Palestine Archaeological Museum, now the Rockefeller Museum

Plate No.	PAM No.	Plate No.	PAM No.	Plate No.	PAM No.	Plate No.	PAM No.	Plate No.	PAM No.
287	41.412	343	41.519	401	41.700	459	41.821	516	41.931
288	41.422	344	41.520	402	41.701	460	41.822	517	41.932
289	41.423	345	41.563	403	41.702			518	41.933
290	41.425	346	41.564	404	41.703	461	41.823	519	41.938
		347	41.565	405	41.704	462	41.824	520	41.939
291	41.426	348	41.566	406	41.705	463	41.825		
292	41.427	349	41.586	407	41.706	464	41.826	521	41.940
293	41.435	350	41.587	408	41.707	465	41.827	522	41.941
294	41.436			409	41.708	466	41.833	523	41.942
295	41.437	351	41.588	410	41.709	467	41.843	524	41.944
296	41.438	352	41.589			468	41.844	525	41.945
297	41.439	353	41.591	411	41.710	469	41.845	526	41.946
298	41.440	354	41.593	412	41.712	470	41.849	527	41.947
299	41.441	355	41.594	413	41.713			528	41.948
300	41.442	356	41.595	414	41.714	471	41.850	529	41.949
		357	41.636	415	41.715	472	41.851	530	41.951
301	41.443	358	41.637	416	41.718	473	41.852		
302	41.444	359	41.638	417	41.720	474	41.853	531	41.952
303	41.450	360	41.639	418	41.742	475	41.854	532	41.954
304	41.451			419	41.743	476	41.855	533	41.955
305	41.452	361	41.640	420	41.744	477	41.856	534	41.956
306	41.453	362	41.641			478	41.857	535	41.964
307	41.454	363	41.642	421	41.759	479	41.858	536	41.965
308	41.455	364	41.643	422	41.760	480	41.859	537	41.966
309	41.456	365	41.644	423	41.761			538	41.967
310	41.457	366	41.645	424	41.762	481	41.860	539	41.972
		367	41.646	425	41.763	482	41.861	540	41.973
311	41.458	368	41.647	426	41.764	483	41.862		
312	41.459	369	41.648	427	41.765	484	41.863	541	41.974
313	41.460	370	41.649	428	41.766	485	41.864	542	41.975
314	41.461			429	41.767	486	41.865	543	41.976
315	41.462	371	41.650	430	41.768	487	41.866	544	41.978
316	41.463	372	41.656			488	41.867	545	41.979
317	41.464	373	41.657	431	41.769	489	41.868	546	41.980
318	41.465	374	41.658	432	41.770	490	41.869	547	41.981
319	41.466	375	41.659	433	41.771			548	41.983
320	41.467	376	41.660	434	41.772	491	41.886	549	41.984
		377	41.661	435	41.773	492	41.887	550	41.985
321	41.468	378	41.662	436	41.774	493	41.888		
322	41.477	379	41.663	437	41.775	494	41.889	551	41.986
323	41.478	380	41.664	438	41.776	495	41.890	552	41.987
324	41.479			439	41.777	496	41.891	553	41.988
325	41.481	381	41.665	440	41.778	497	41.892	554	41.989
326	41.482	382	41.666			498	41.893	555	41.990
327	41.483	383	41.675	441	41.779	499	41.894	556	41.991
328	41.499	384	41.676	442	41.780	500	41.895	557	41.992
329	41.502	385	41.677	443	41.781			558	41.993
330	41.503	386	41.678	444	41.782	501	41.903	559	41.995
		387	41.679	445	41.783	502	41.904	560	41.996
331	41.504	388	41.684	446	41.784	503	41.905		
332	41.505	389	41.686	447	41.785	504	41.906	561	41.997
333	41.506	390	41.687	448	41.786	505	41.907	562	41.998
334A	41.507			449	41.787	506	41.908	563	41.999
334B	41.508	391	41.690	450	41.788	507	41.909	564	42.000
335	41.509	392	41.690A			508	41.910	565	42.001
336	41.512	393	41.692	451	41.789	509	41.911	566	42.002
337	41.513	394	41.693	452	41.790	510	41.913	567	42.003
338	41.514	395	41.694	453	41.791			568	42.004
339	41.515	396	41.695	454	41.792	511	41.914	569	42.005
340	41.516	397	41.696	455	41.798	512	41.915	570	42.006
		398	41.697	456	41.799	513	41.916		
341	41.517	399	41.698	457	41.816	514	41.917	571	42.007
342	41.518	400	41.699	458	41.820	515	41.918	572	42.008

Plate No.	PAM No.	Plate No.	PAM No.	Plate No.	PAM No.	Plate No.	PAM No.	Plate No.	PAM No.
573	42.009	631	42.070	689	42.187	746	42.267	803	42.378
574	42.010	632	42.071	690	42.188	747	42.268	804	42.379
575	42.011	633	42.072			748	42.269	805	42.380
576	42.012	634	42.073	691	42.189	749	42.270	806	42.381
577	42.013	635	42.074	692	42.190	750	42.271	807	42.382
578	42.014	636	42.075	693	42.191			808	42.383
579	42.015	637	42.076	694	42.192	751	42.272	809	42.384
580	42.016	638	42.077	695	42.193	752	42.273	810	42.385
		639	42.078	696	42.194	753	42.274		
581	42.017	640	42.079	697	42.196	754	42.275	811	42.386
582	42.018			698	42.197	755	42.276	812	42.387
583	42.019	641	42.081	699	42.198	756	42.277	813	42.388
584	42.020	642	42.082	700	42.199	757	42.278	814	42.389
585	42.021	643	42.085			758	42.279	815	42.390
586	42.022	644	42.086	701	42.200	759	42.280	816	42.391
587	42.023	645	42.087	702	42.201	760	42.281	817	42.392
588	42.024	646	42.088	703	42.202			818	42.393
589	42.025	647	42.089	704	42.203	761	42.282	819	42.394
590	42.026	648	42.090	705	42.204	762	42.283	820	42.395
		649	42.100	706	42.205	763	42.284		
591	42.027	650	42.132	707	42.206	764	42.285	821	42.396
592	42.028			708	42.207	765	42.286	822	42.397
593	42.029	651	42.136	709	42.208	766	42.287	823	42.398
594	42.030	652	42.137	710	42.209	767	42.288	824	42.399
595	42.031	653	42.143			768	42.289	825	42.400
596	42.032	654	42.144	711	42.210	769	42.324	826	42.401
597	42.033	655	42.145	712	42.211	770	42.325	827	42.402
598	42.034	656	42.146	713	42.212			828	42.403
599	42.035	657	42.147	714	42.213	771	42.326	829	42.404
600	42.036	658	42.151	715	42.214	772	42.327	830	42.405
		659	42.152	716	42.215	773	42.328		
601	42.037	660	42.153	717	42.216	774	42.330	831	42.406
602	42.038			718	42.217	775	42.331	832	42.407
603	42.039	661	42.154	719	42.218	776	42.332	833	42.408
604	42.040	662	42.155	720	42.219	777	42.333	834	42.409
605	42.041	663	42.156			778	42.334	835	42.410
606	42.042	664	42.157	721	42.220	779	42.335	836	42.411
607	42.043	665	42.158	722	42.221	780	42.338A	837	42.412
608	42.044	666	42.159	723	42.222			838	42.413
609	42.045	667	42.160	724	42.223	781	42.356	839	42.414
610	42.046	668	42.161	725	42.224	782	42.357	840	42.415
		669	42.162	726	42.225	783	42.358		
611	42.047	670	42.163	727	42.226	784	42.359	841	42.416
612	42.048			728	42.232	785	42.360	842	42.417
613	42.049	671	42.164	729	42.233	786	42.361	843	42.418
614	42.050	672	42.165	730	42.239	787	42.362	844	42.419
615	42.051	673	42.166			788	42.363	845	42.420
616	42.052	674	42.167	731	42.240	789	42.364	846	42.421
617	42.053	675	42.168	732	42.241	790	42.365	847	42.422
618	42.055	676	42.169	733	42.242			848	42.423
619	42.056	677	42.170	734	42.243	791	42.366	849	42.424
620	42.057	678	42.171	735	42.244	792	42.367	850	42.425
		679	42.172	736	42.245	793	42.368		
621	42.058	680	42.173	737	42.246	794	42.369	851	42.426
622	42.059			738	42.247	795	42.370	852	42.427
623	42.060	681	42.174	739	42.260	796	42.371	853	42.428
624	42.061	682	42.175	740	42.261	797	42.372	854	42.429
625	42.062	683	42.176			798	42.373	855	42.430
626	42.064	684	42.177	741	42.262	799	42.374	856	42.431
627	42.066	685	42.182	742	42.263	800	42.375	857	42.435
628	42.067	686	42.184	743	42.264			858	42.436
629	42.068	687	42.185	744	42.265	801	42.376	859	42.438
630	42.069	688	42.186	745	42.266	802	42.377	860	42.439

PLATE 20

PLATE 19A

PLATE 19B

PLATE 21

PLATE 22

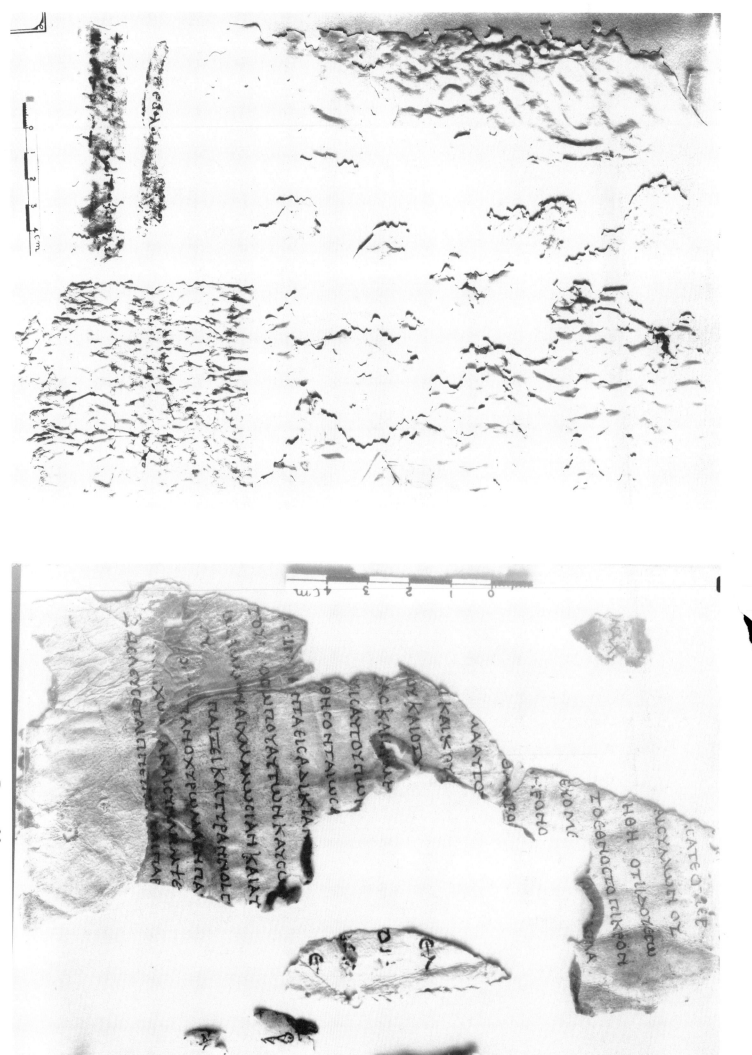

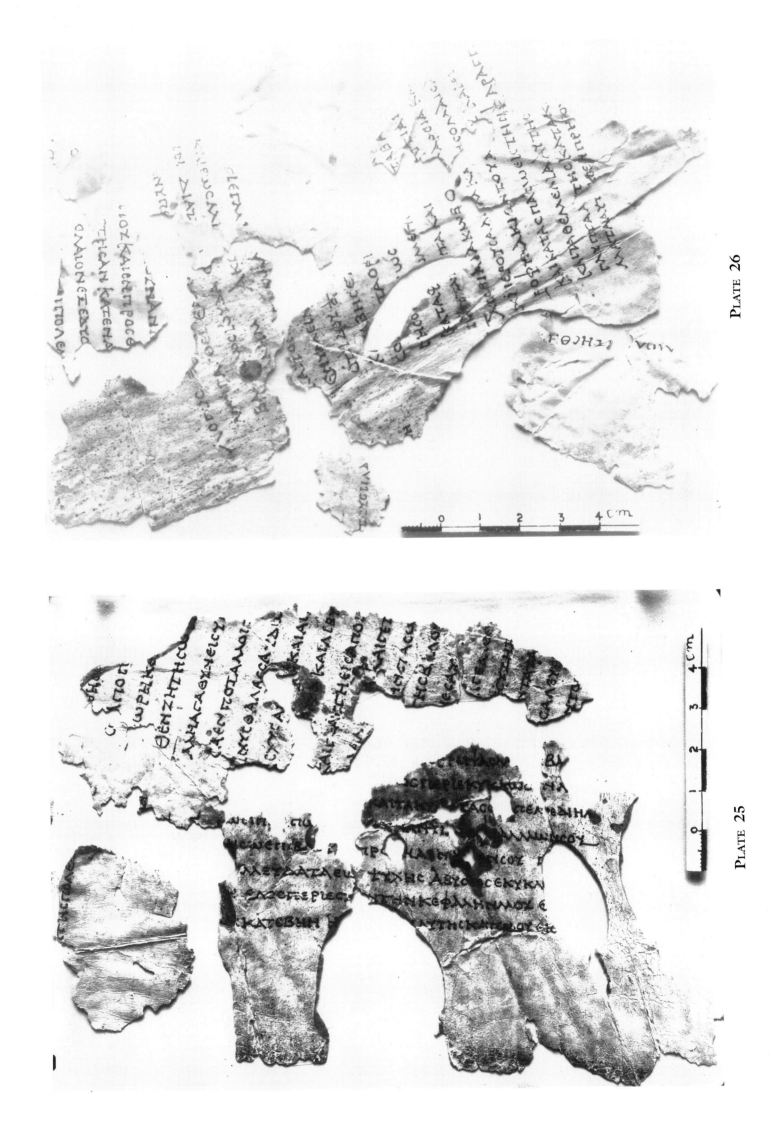

PLATE 26

PLATE 25

PLATE 23

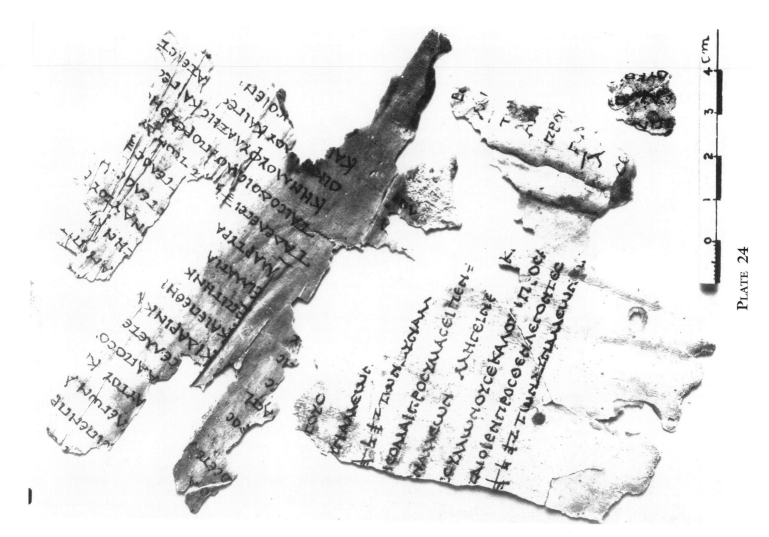

PLATE 24

PLATE 27

PLATE 28

PLATE 29

PLATE 30

PLATE 32

PLATE 31

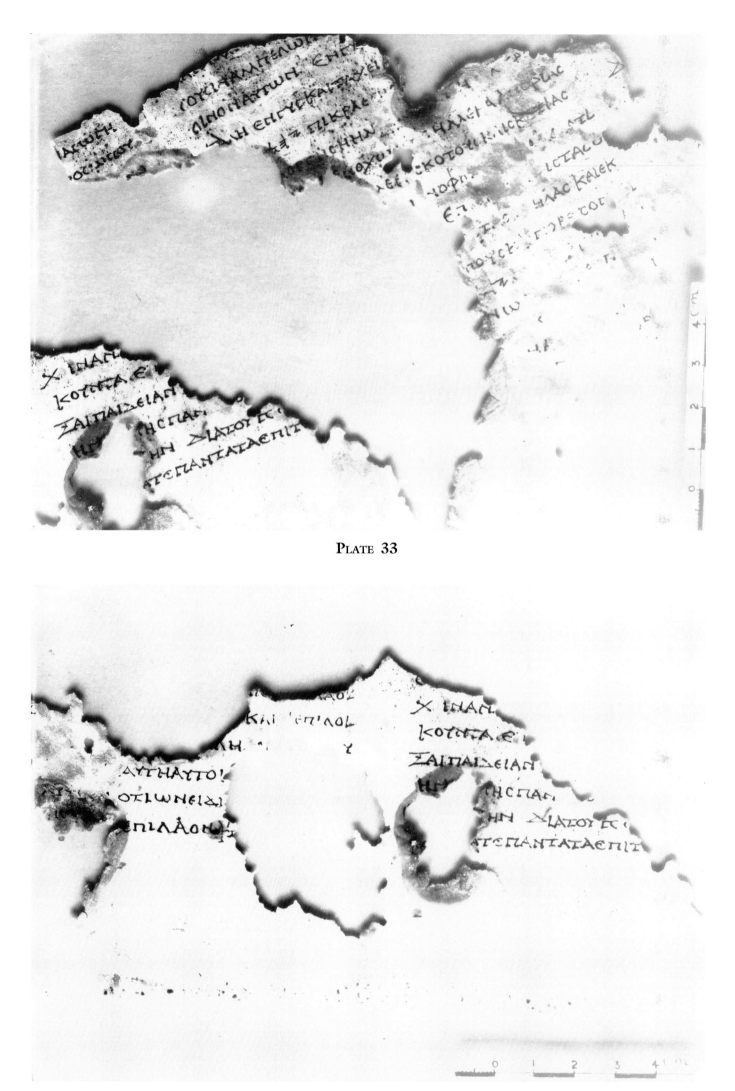

PLATE 33

PLATE 34

Plate 35

Plate 36

PLATE 38

PLATE 37

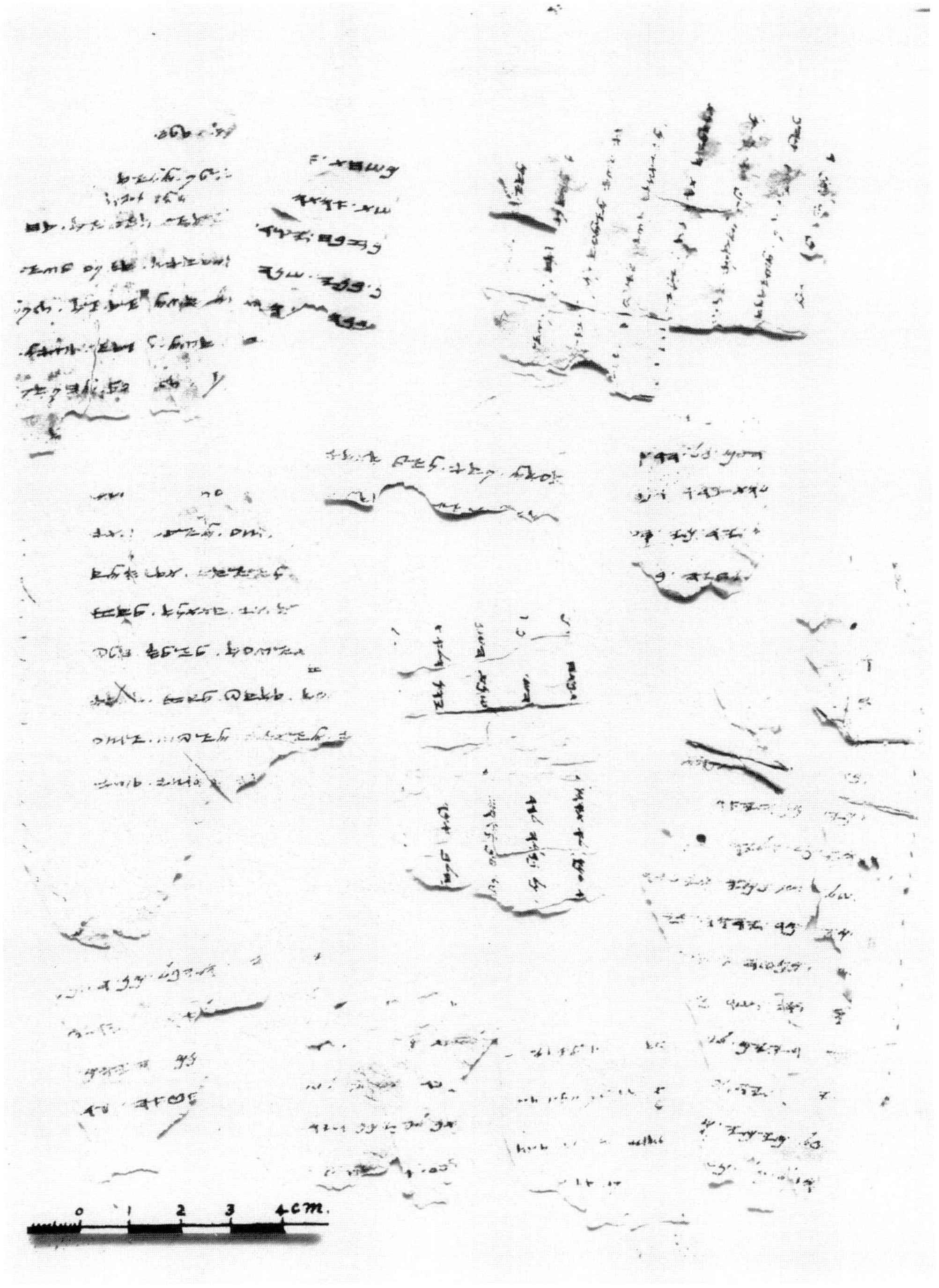

Plate 39

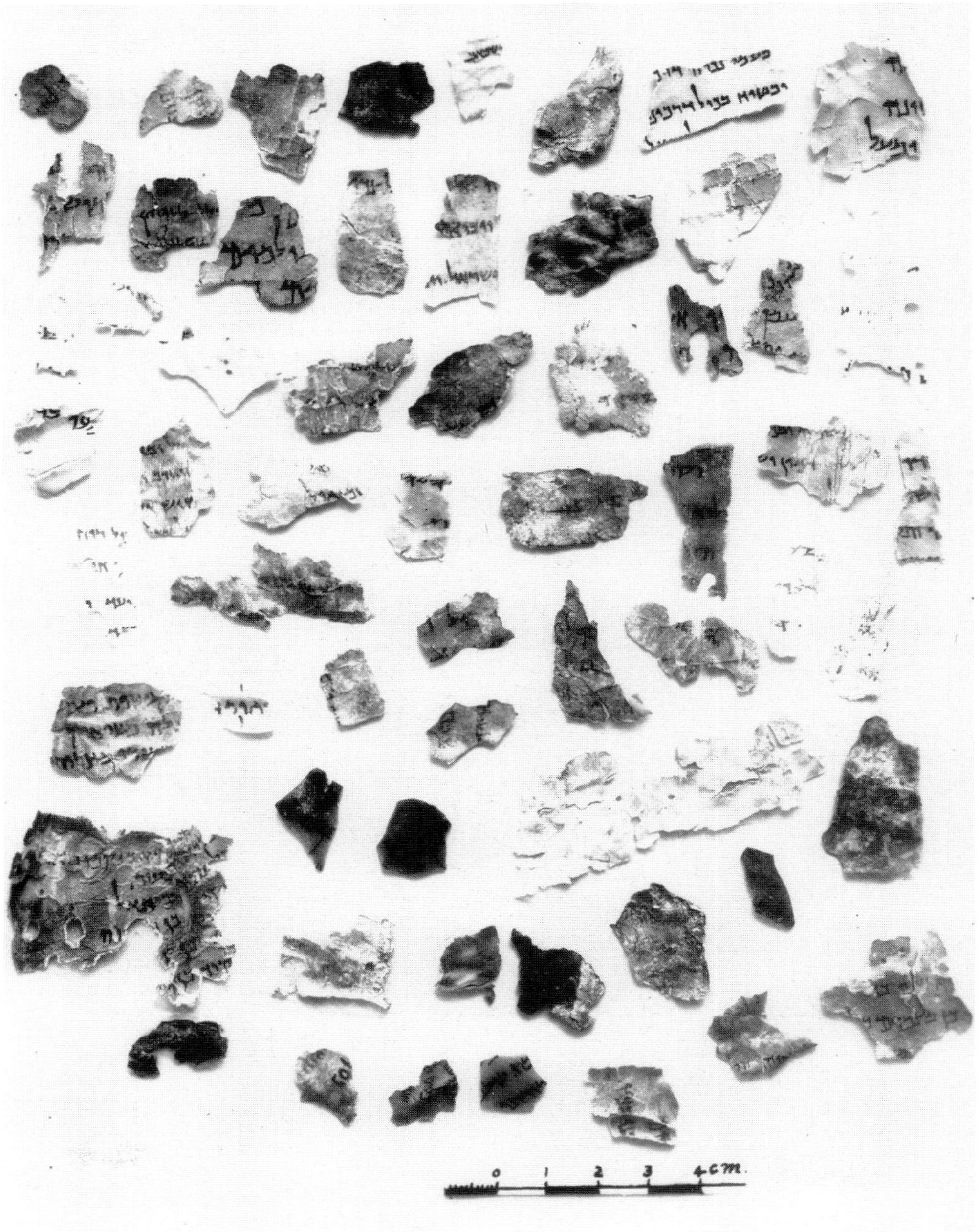

Plate 40

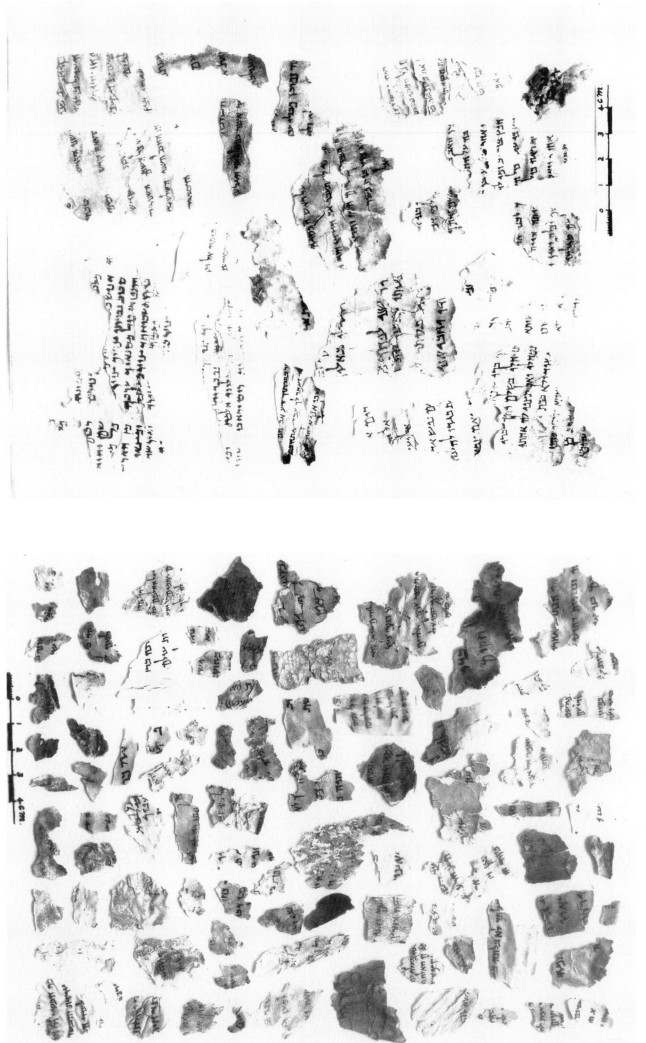

PLATE 42

PLATE 41

PLATE 44

PLATE 43

PLATE 46

PLATE 45

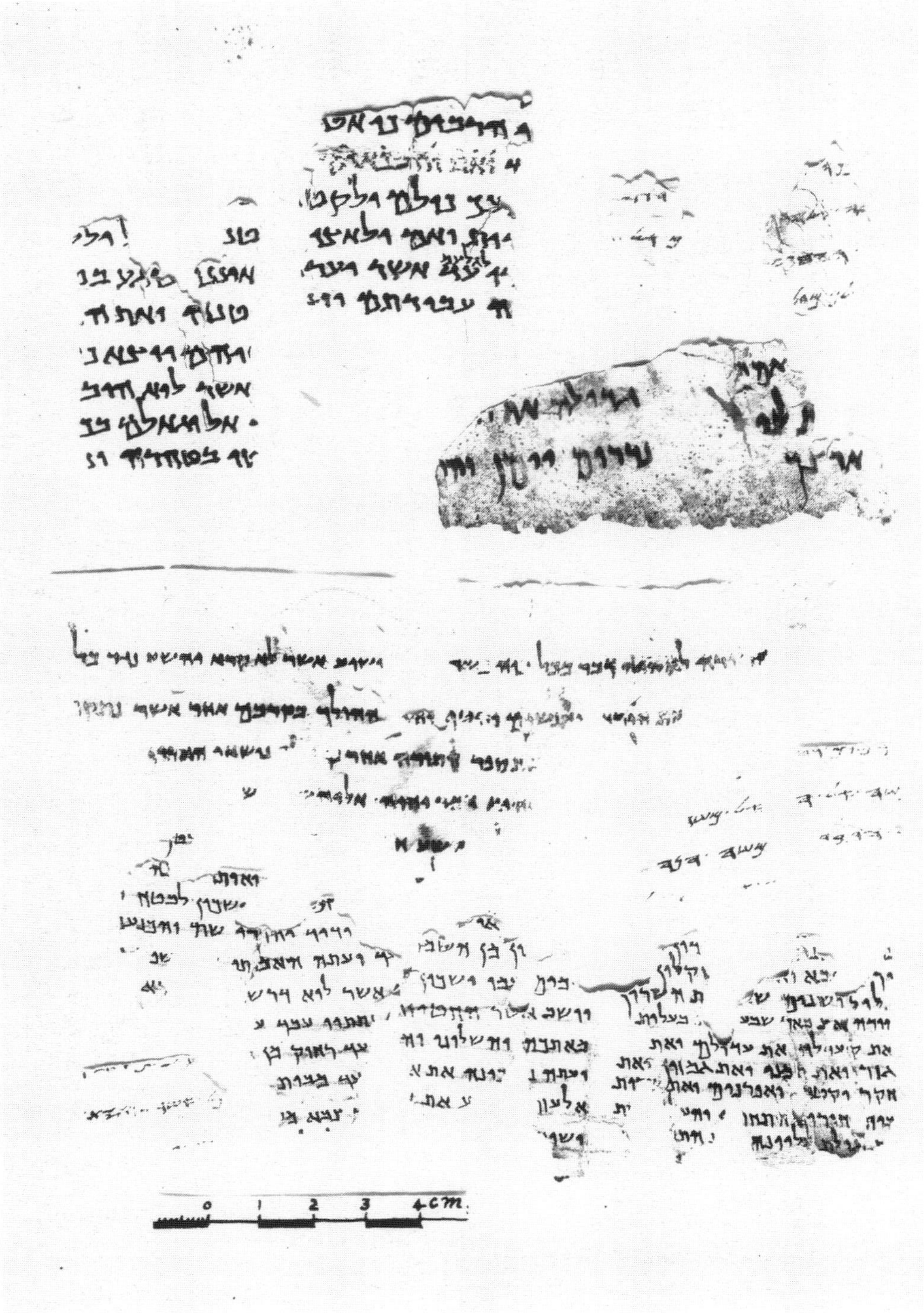

PLATE 47

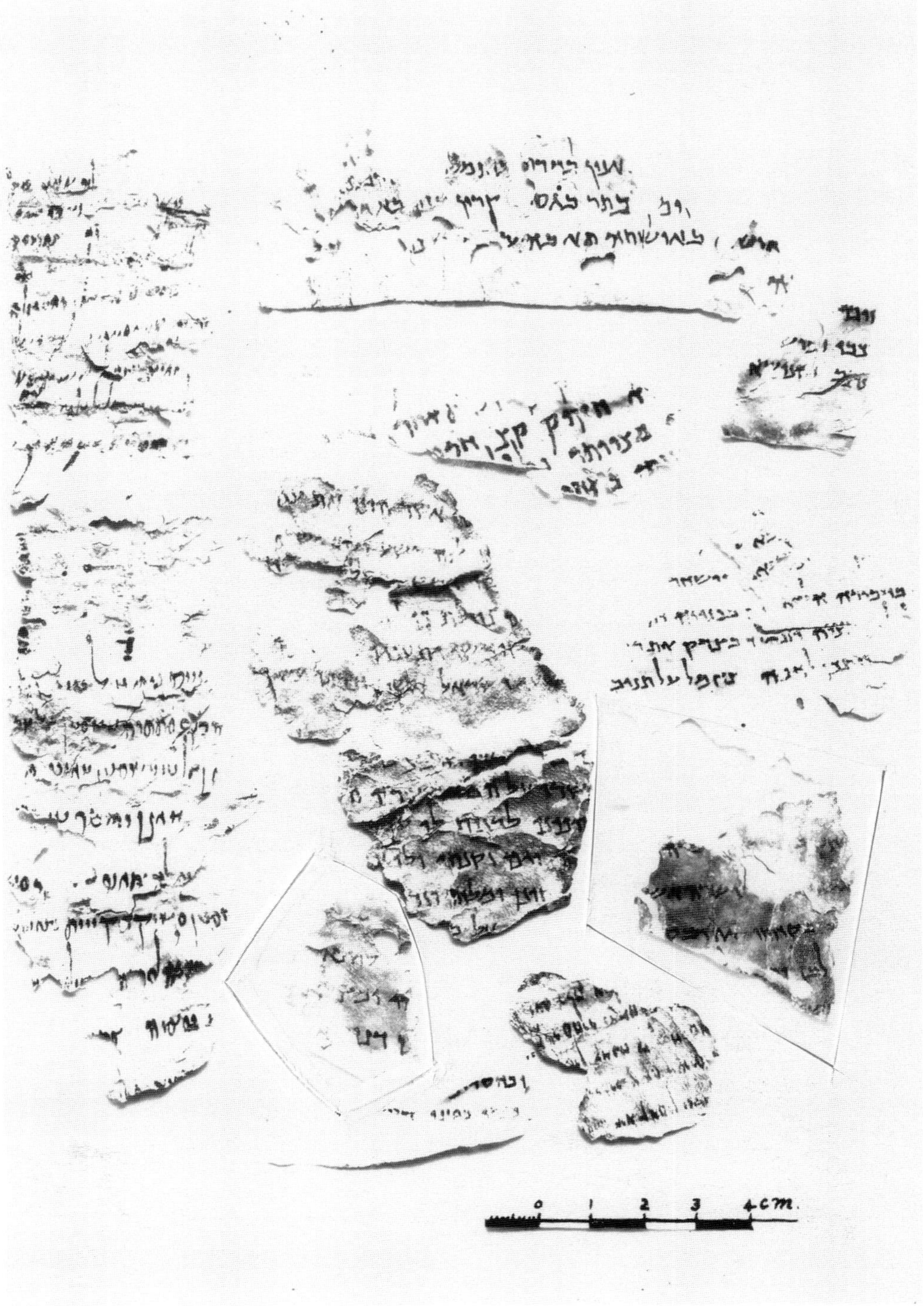

PLATE 48

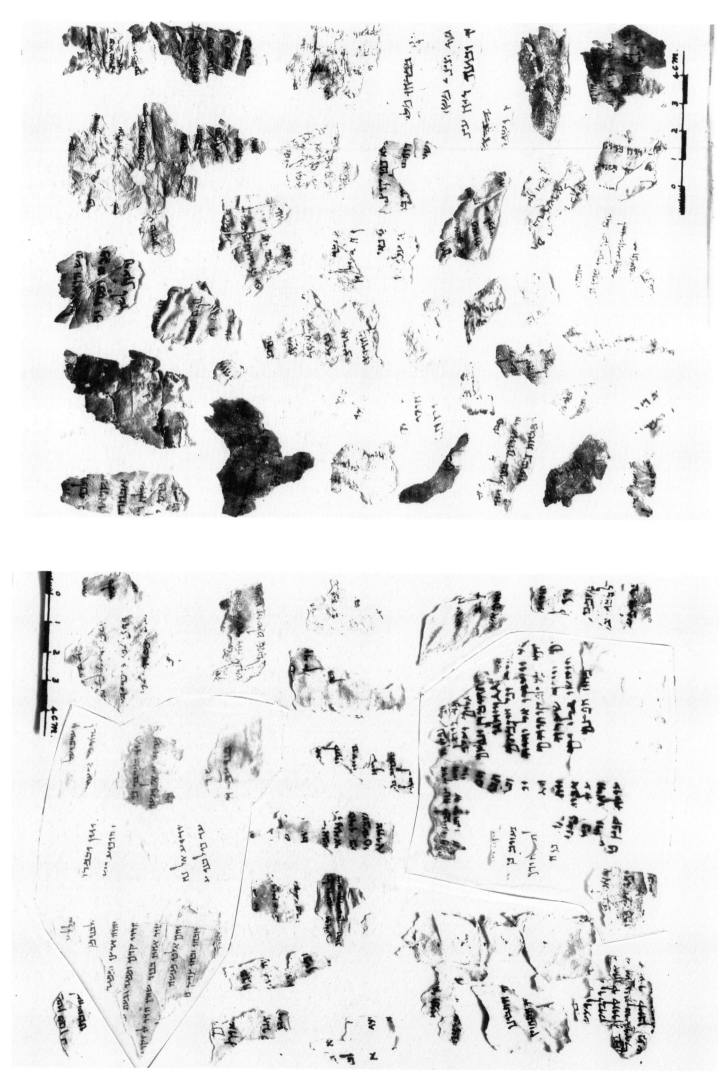

PLATE 49

PLATE 50

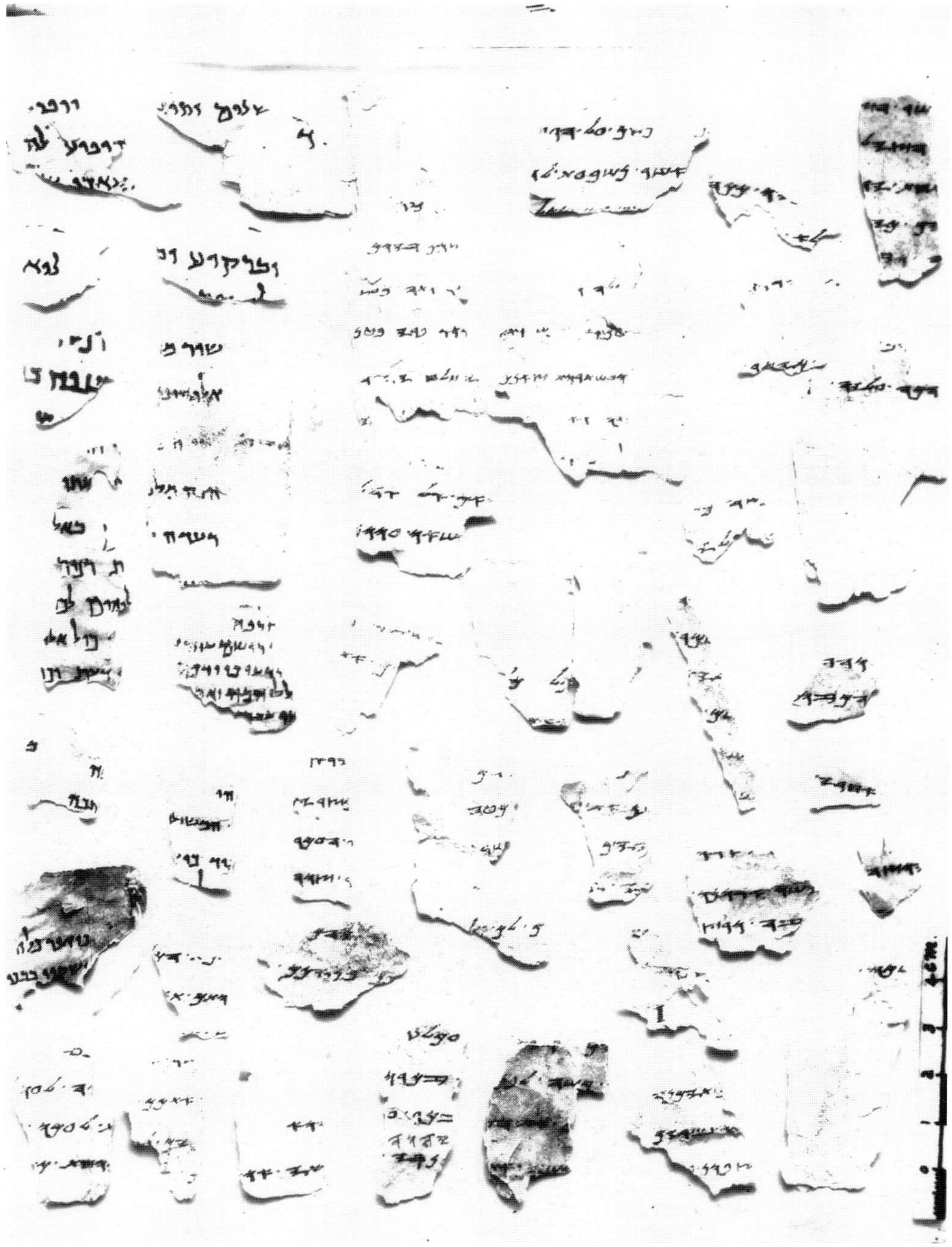

PLATE 51

PLATE 52

PLATE 54

PLATE 53

PLATE 56

PLATE 55

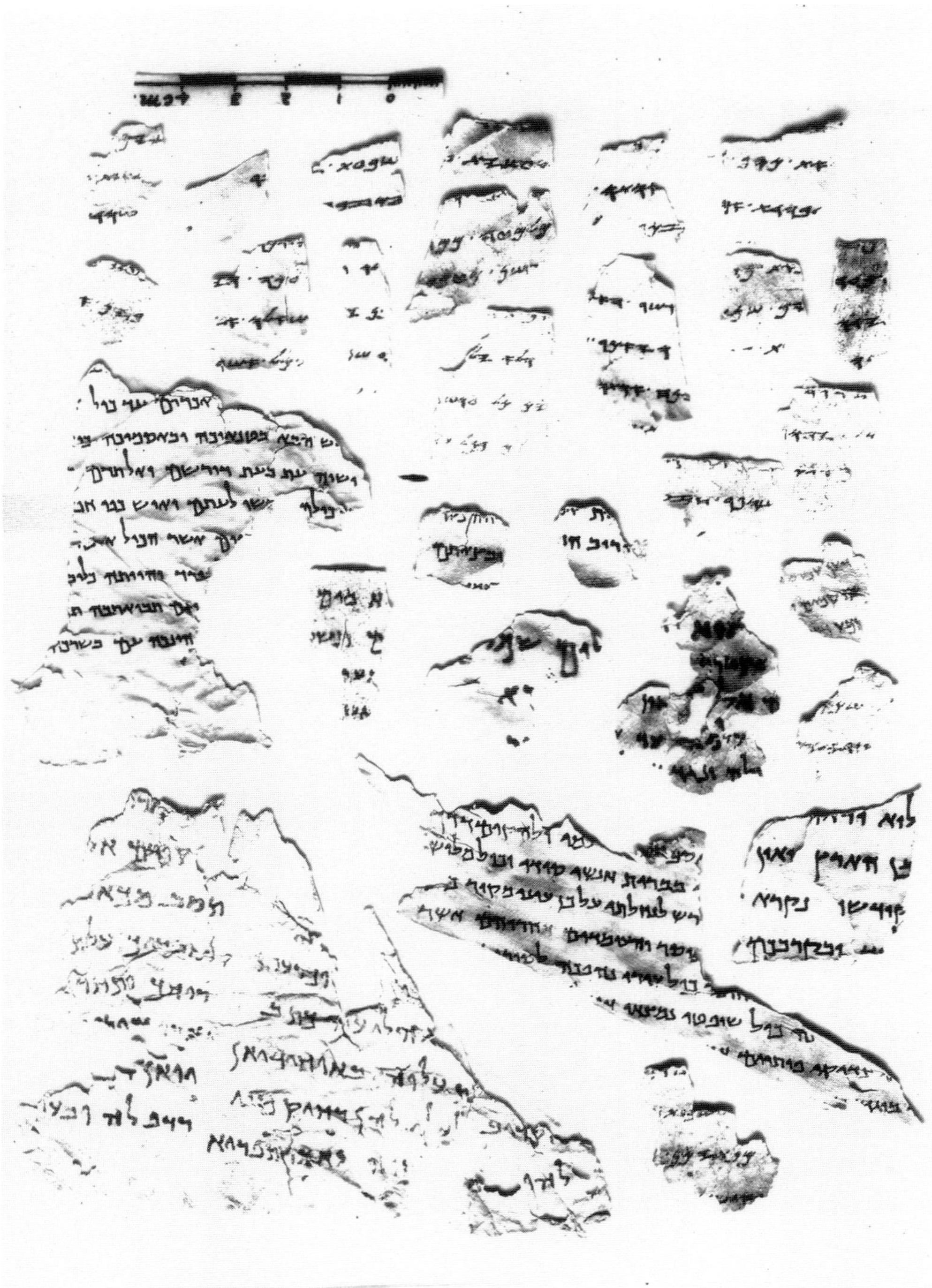

PLATE 57

PLATE 58

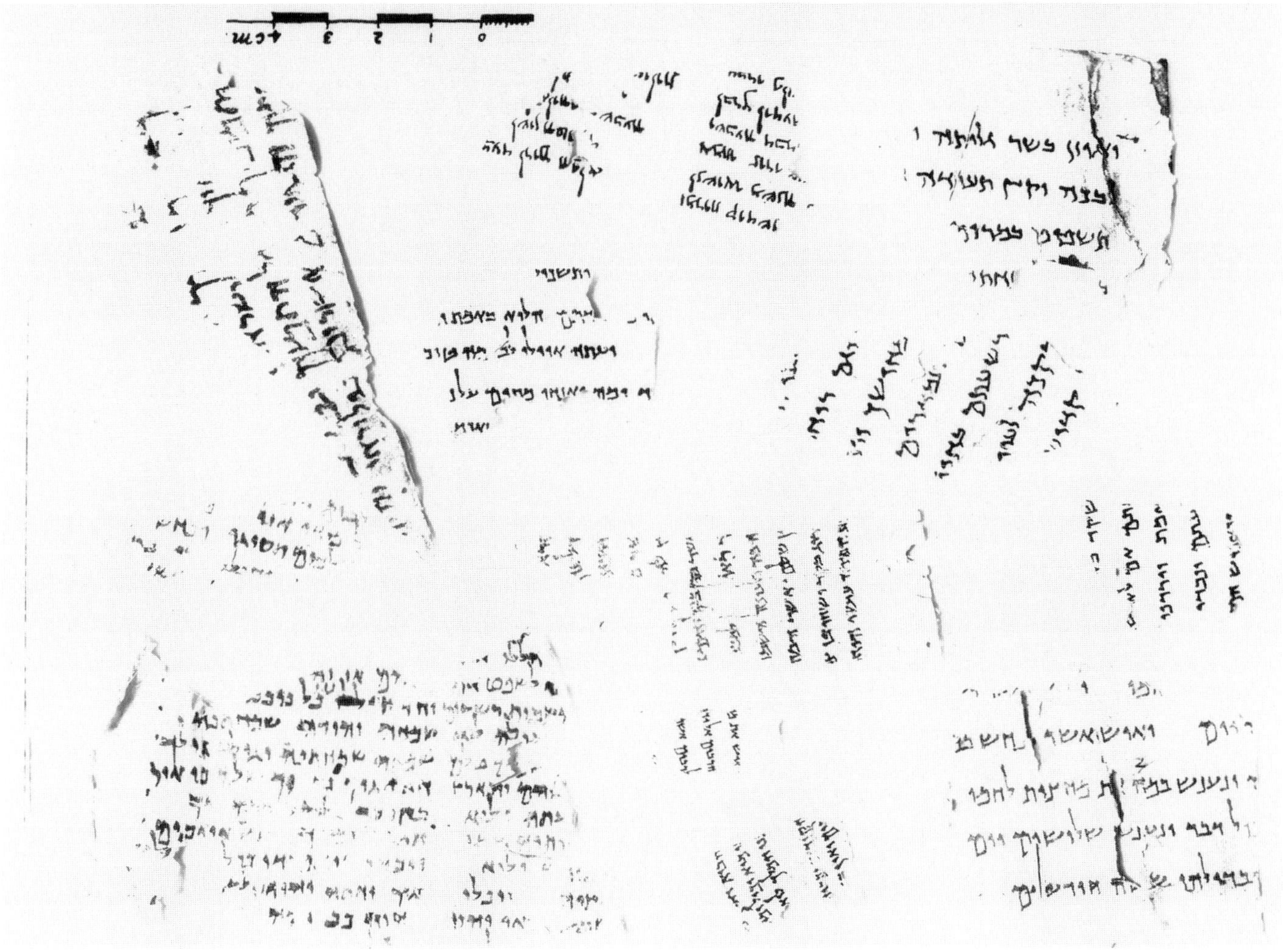

PLATE 59

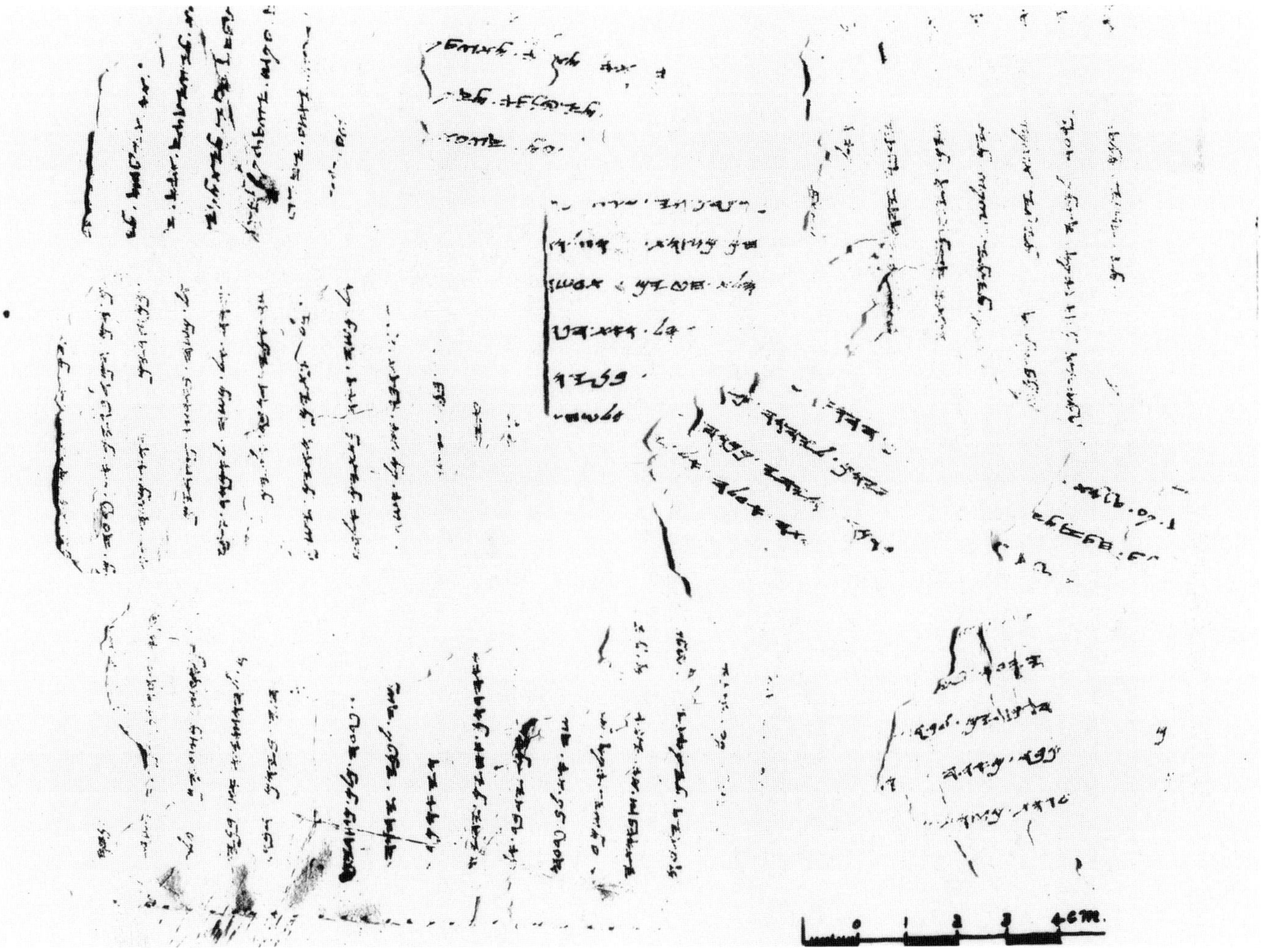

PLATE 60

PLATE 61

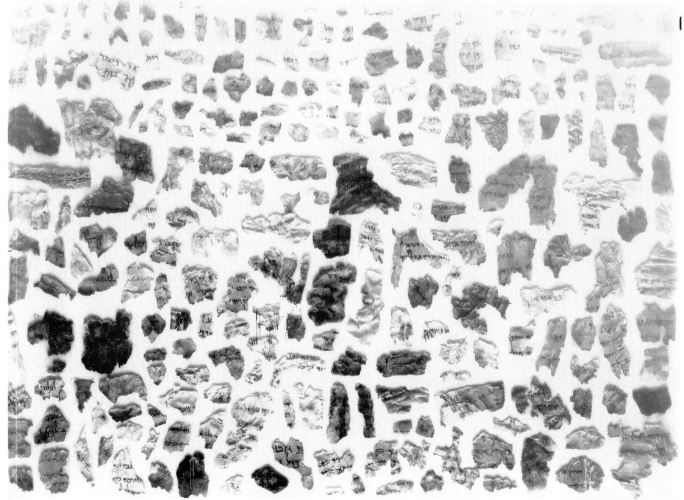

PLATE 62

PLATE 63

PLATE 64

PLATE 65

PLATE 66

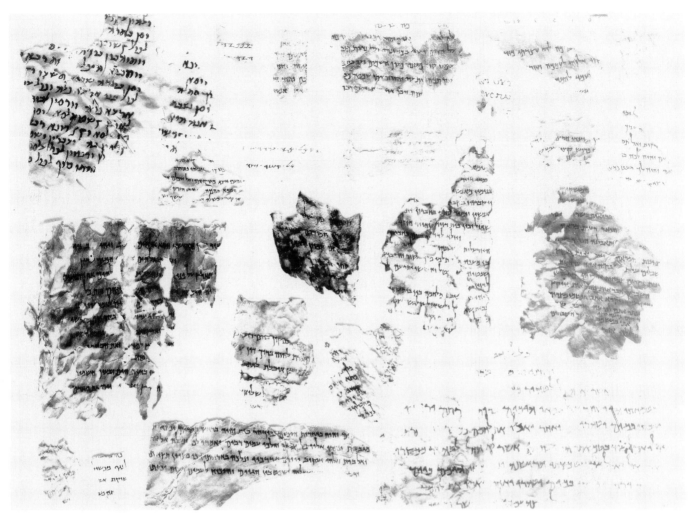

PLATE 83

PLATE 84

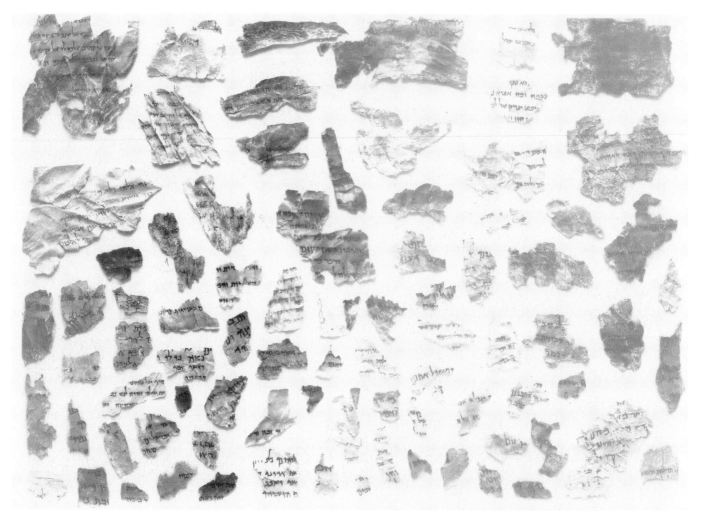

PLATE 85

PLATE 86

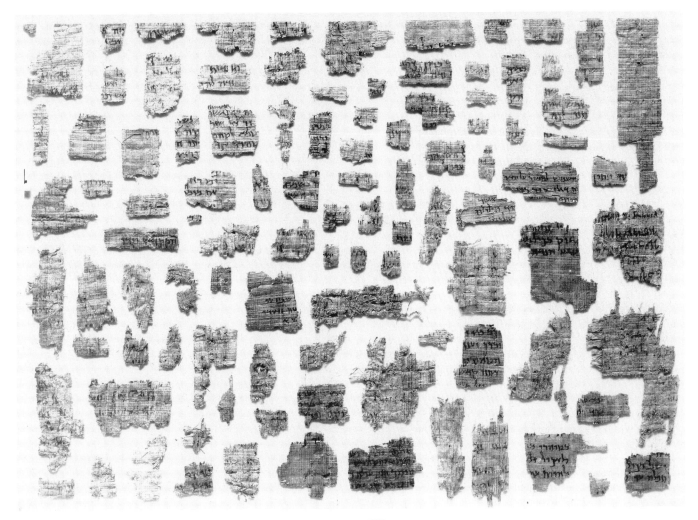

PLATE 87

PLATE 88

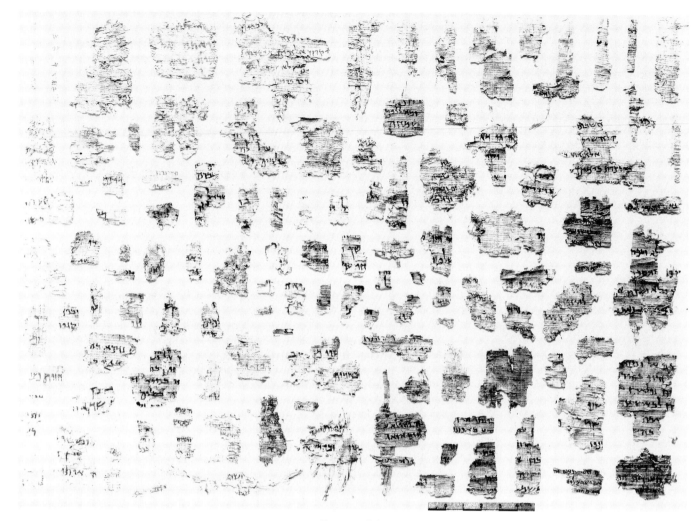

PLATE 89

PLATE 90

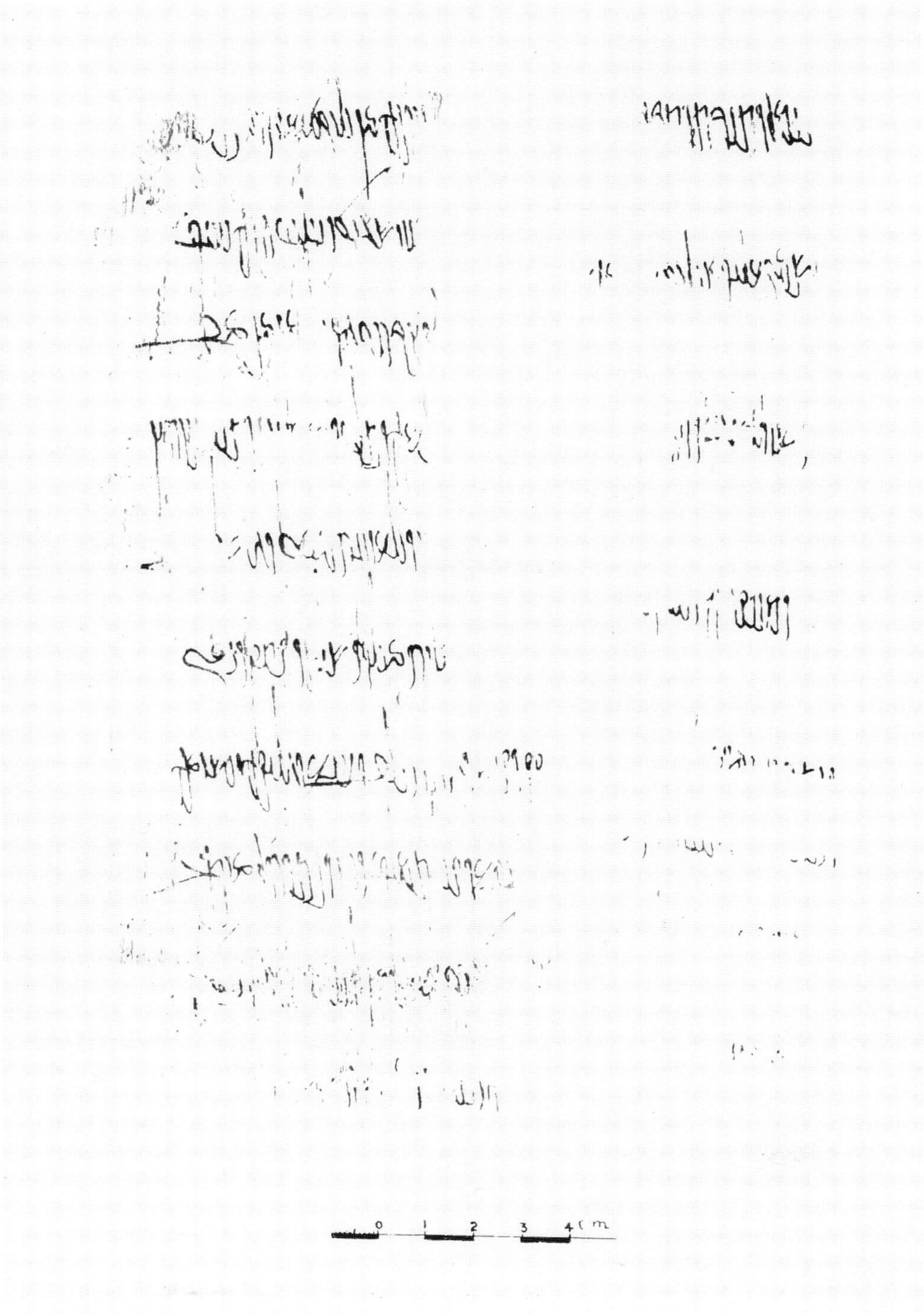

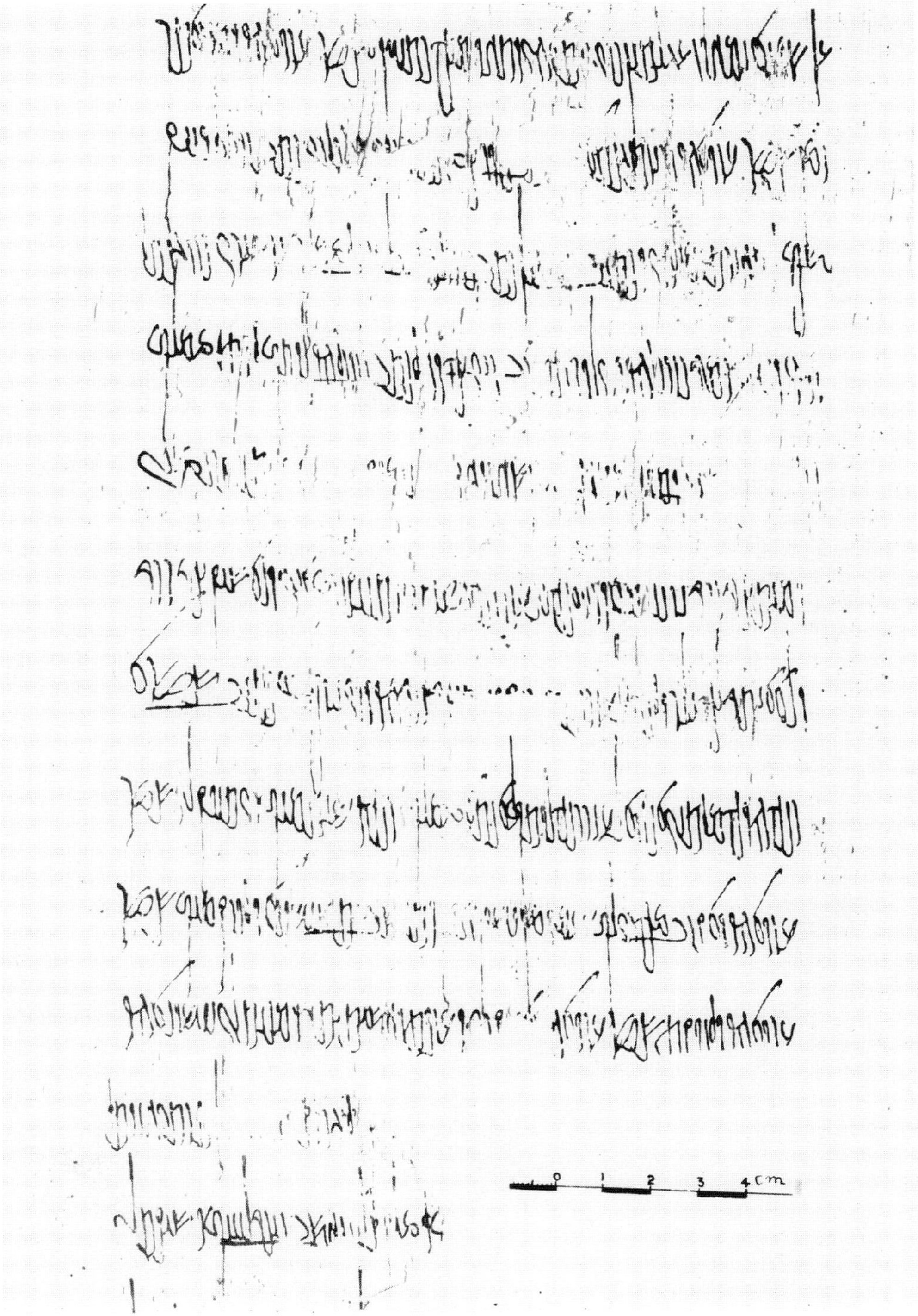

PLATE 100

PLATE 99

PLATE 101

PLATE 102

PLATE 103

PLATE 104

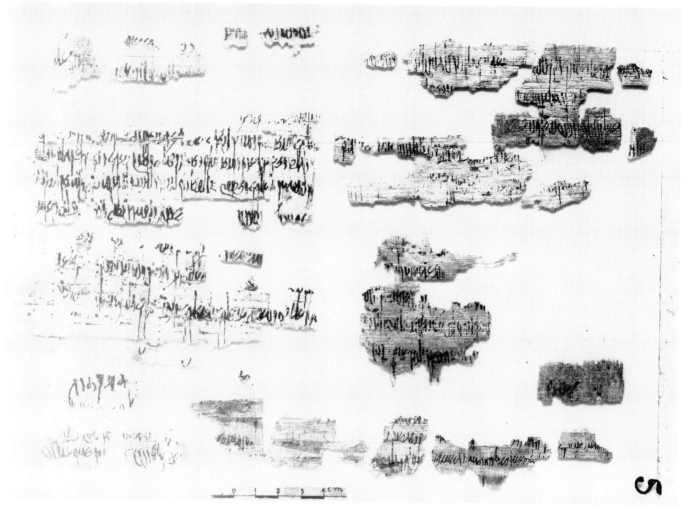

PLATE 105

PLATE 106

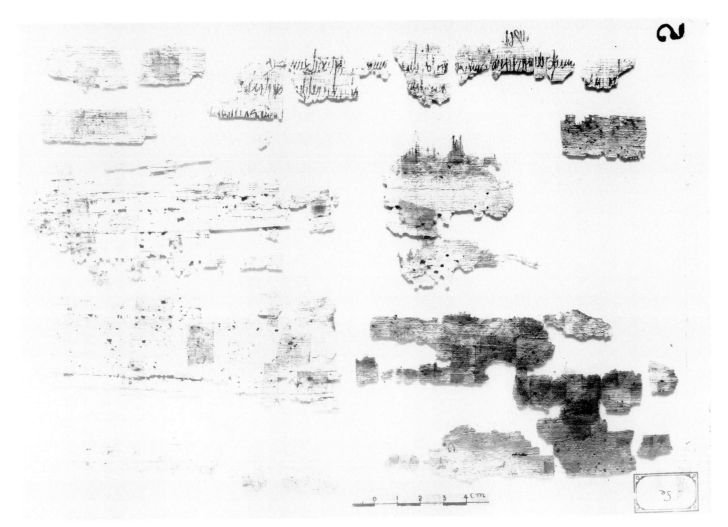

PLATE 107

PLATE 108

PLATE 109

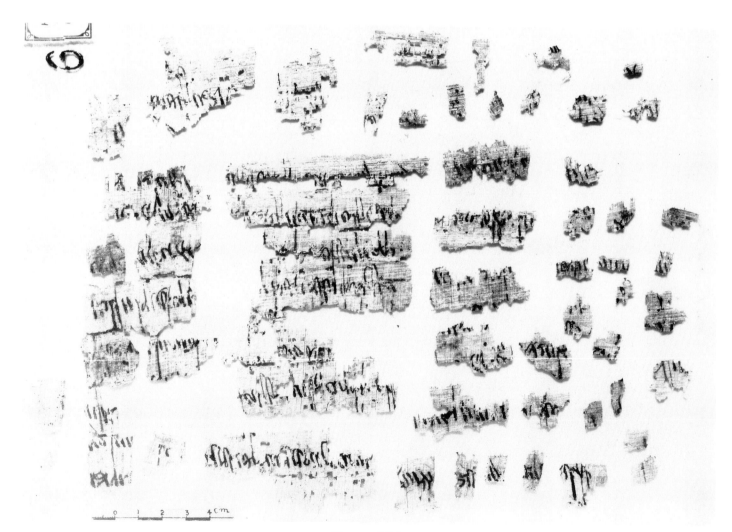

PLATE 110

PLATE 111

PLATE 113

PLATE 112

PLATE 114

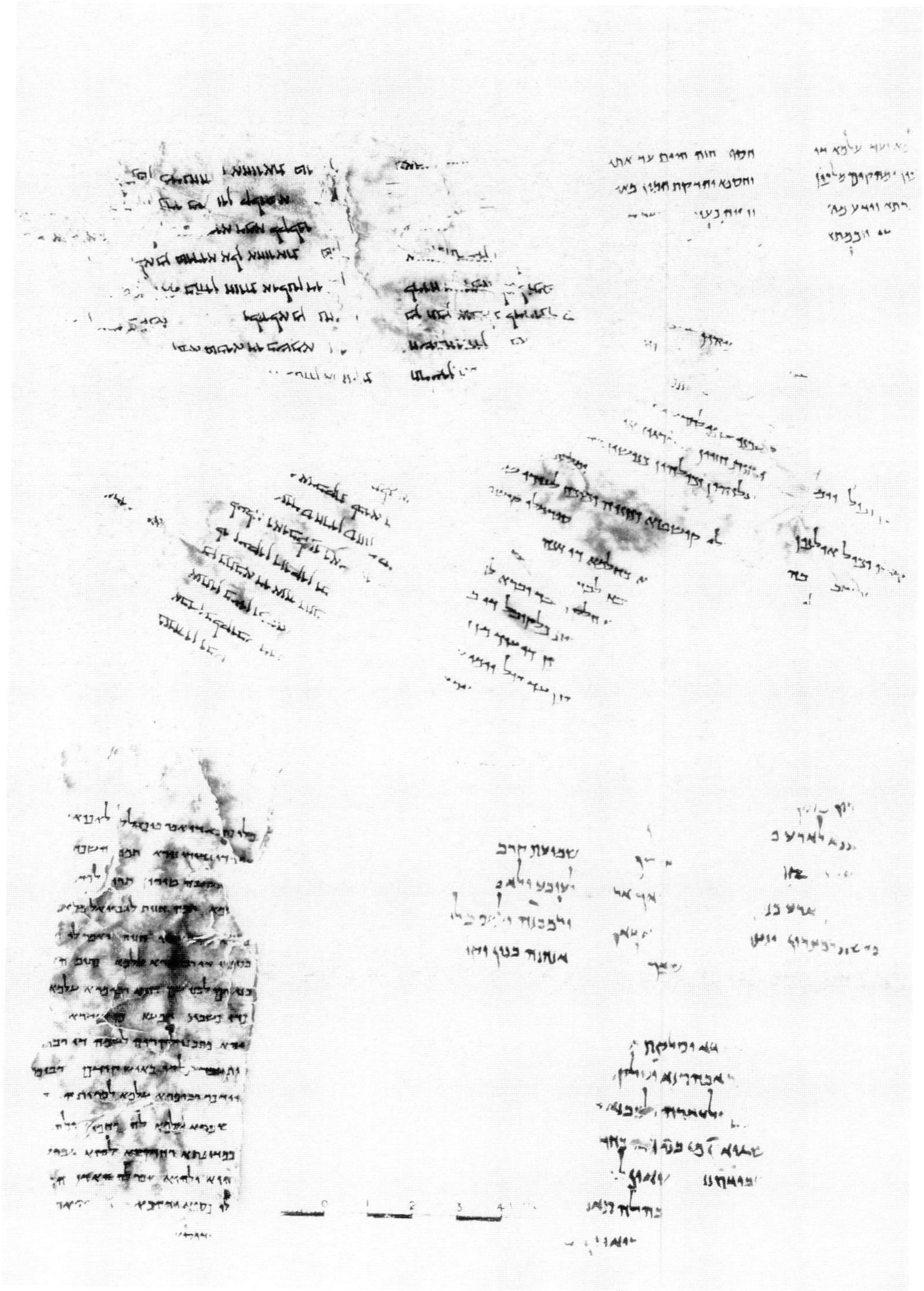

PLATE 115

PLATE 116

PLATE 117

PLATE 119

PLATE 118

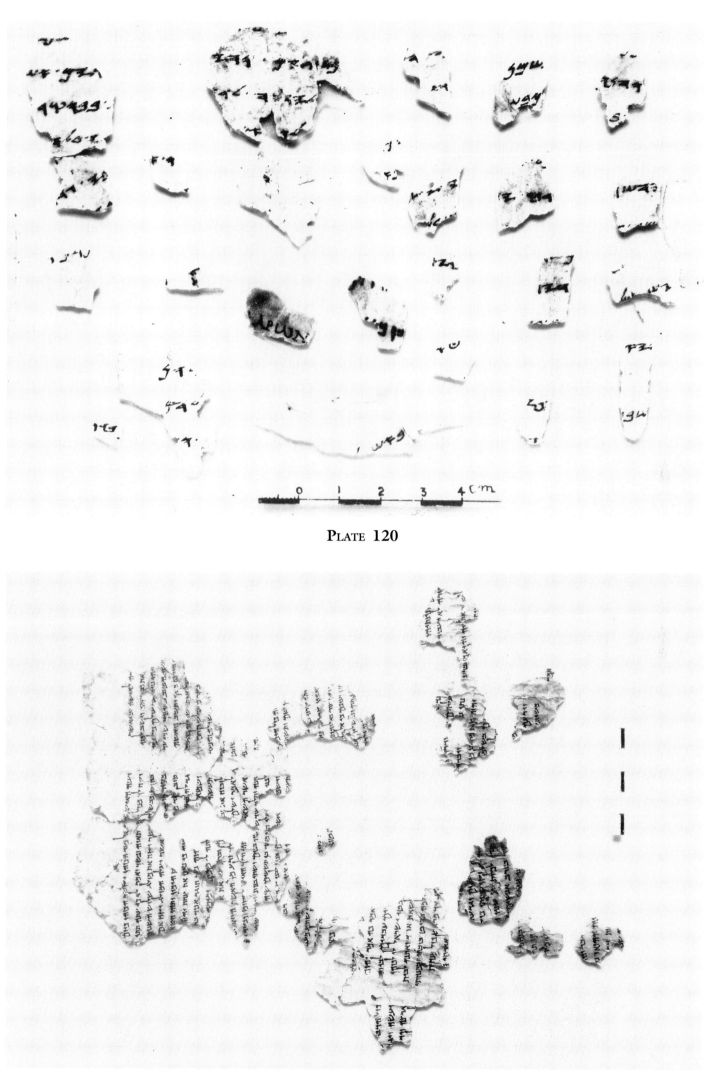

PLATE 120

PLATE 121

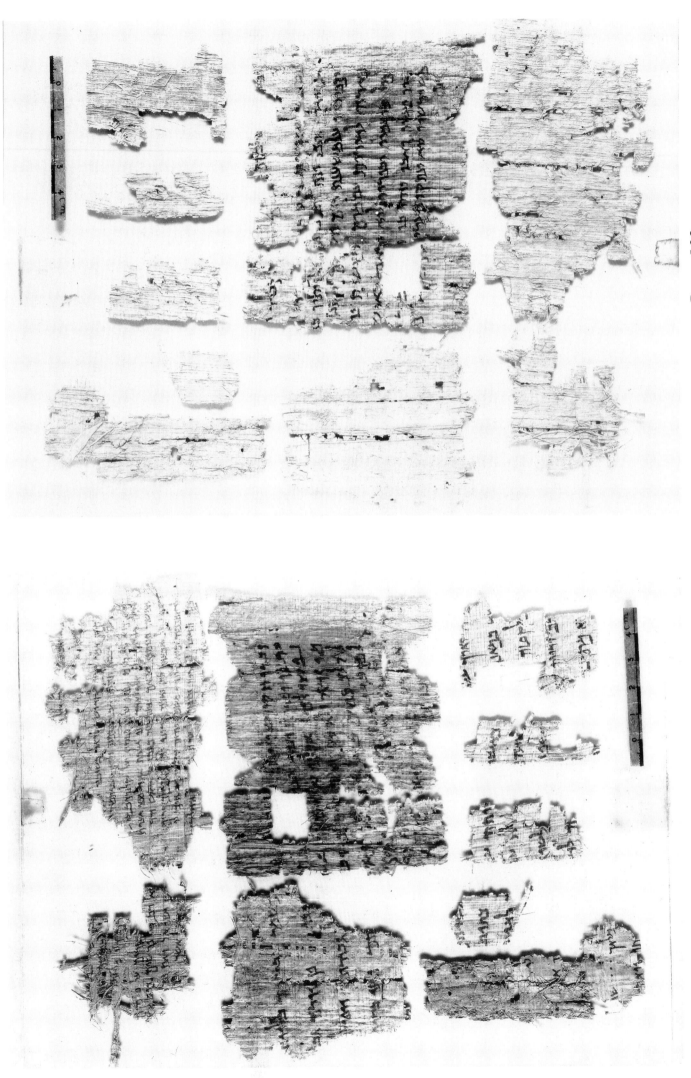

PLATE 123

PLATE 122

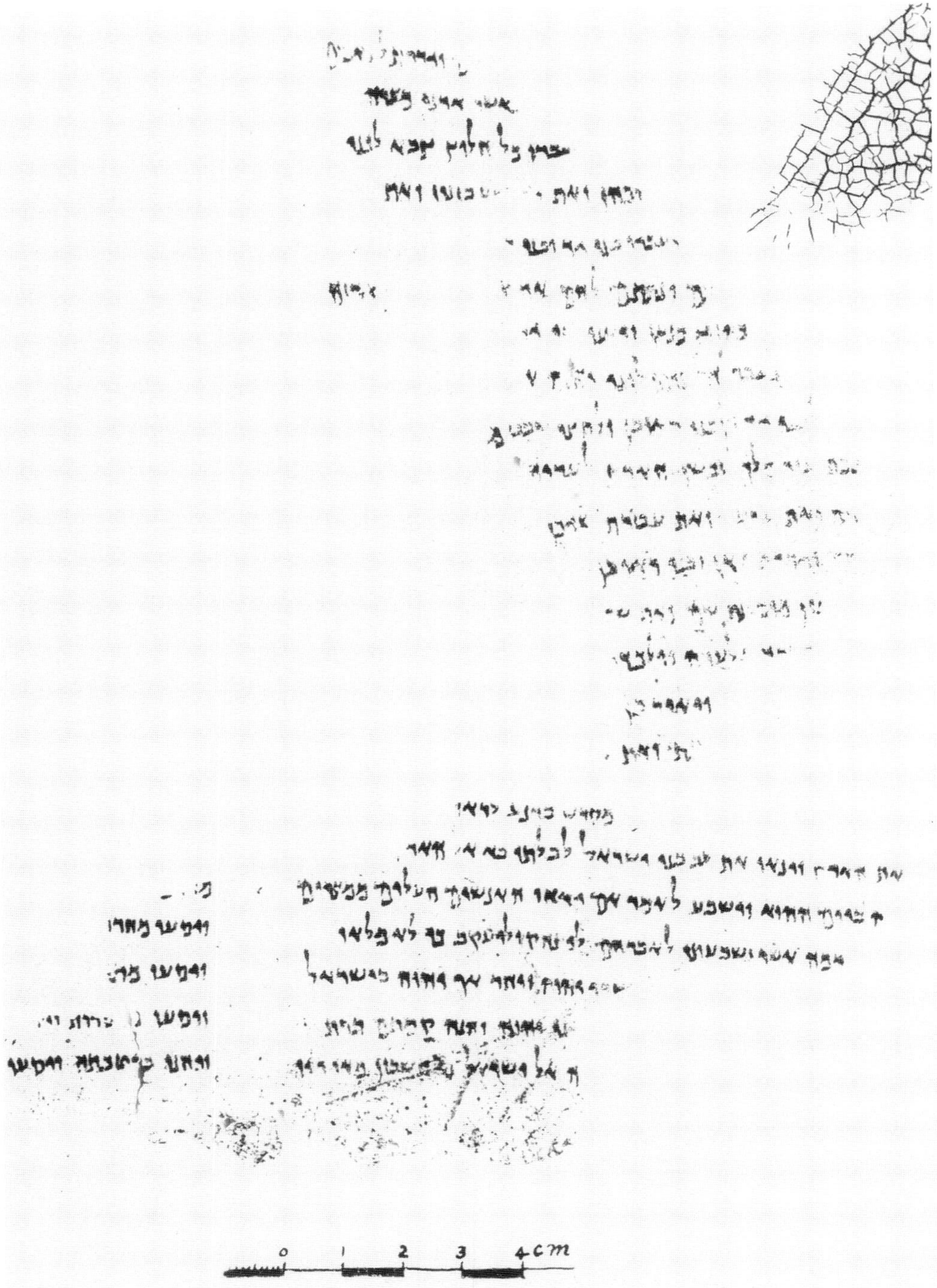

PLATE 163

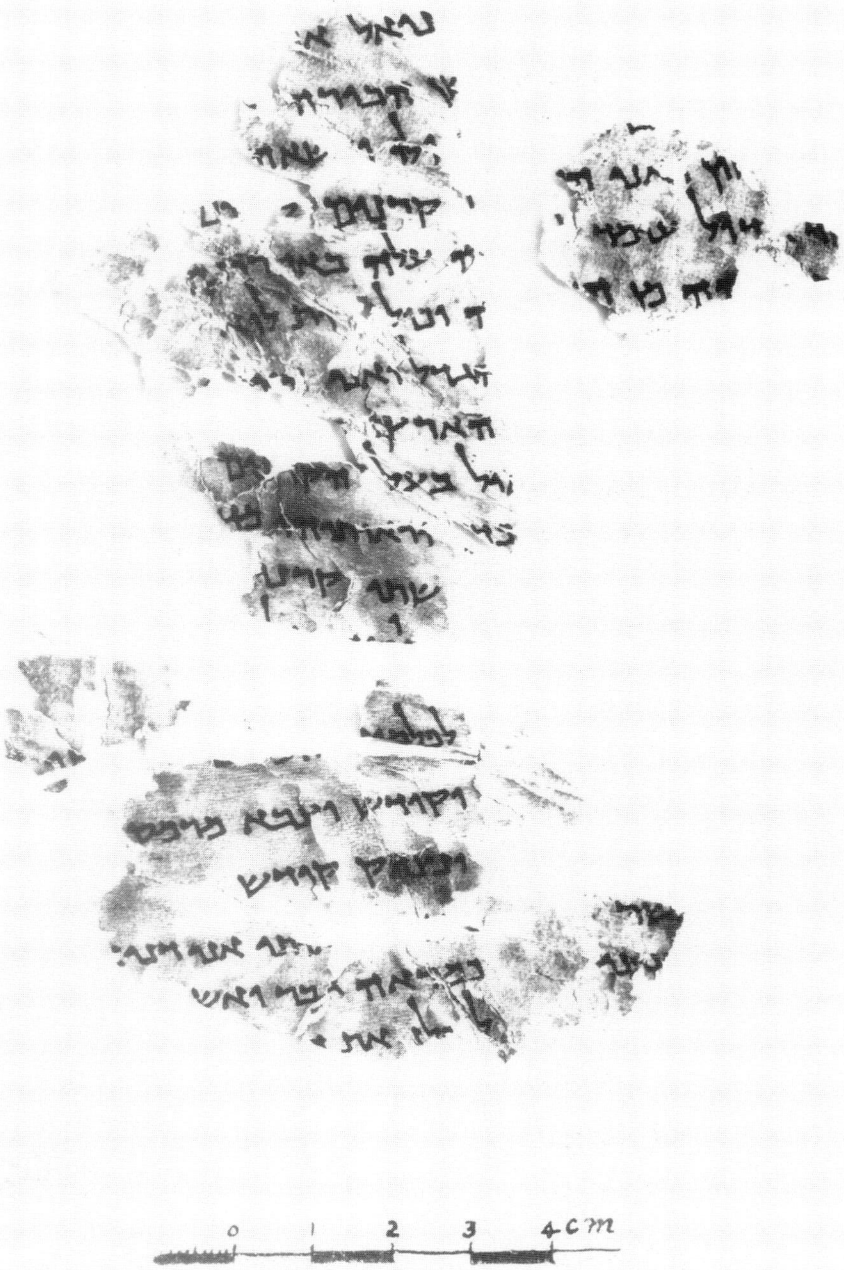

PLATE 164

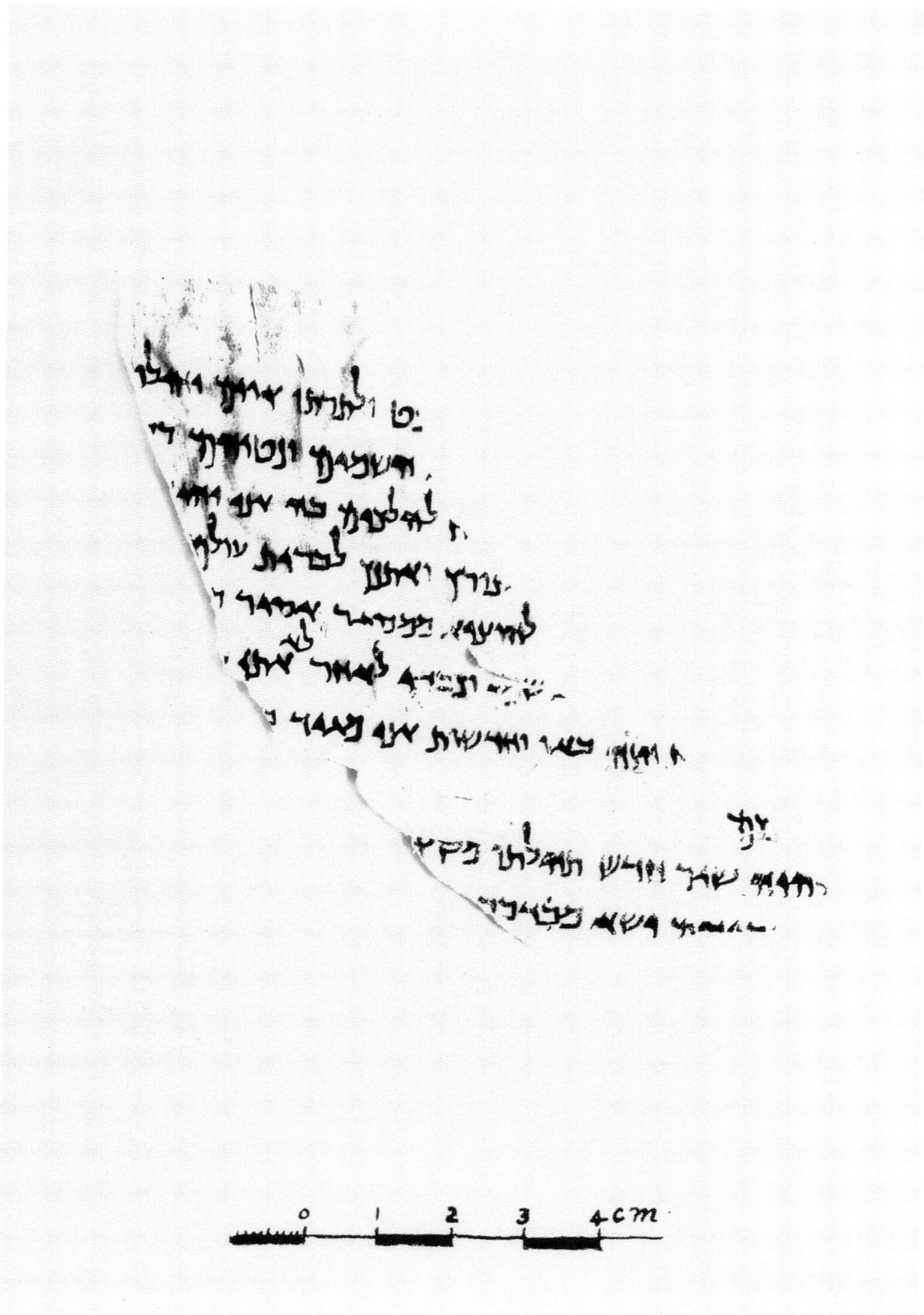

PLATE 165

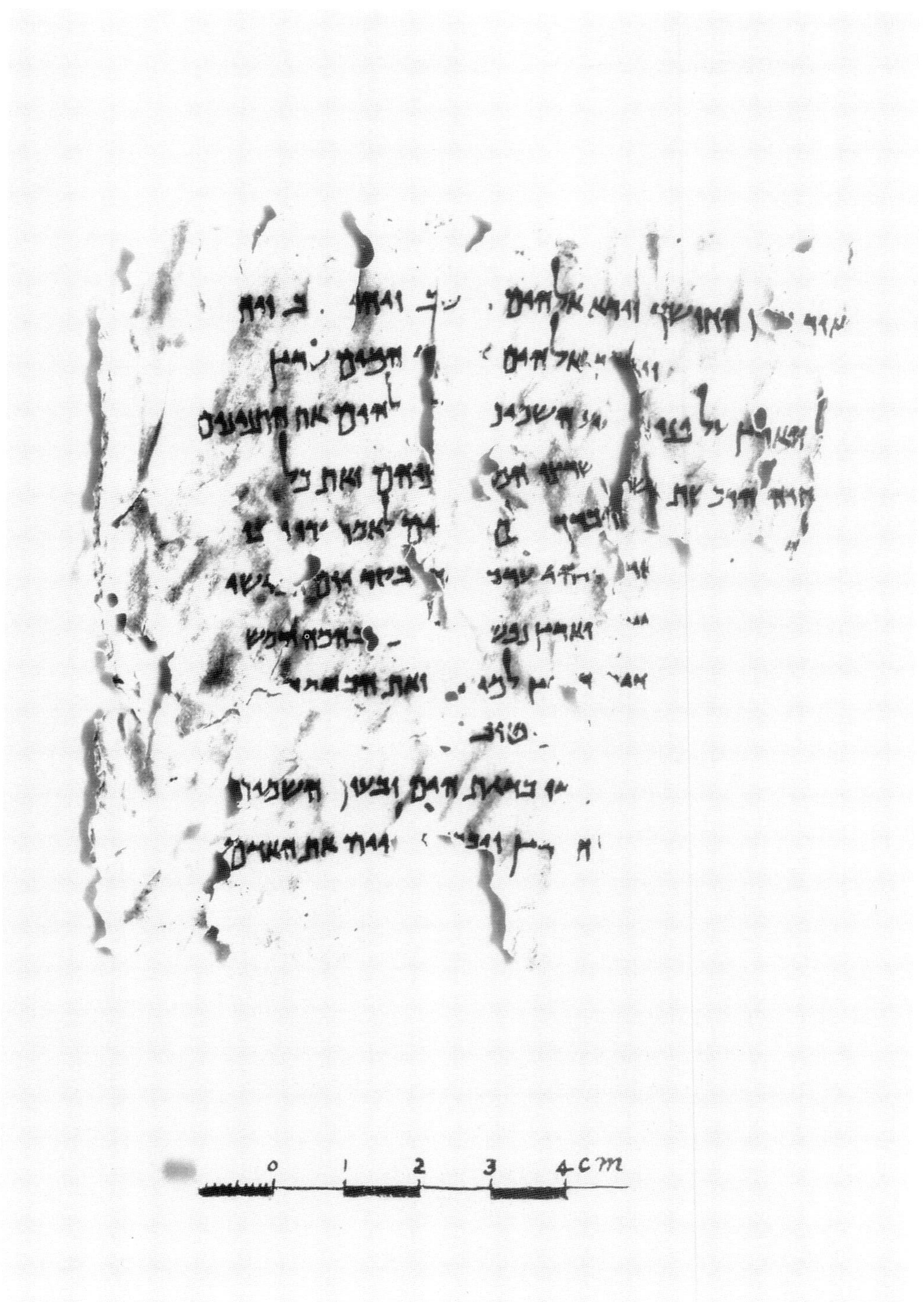

PLATE 168

PLATE 167

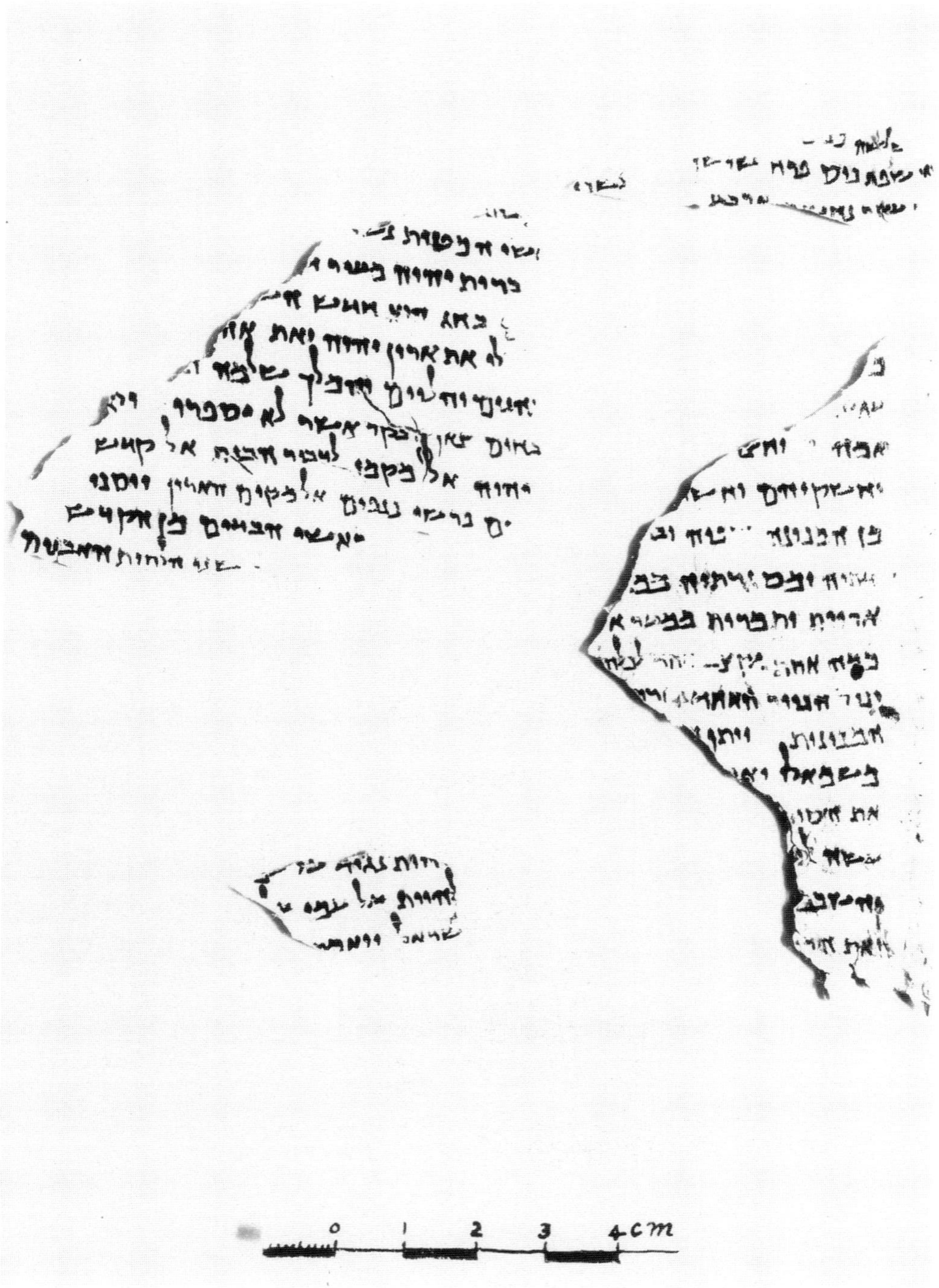

PLATE 169

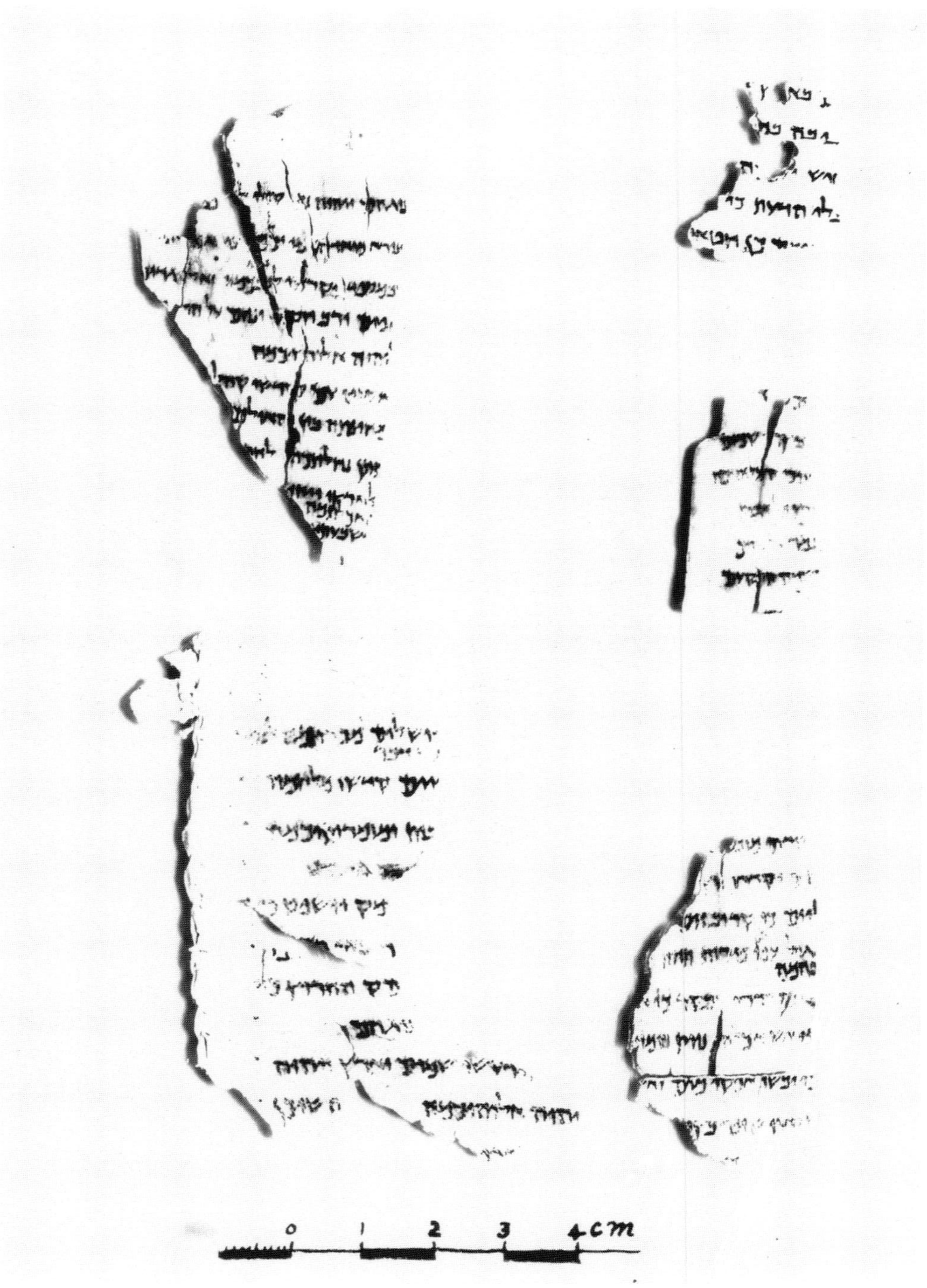

PLATE 170

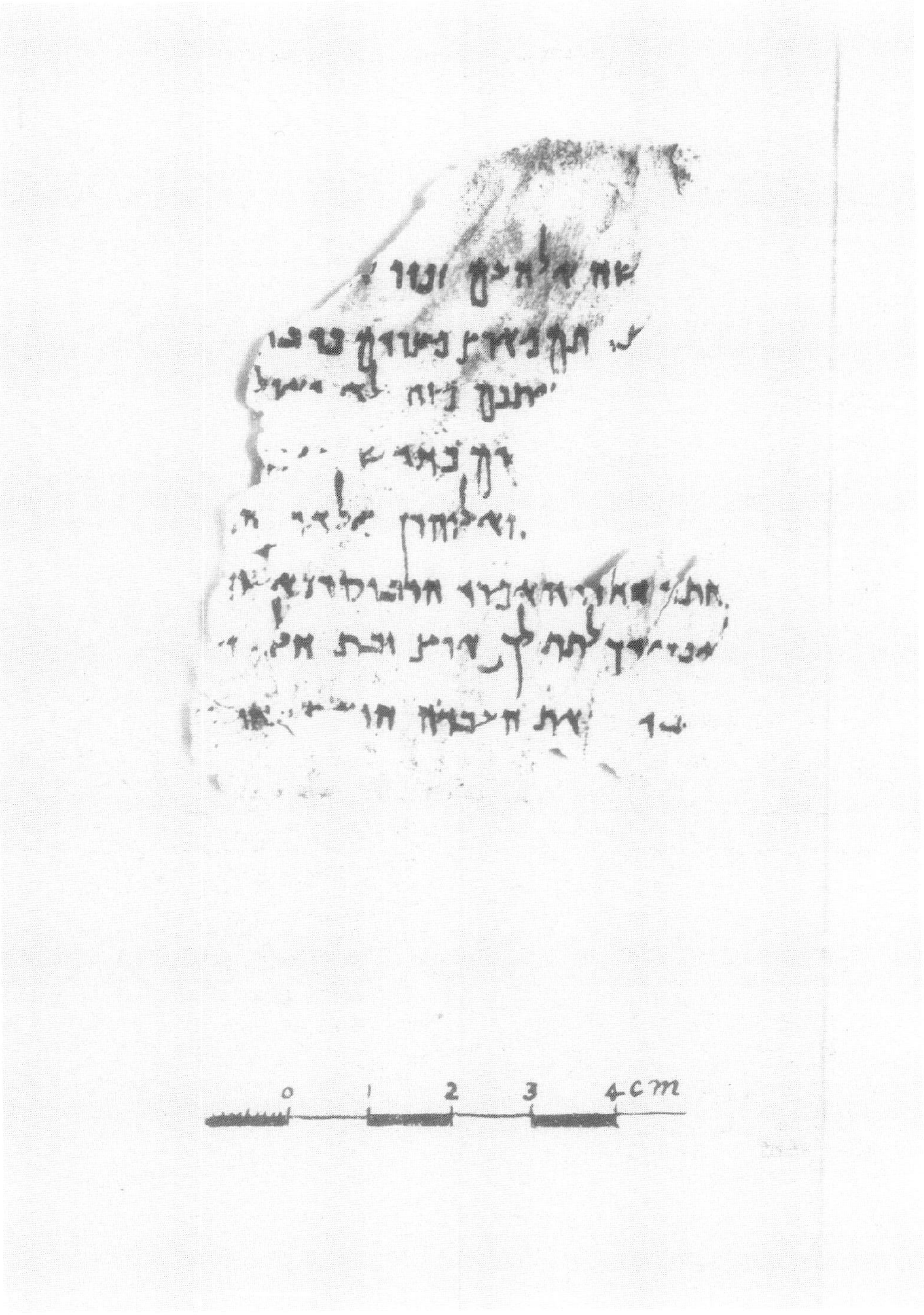

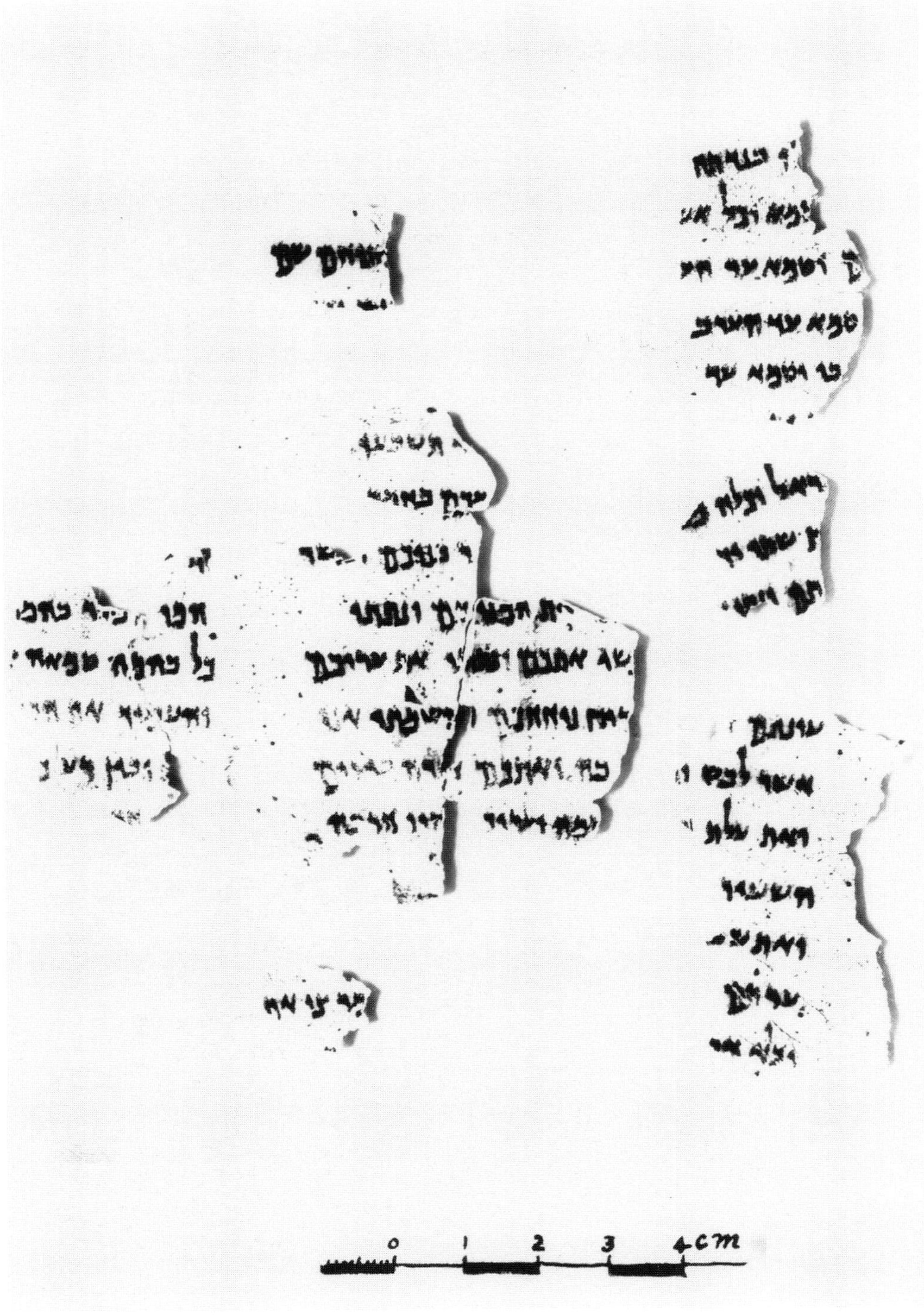

PLATE 172

PLATE 171

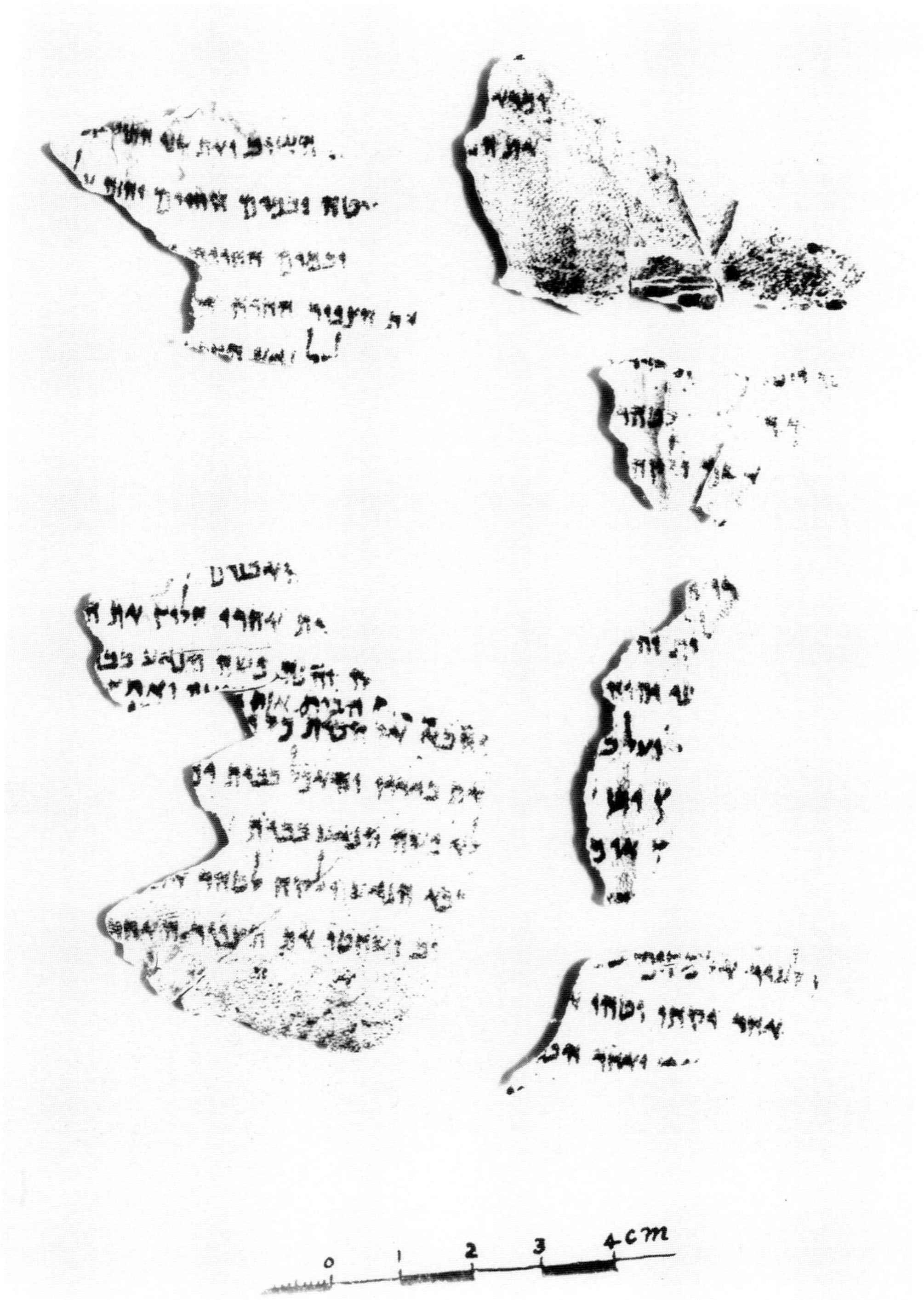

Plate 173

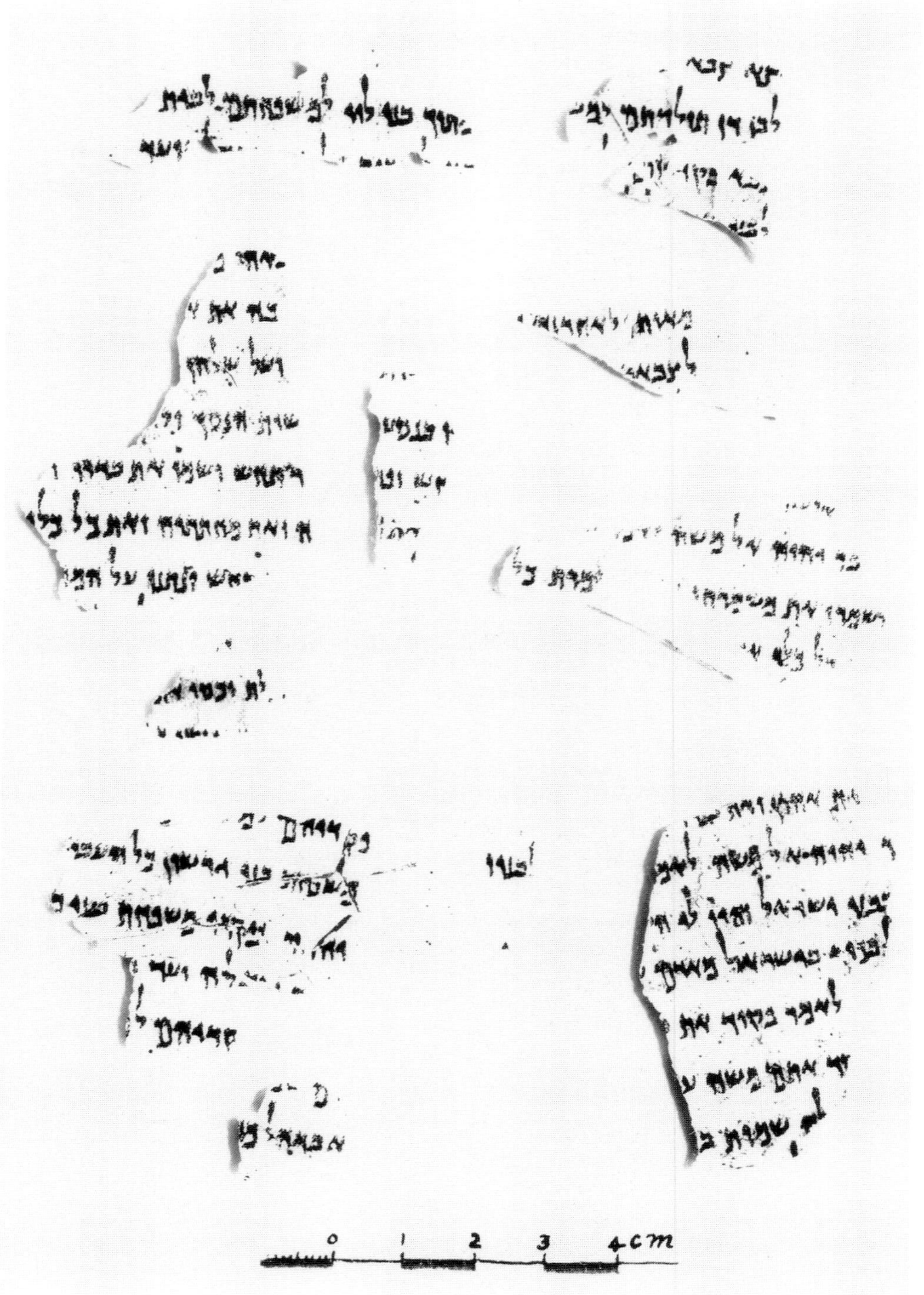

Plate 174

PLATE 215

PLATE 216

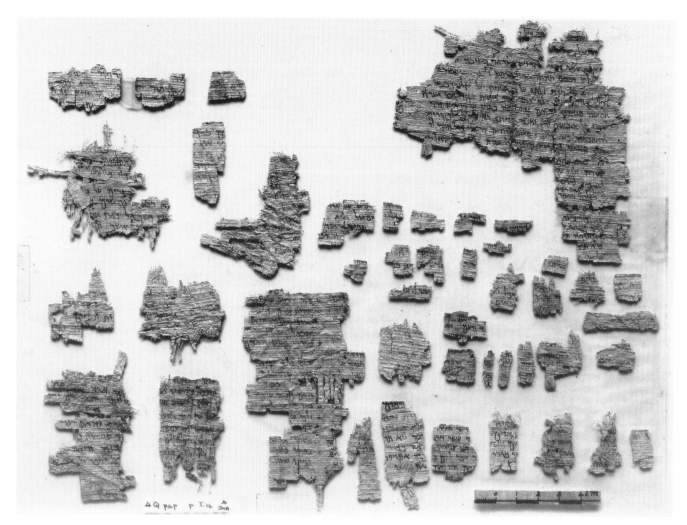

PLATE 217

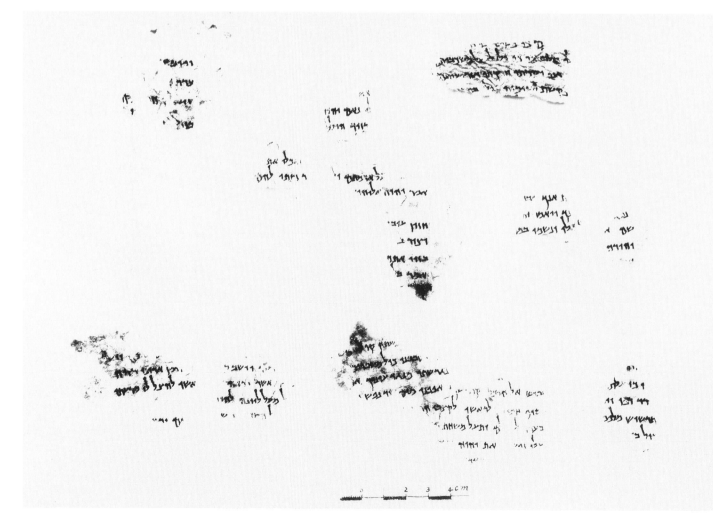

PLATE 218

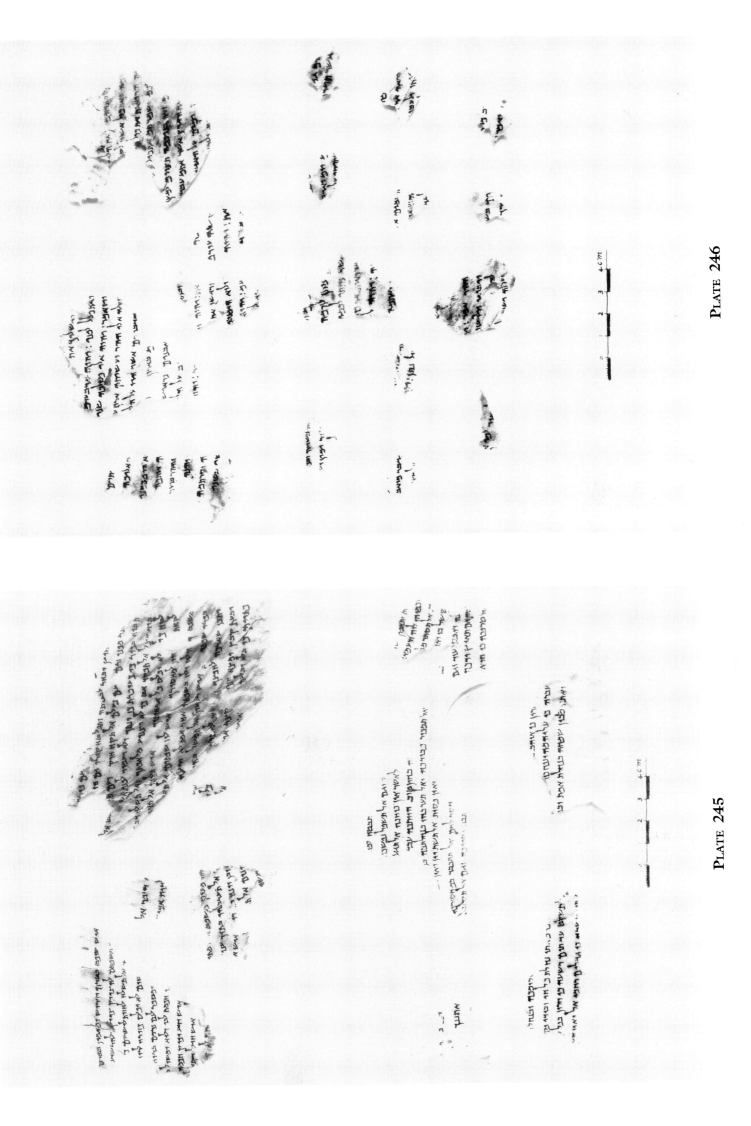

PLATE 245

PLATE 246

PLATE 247

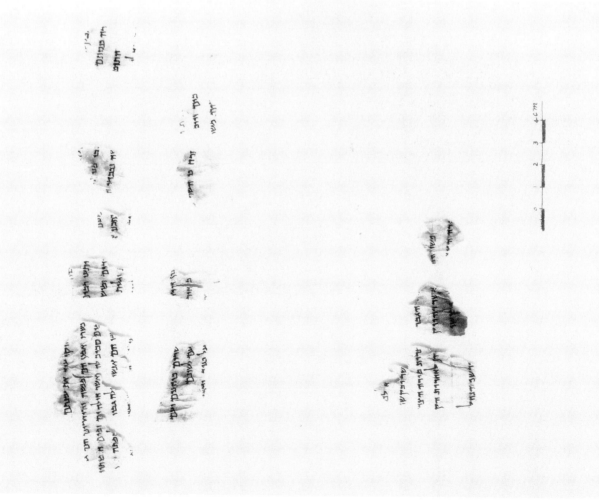

PLATE 248

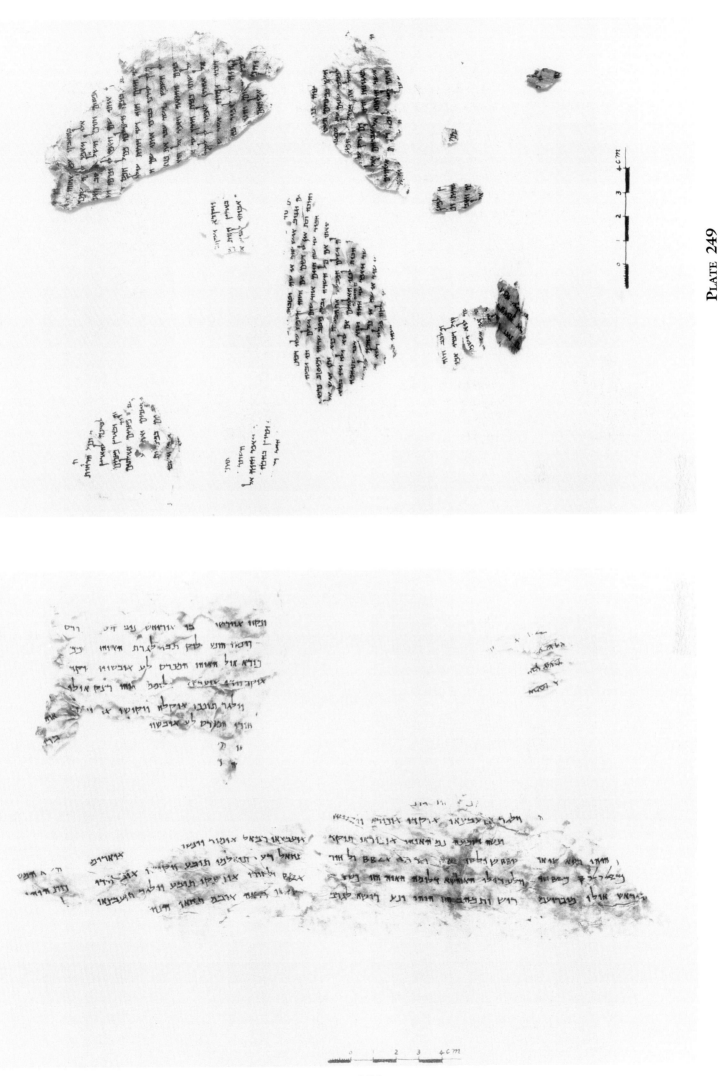

PLATE 249

PLATE 250

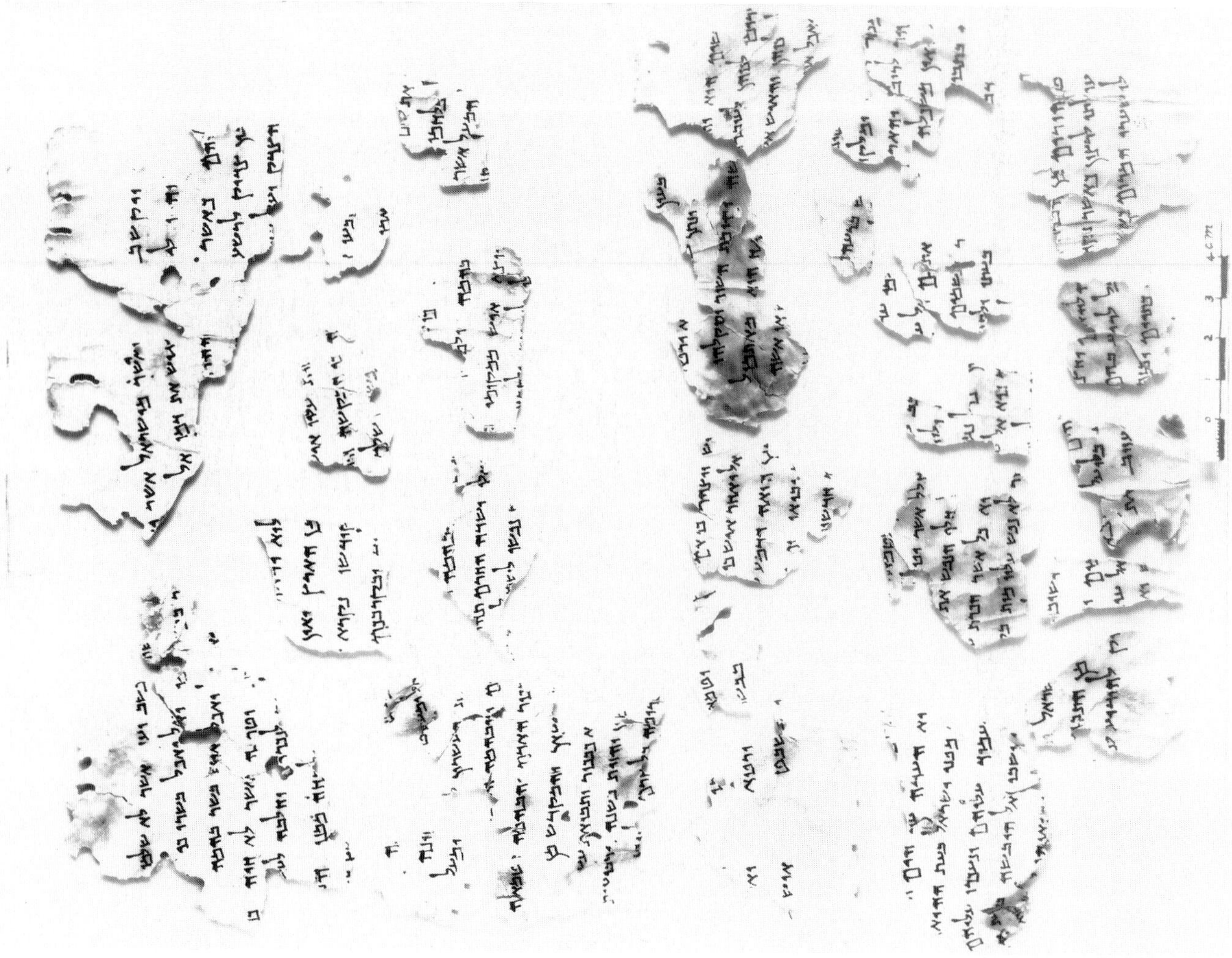

PLATE 251

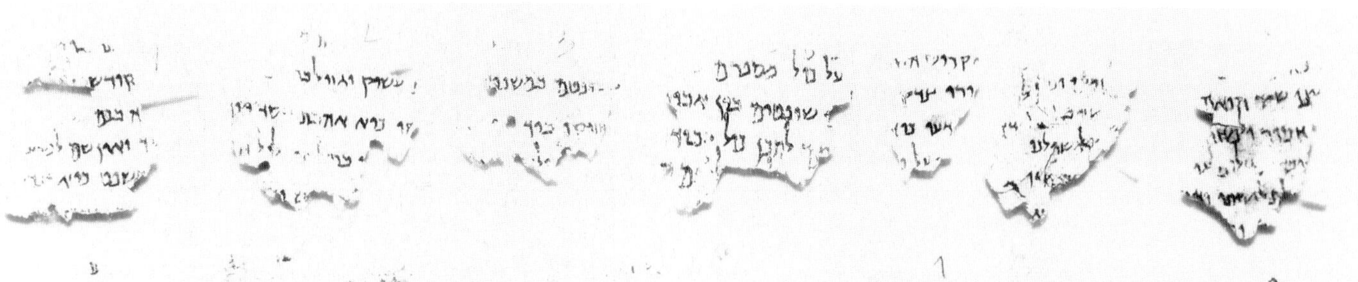

PLATE 252

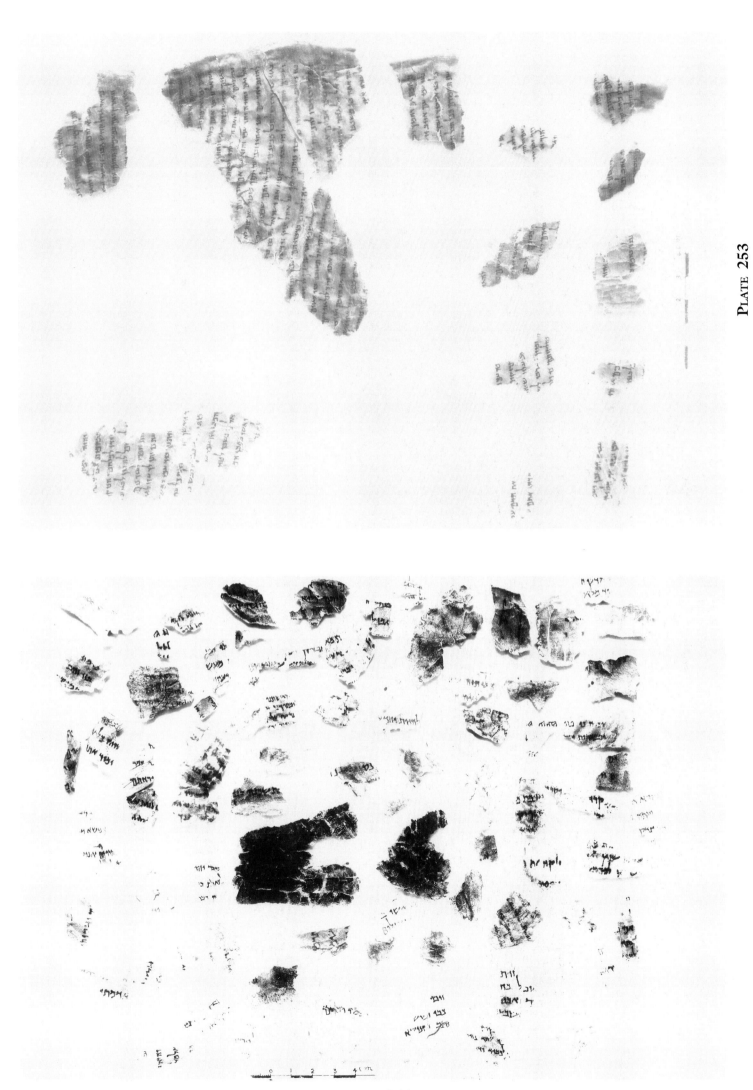

PLATE 253

PLATE 254

PLATE 255

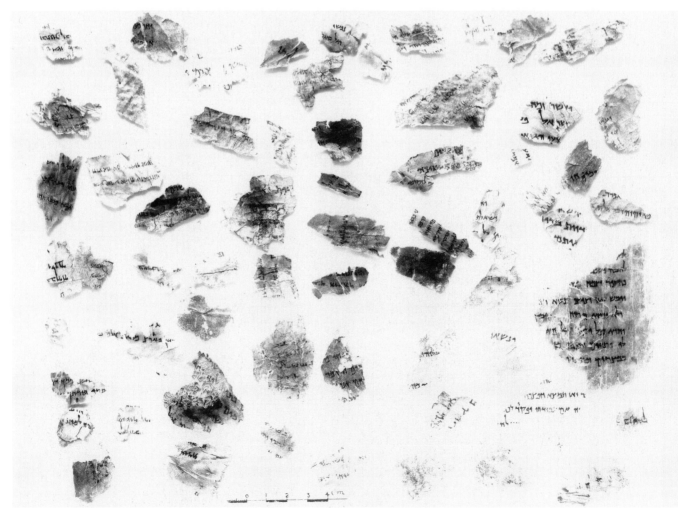

PLATE 256

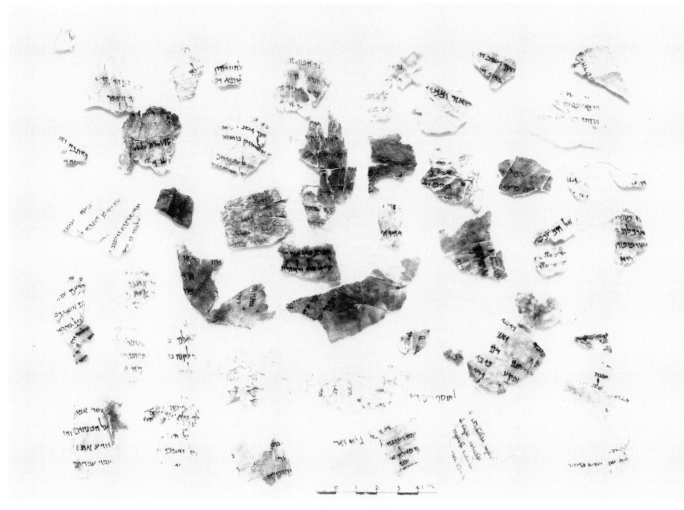

PLATE 257

PLATE 258

PLATE 259

PLATE 260

PLATE 261

PLATE 262

PLATE 263

PLATE 264

PLATE 265

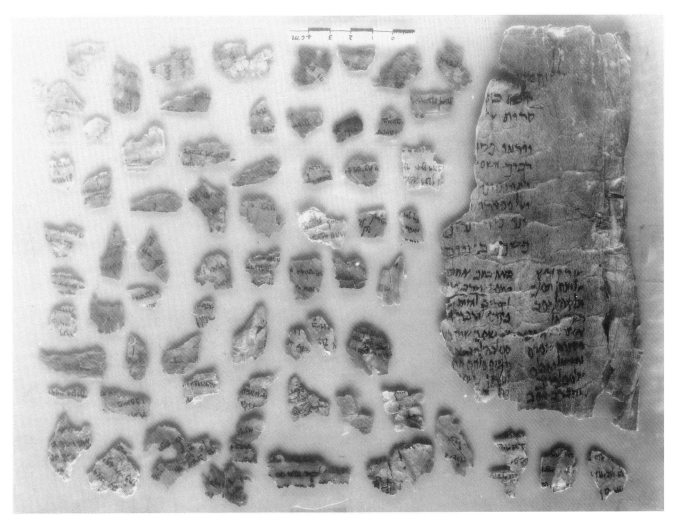

PLATE 266

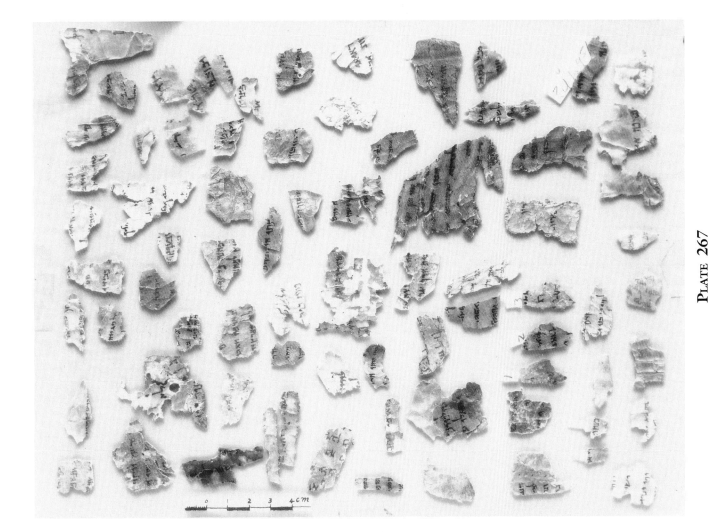

PLATE 267

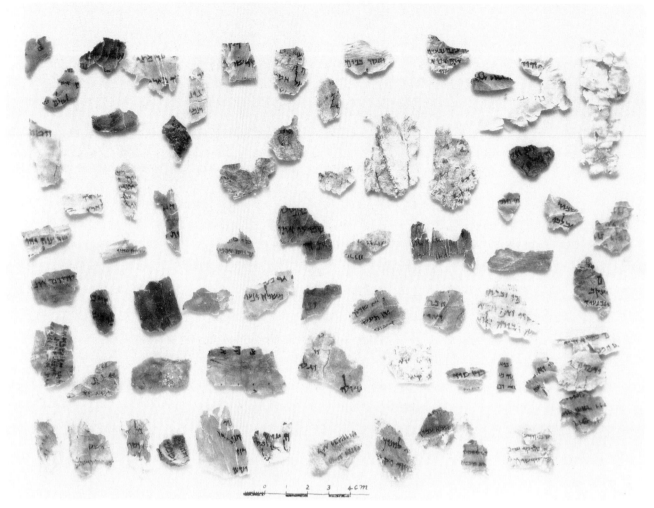

PLATE 268

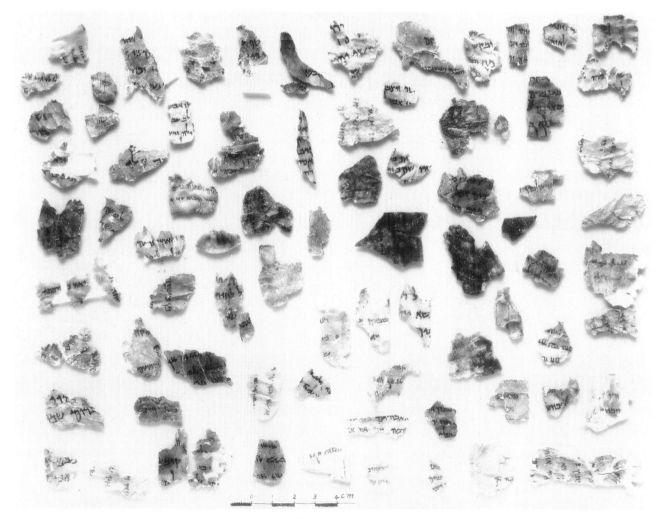

PLATE 269

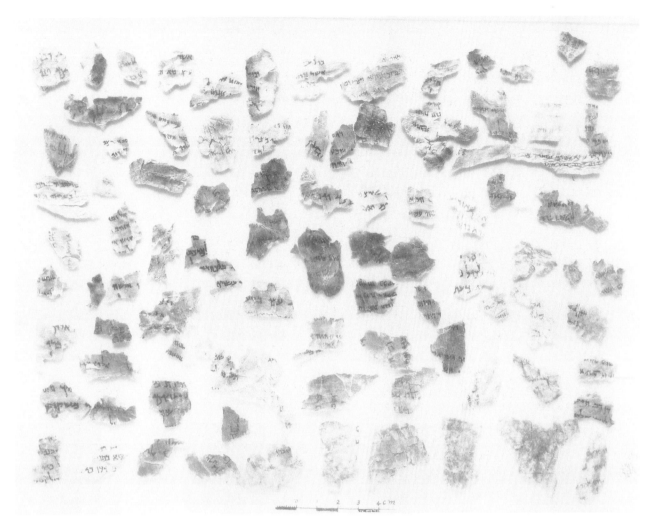

PLATE 270

PLATE 271

PLATE 272

PLATE 273

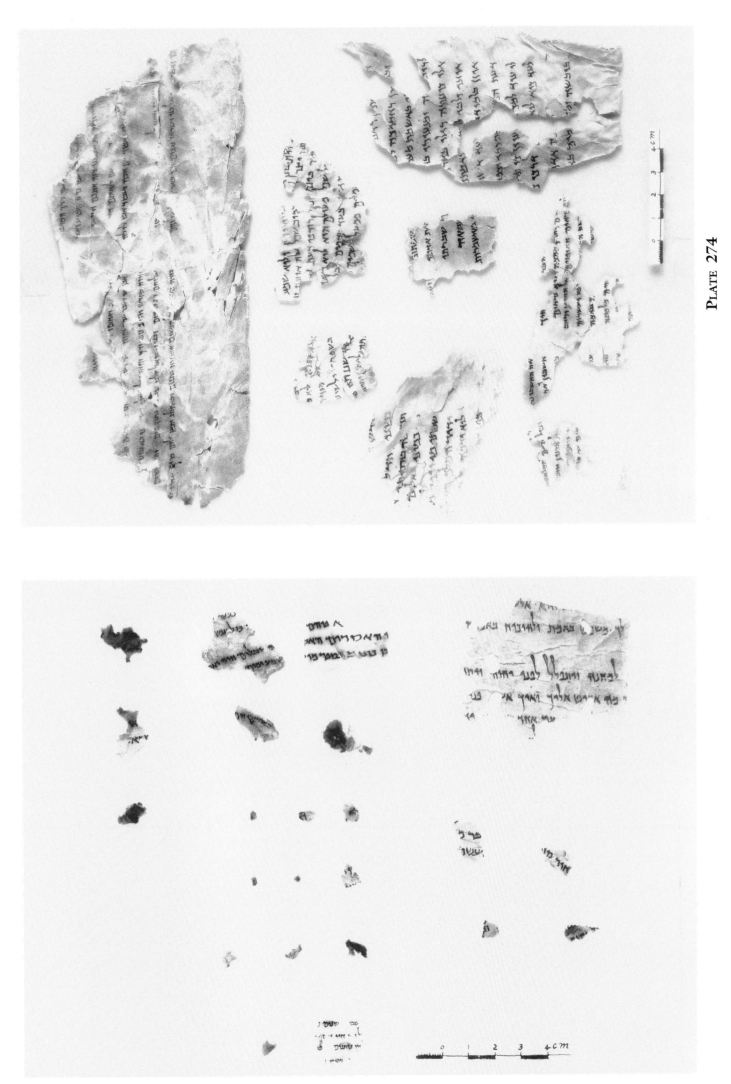

PLATE 274

PLATE 275

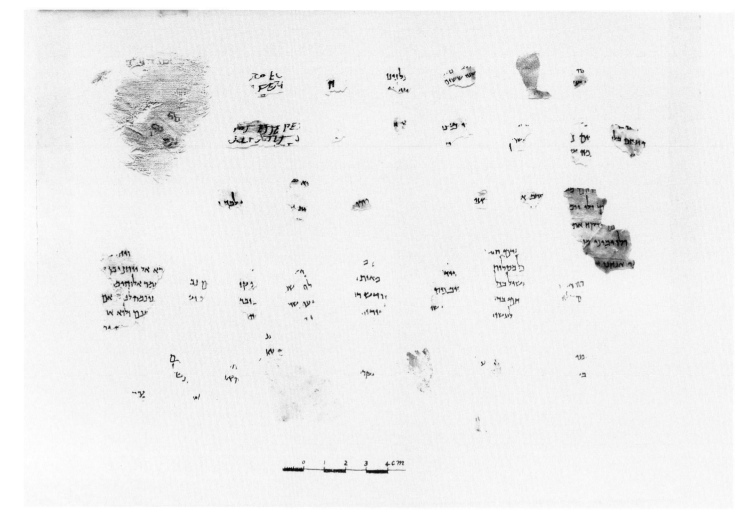

PLATE 276

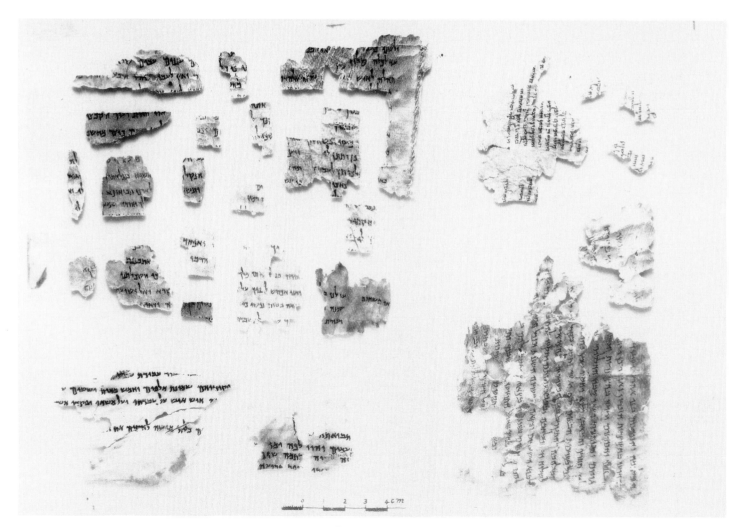

PLATE 277

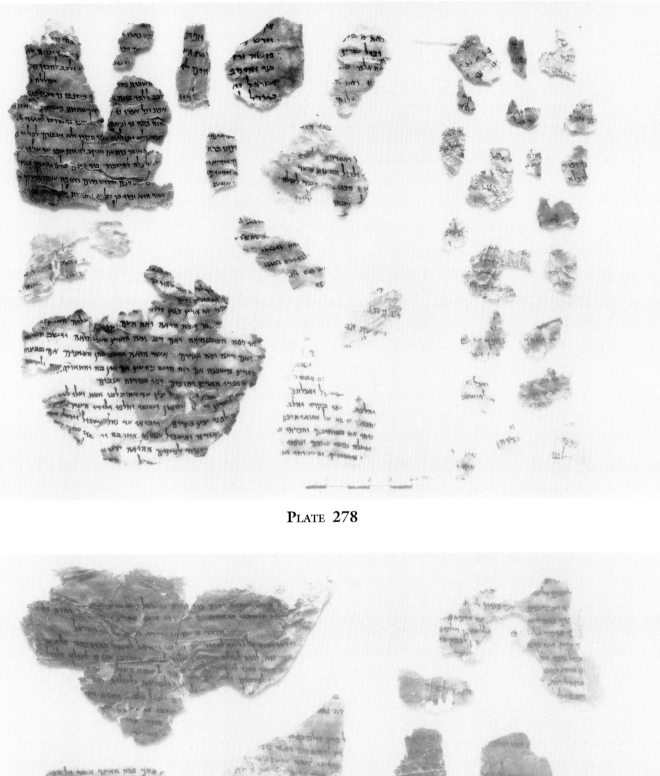

PLATE 278

PLATE 279

PLATE 280

PLATE 281

PLATE 282

PLATE 283

PLATE 284

PLATE 285

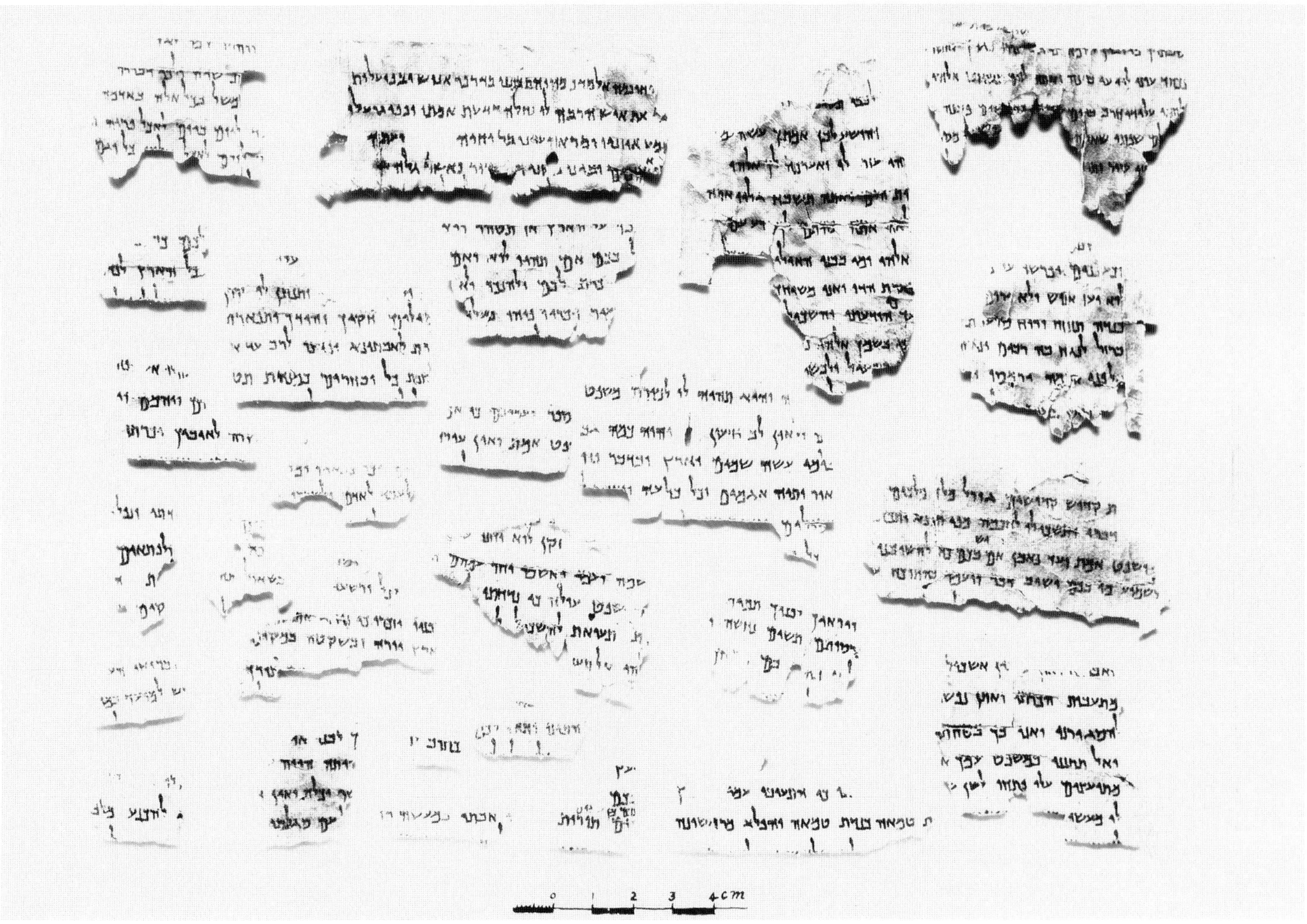

PLATE 286

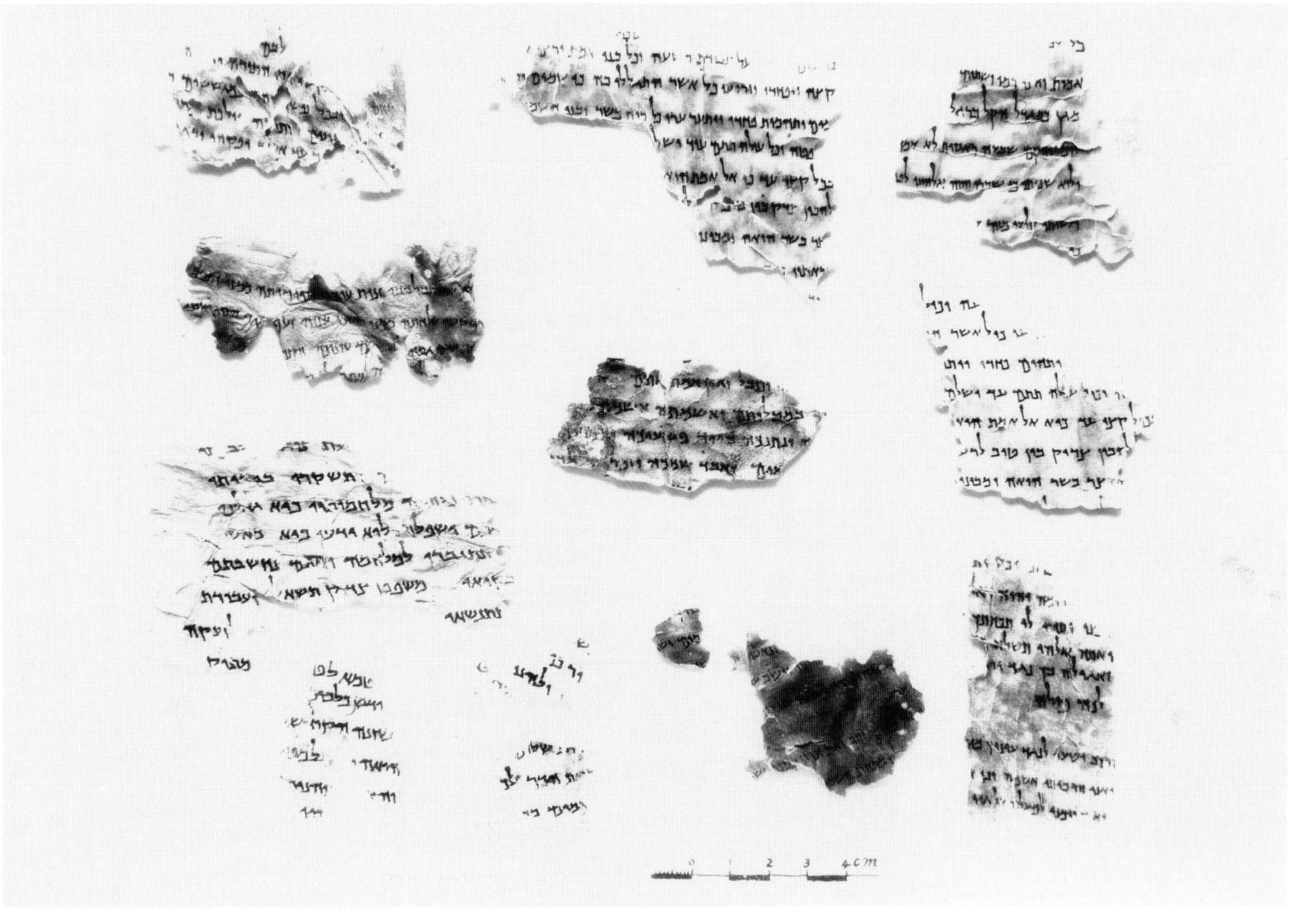

PLATE 287

PLATE 288

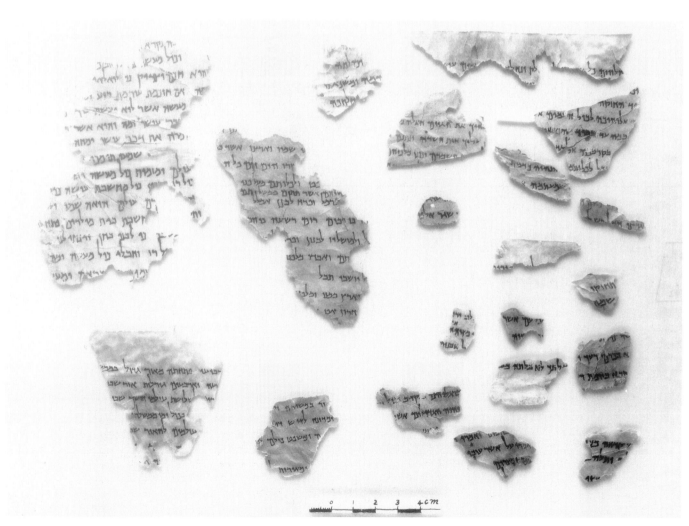

PLATE 289

PLATE 290

PLATE 291

PLATE 292

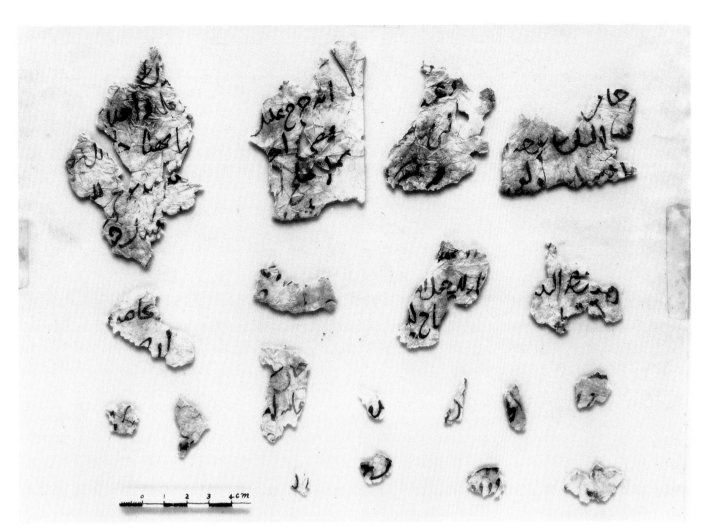

PLATE 293

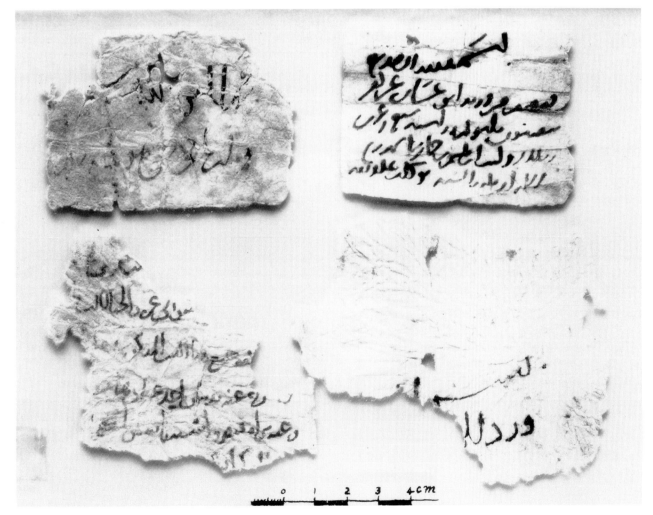

PLATE 294

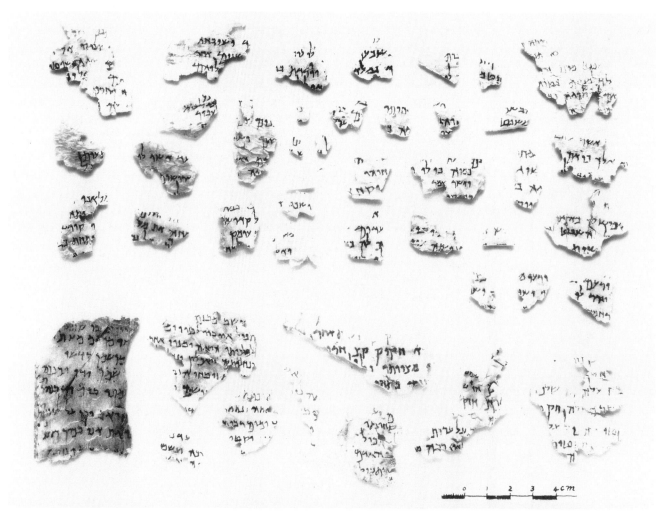

PLATE 295

PLATE 296

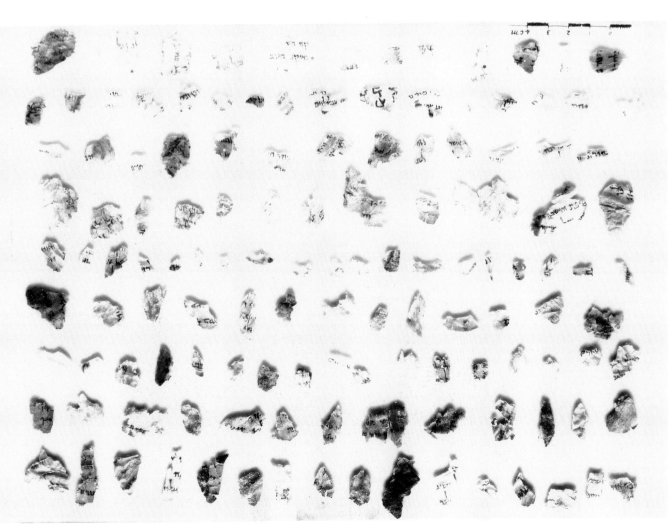

PLATE 309

PLATE 310

PLATE 311

PLATE 312

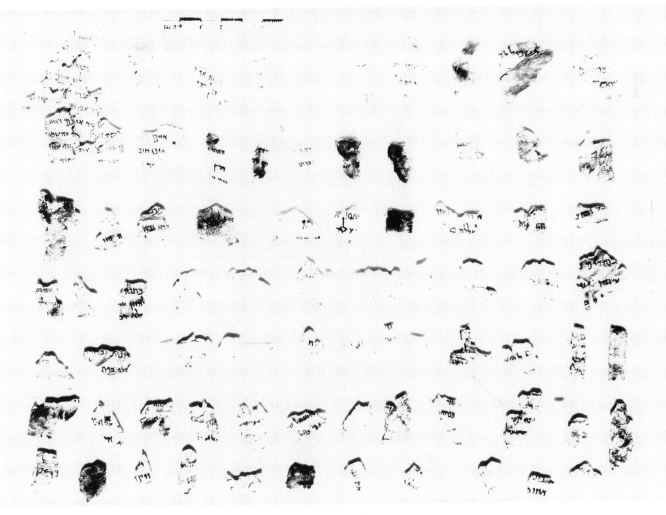

PLATE 313

PLATE 314

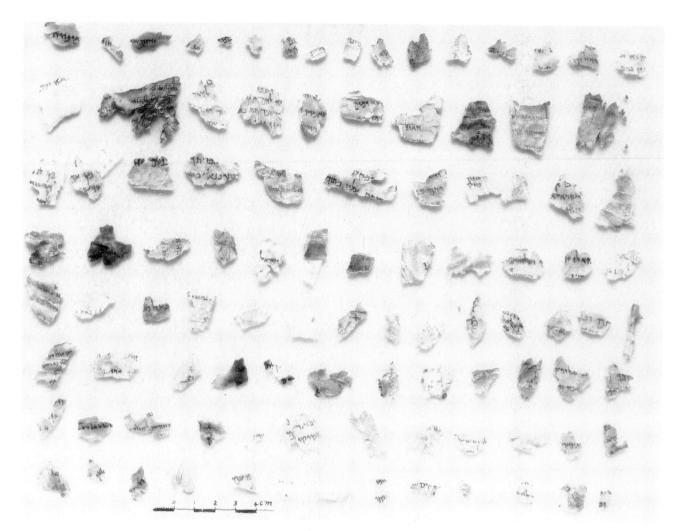

PLATE 315

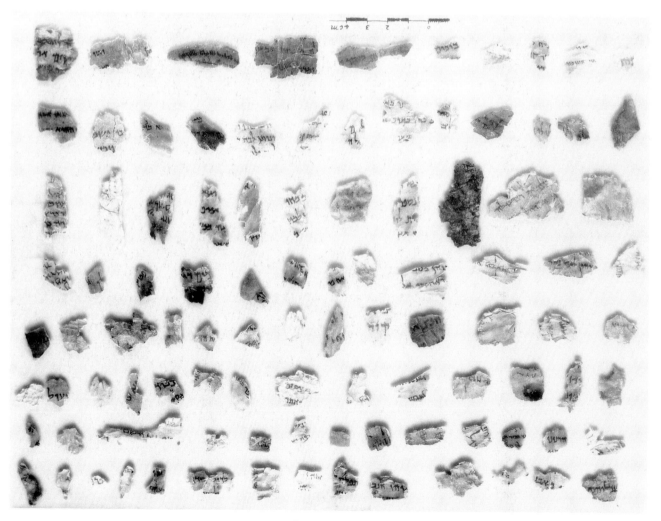

PLATE 316

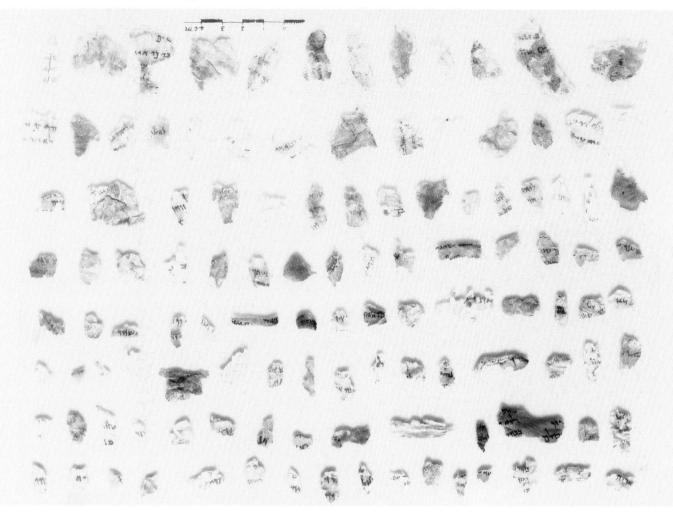

PLATE 317

PLATE 318

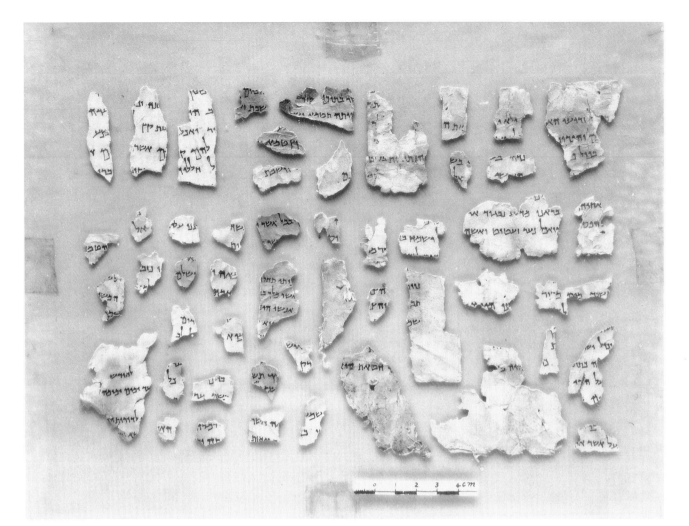

PLATE 319

PLATE 320

PLATE 321

PLATE 322

PLATE 323

PLATE 324

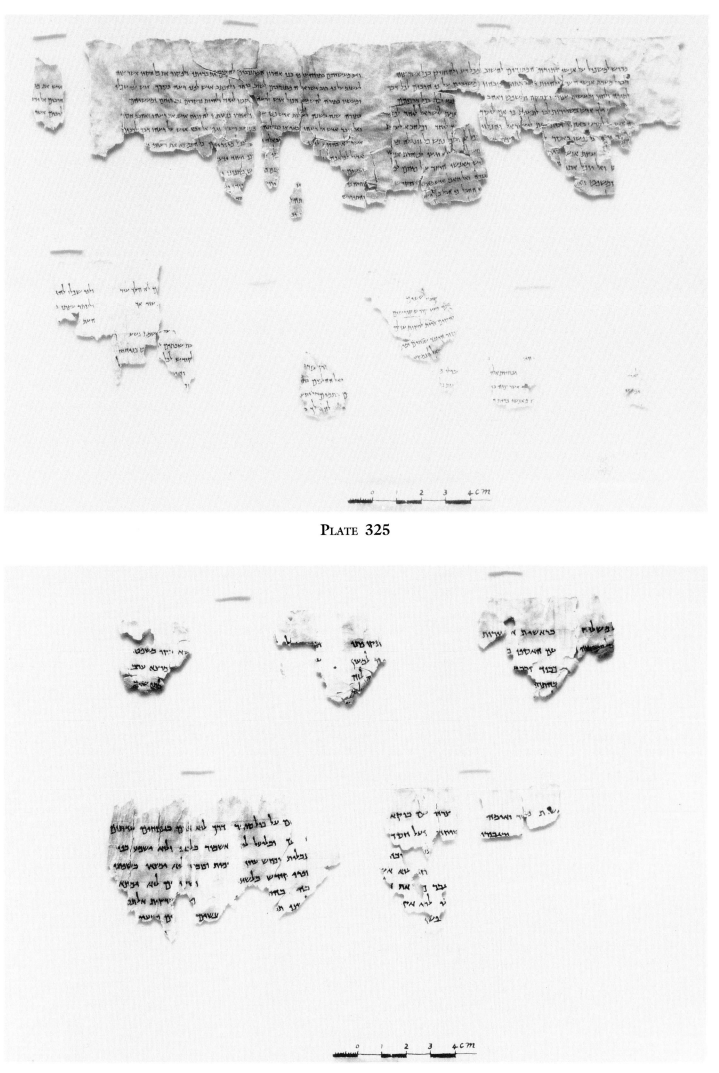

PLATE 325

PLATE 326

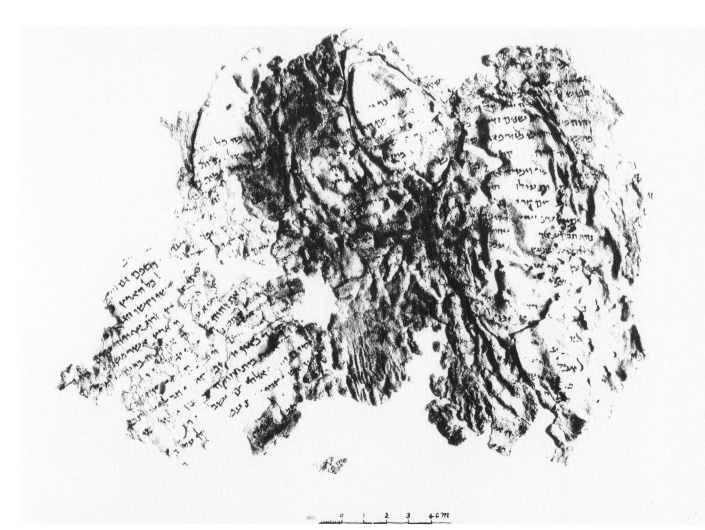

PLATE 327

PLATE 328

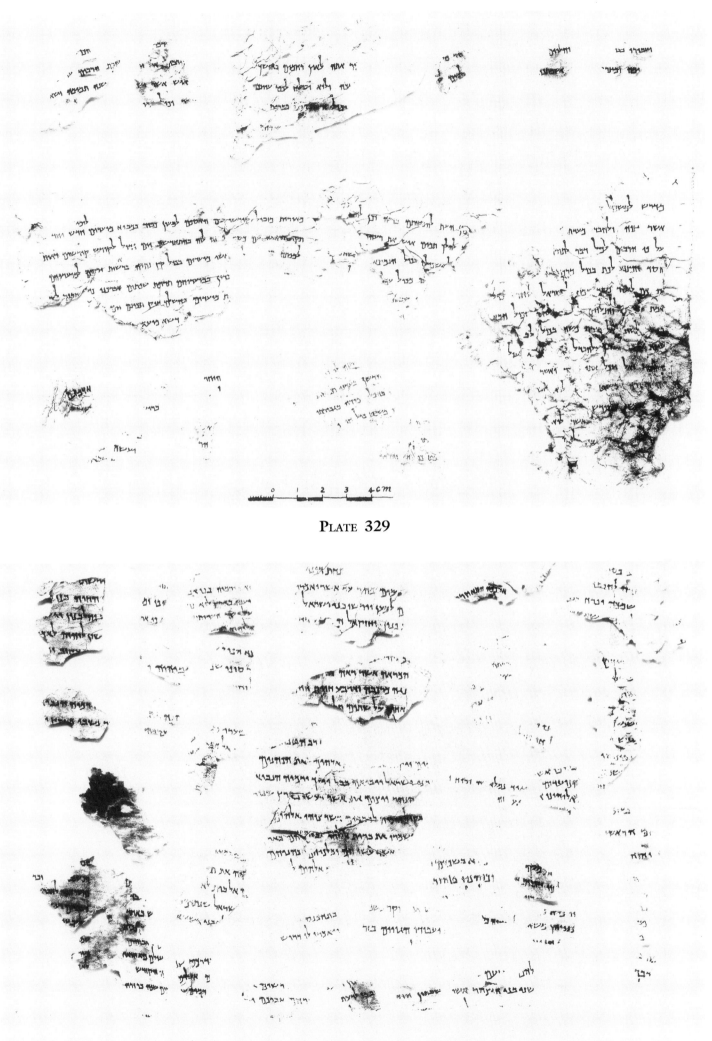

PLATE 329

PLATE 330

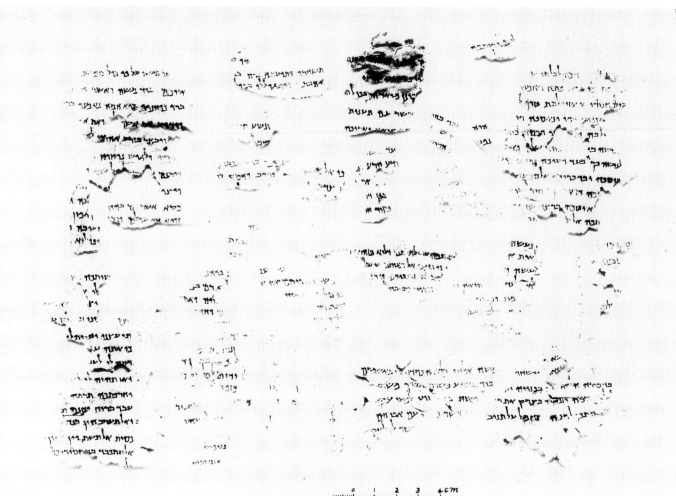

PLATE 331

PLATE 332

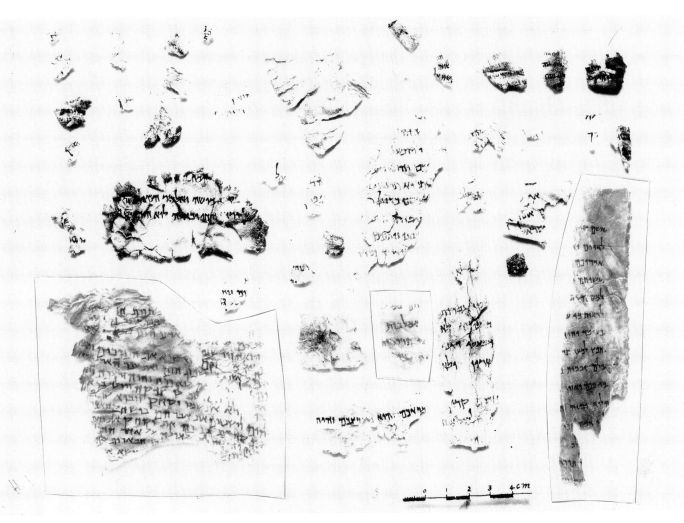

PLATE 341

PLATE 342

PLATE 343

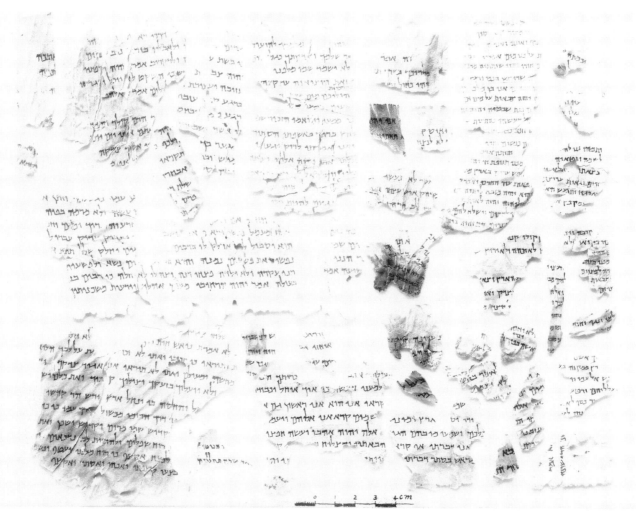

PLATE 344

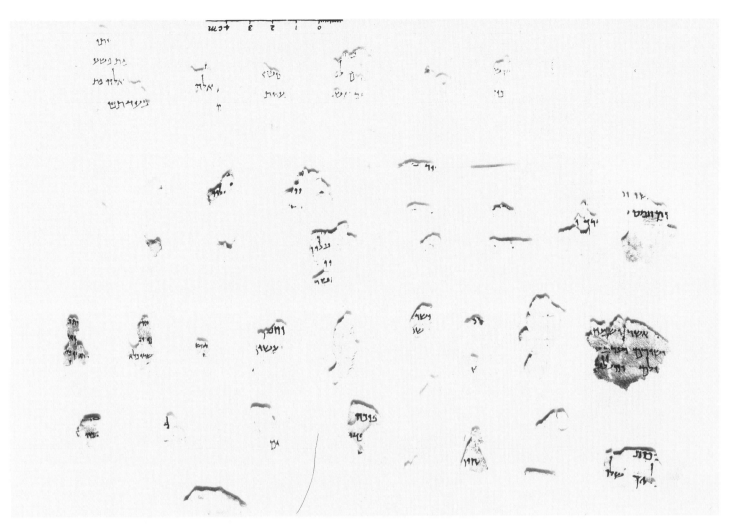

PLATE 345

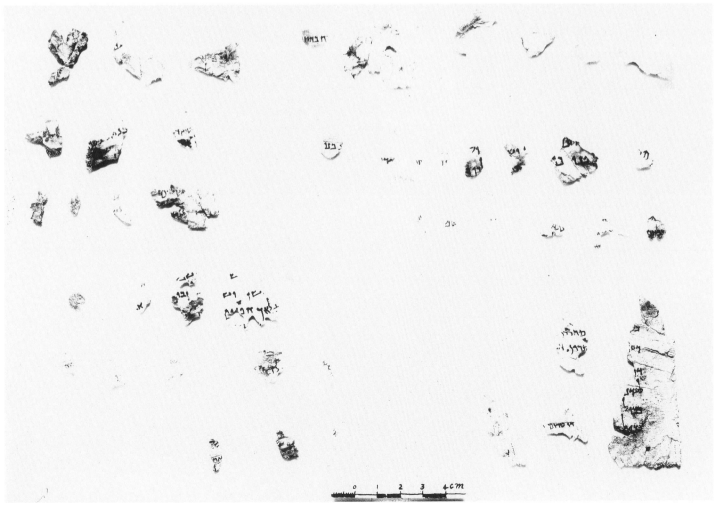

PLATE 346

PLATE 347

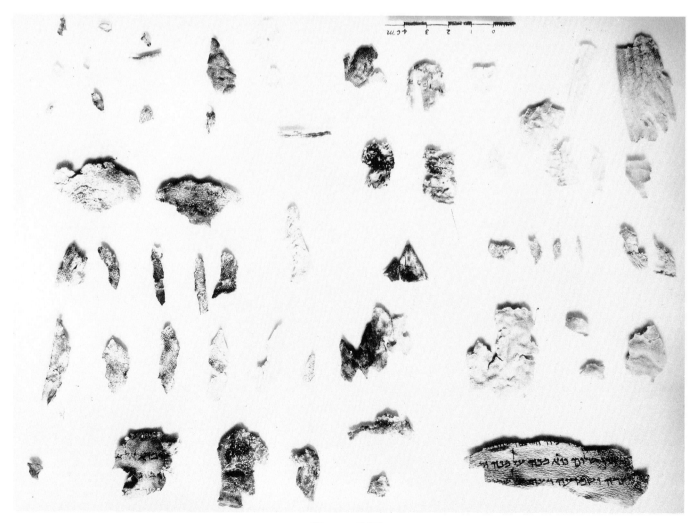

PLATE 348

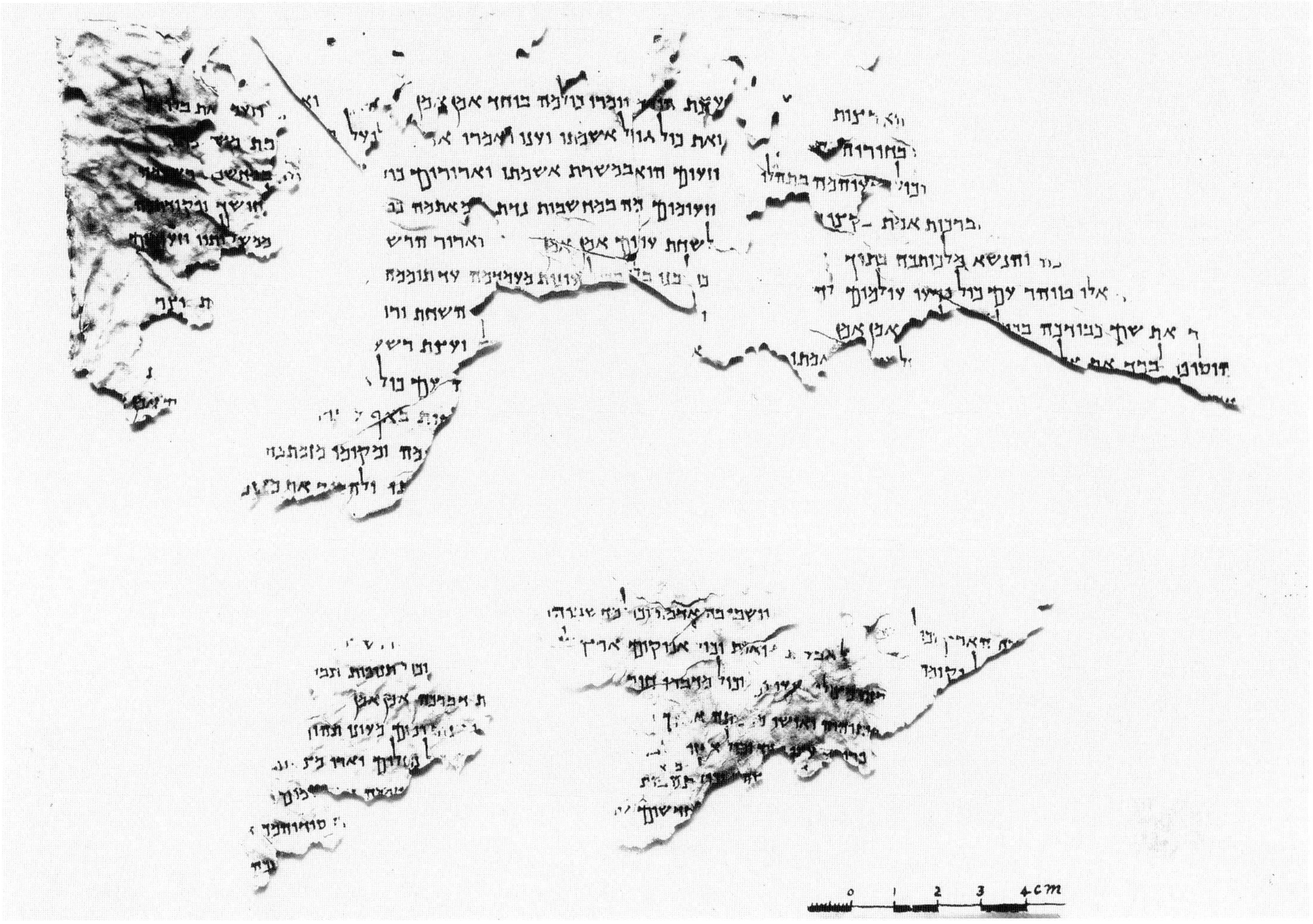

Plate 349

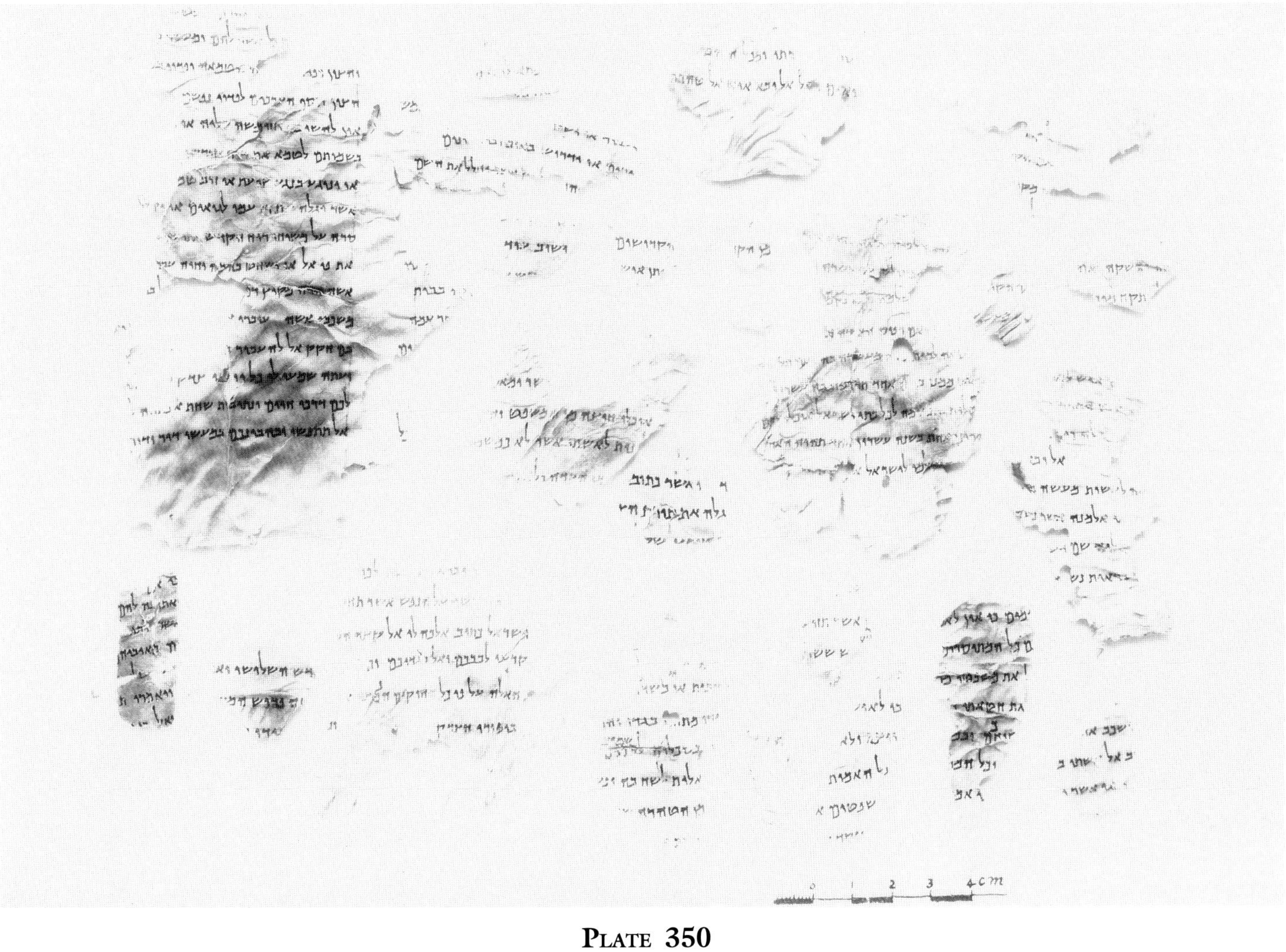

Plate 350

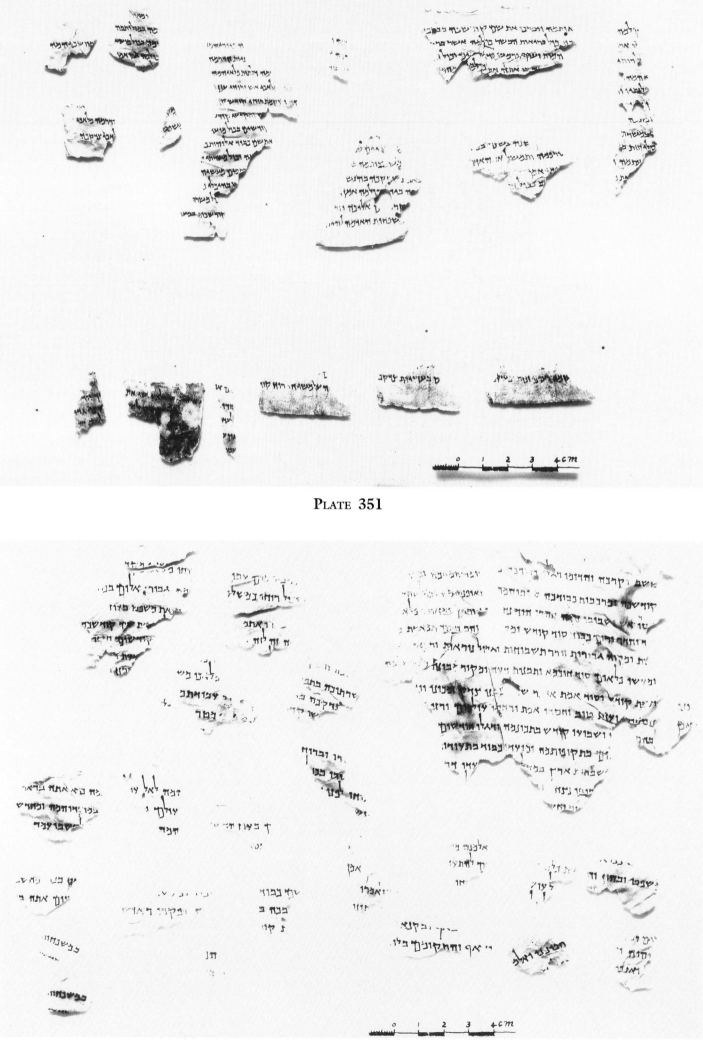

PLATE 351

PLATE 352

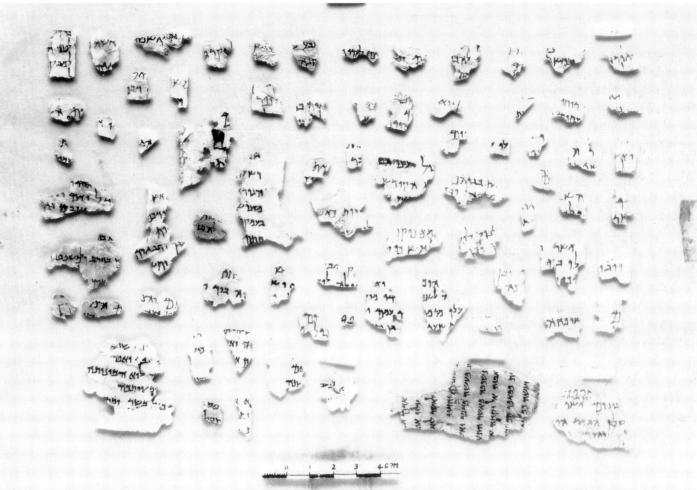

PLATE 380

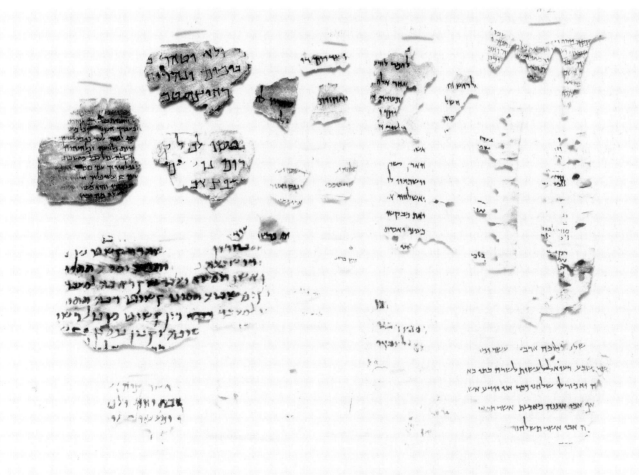

PLATE 381

PLATE 382

PLATE 383

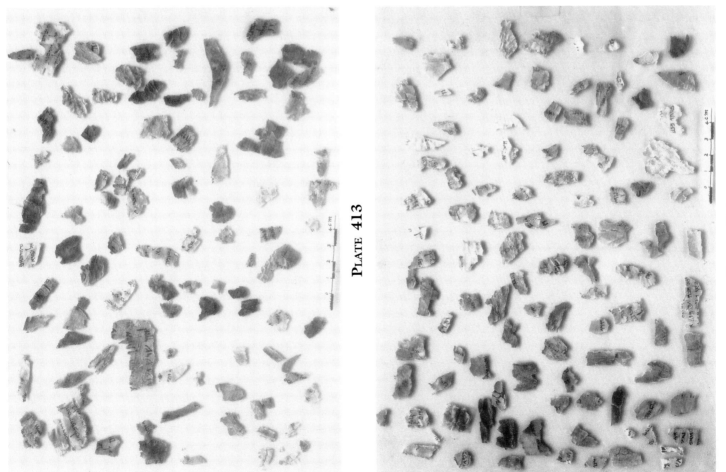

PLATE 412

PLATE 413

PLATE 414

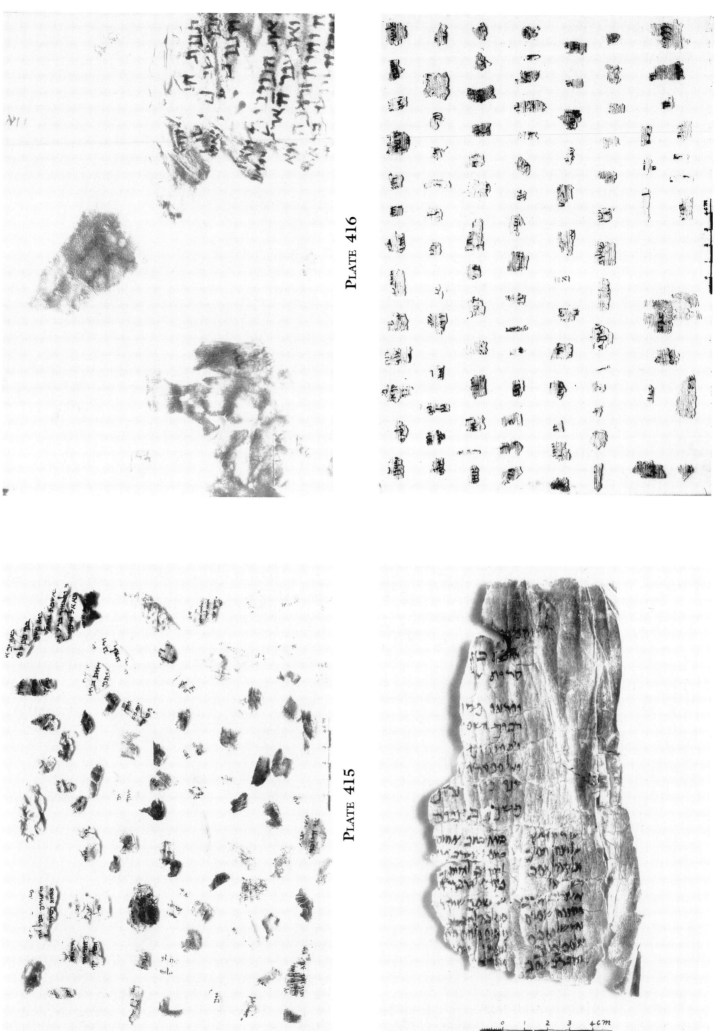

PLATE 416

PLATE 418

PLATE 415

PLATE 417

PLATE 419

PLATE 420

PLATE 421

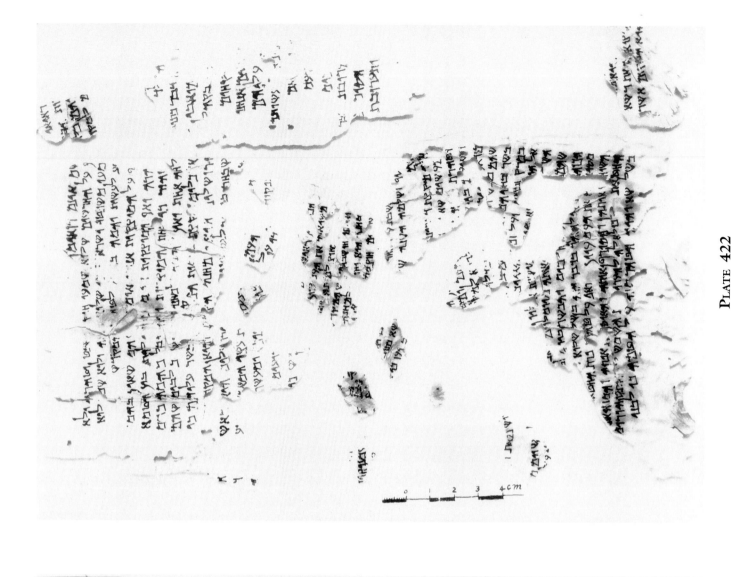

PLATE 422

PLATE 423

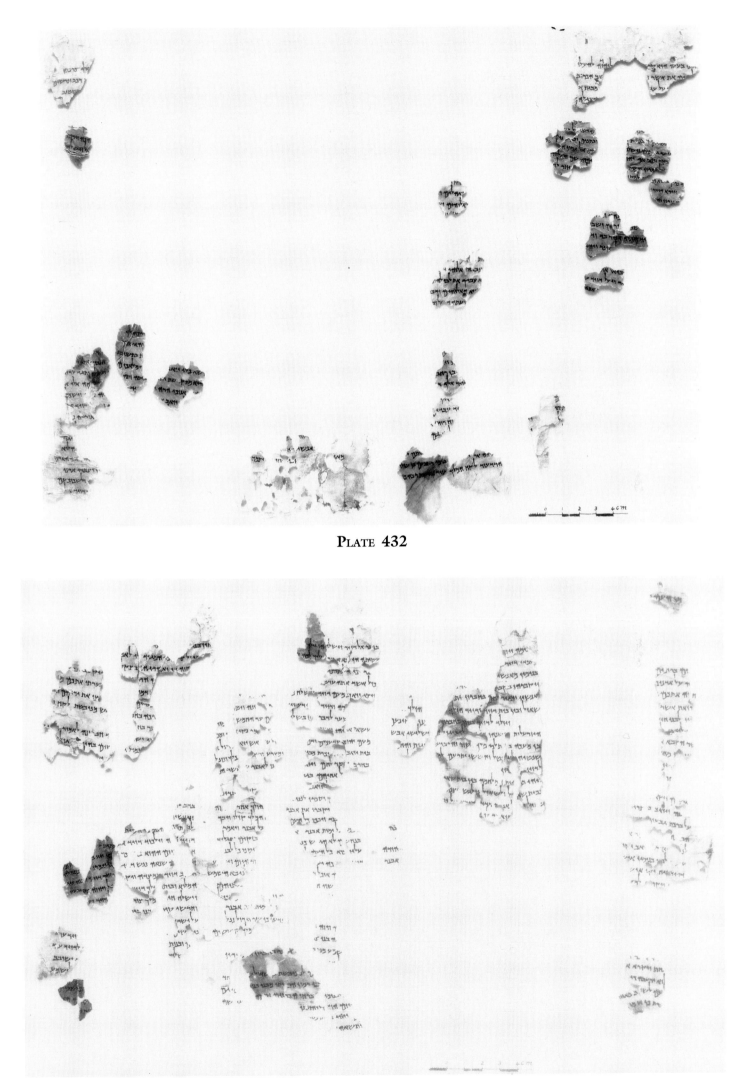

PLATE 432

PLATE 433

PLATE 434

PLATE 435

PLATE 436

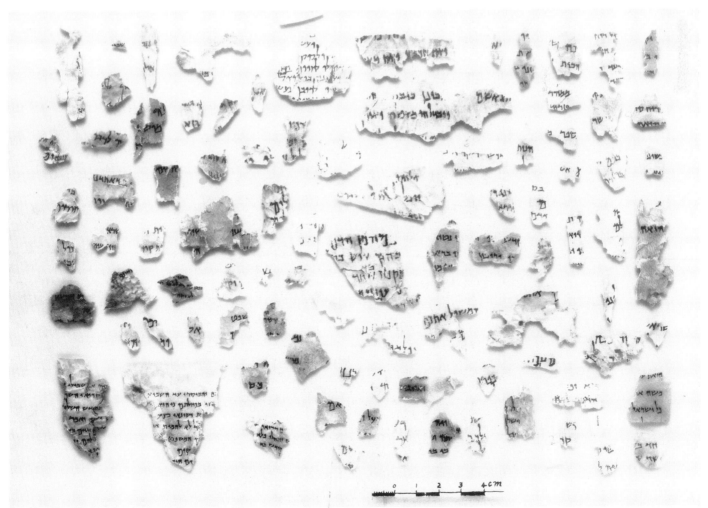

PLATE 437

PLATE 438

PLATE 439

PLATE 440

PLATE 441

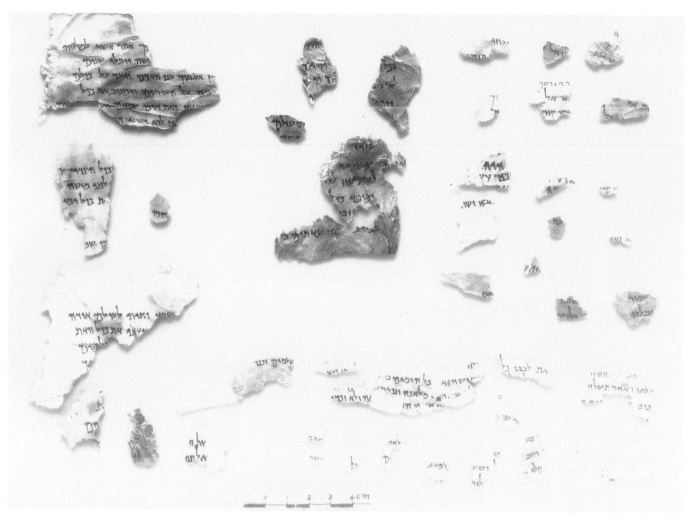

PLATE 442

PLATE 443

PLATE **444**

PLATE **445**

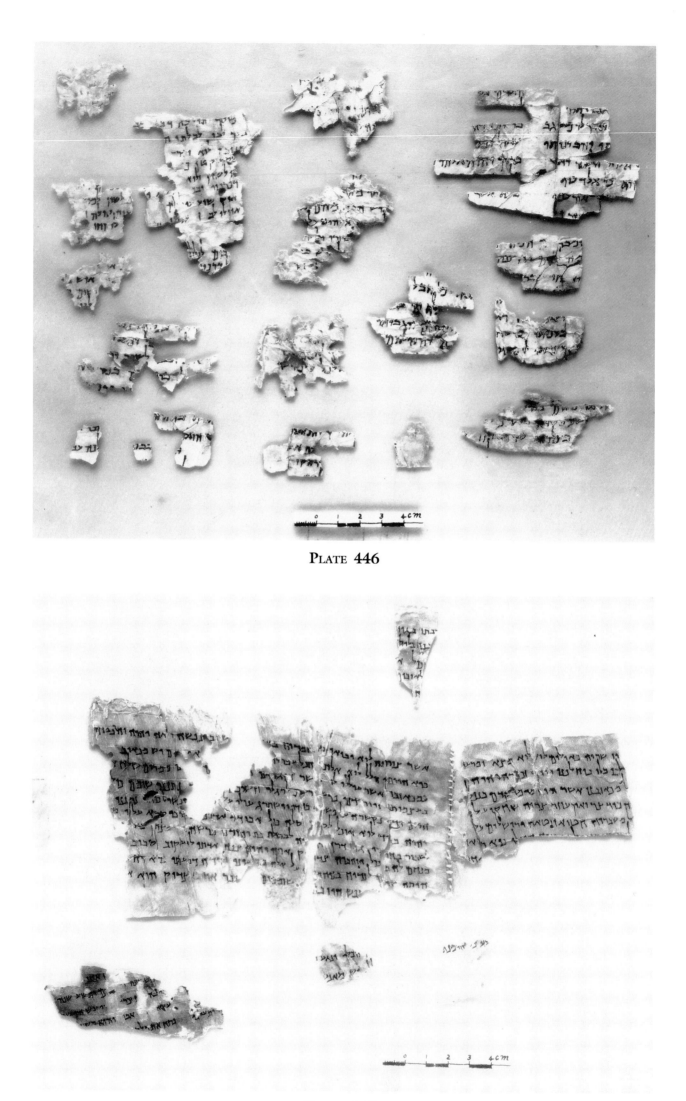

PLATE 446

PLATE 447

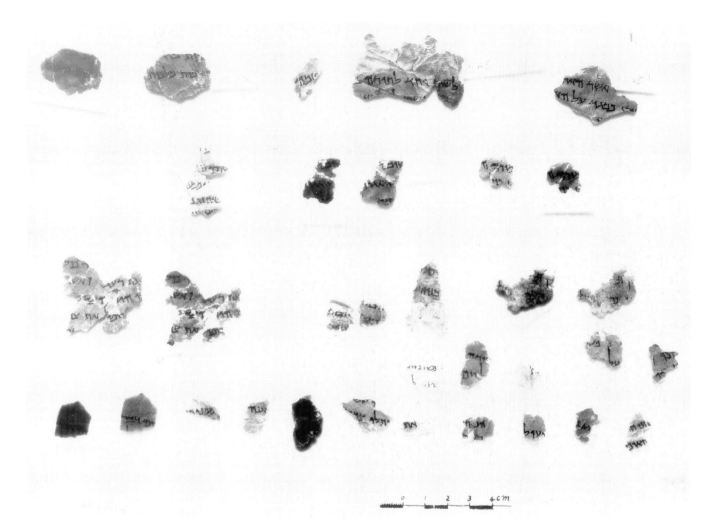

PLATE 456

PLATE 457

PLATE 458

PLATE 459

PLATE 460

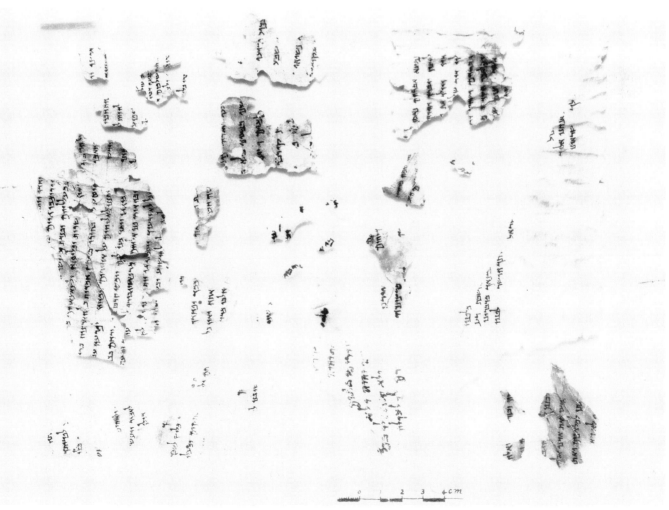

PLATE 461

PLATE 462

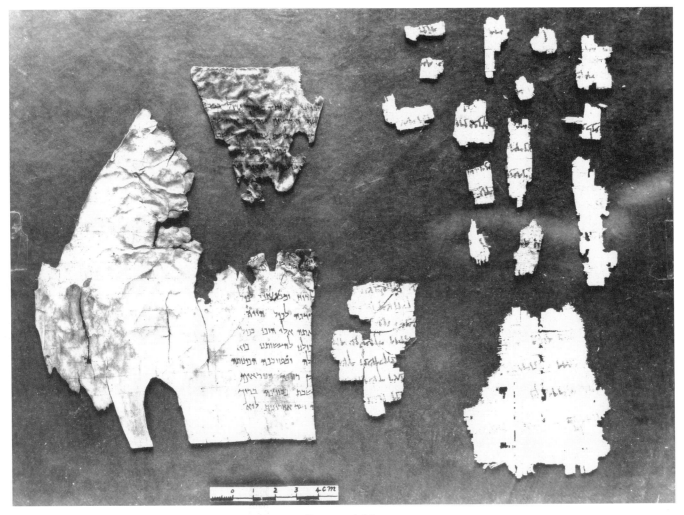

PLATE 463

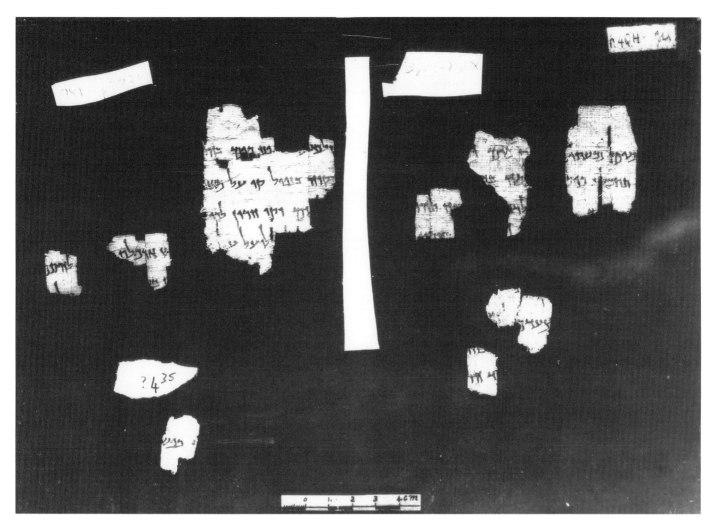

PLATE 464

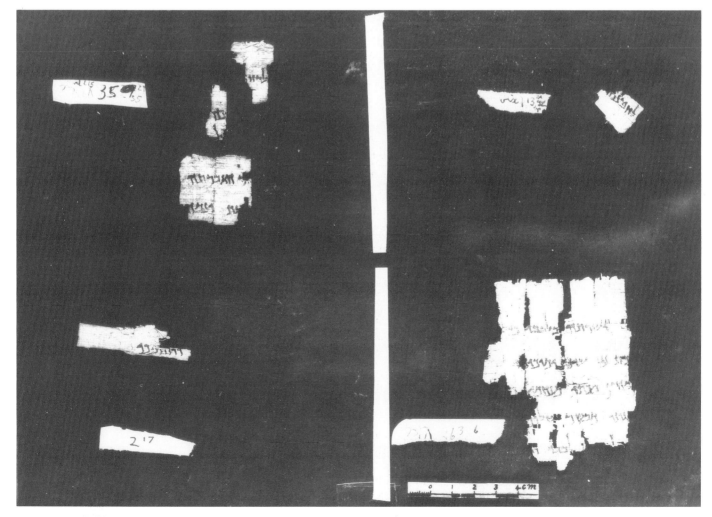

PLATE 465

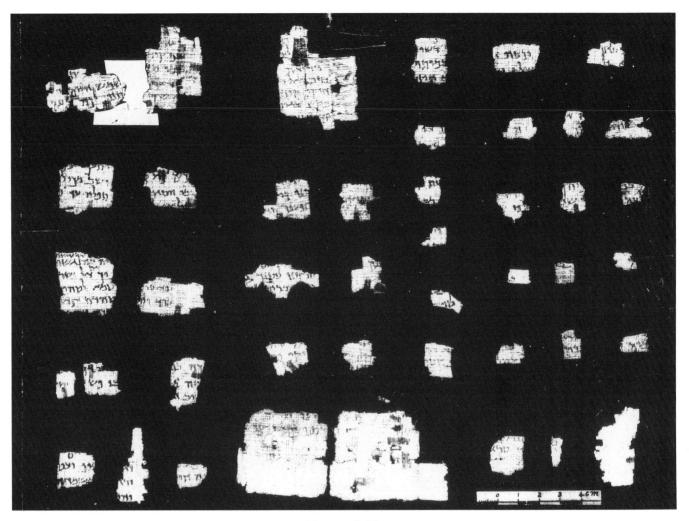

PLATE 466

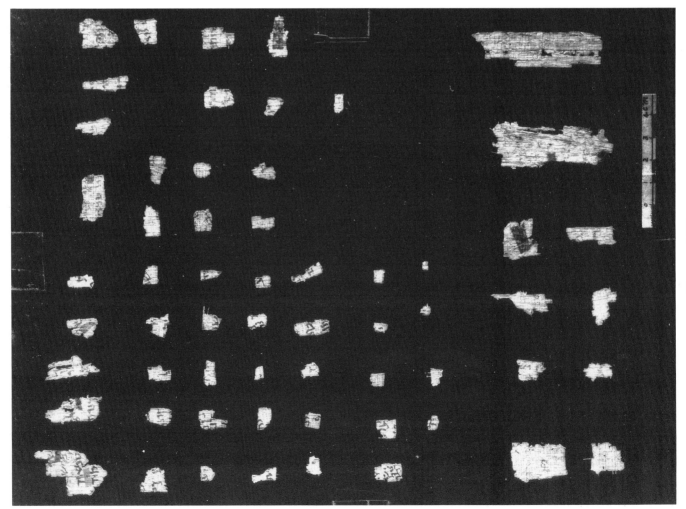

PLATE 467

PLATE 469

PLATE 468

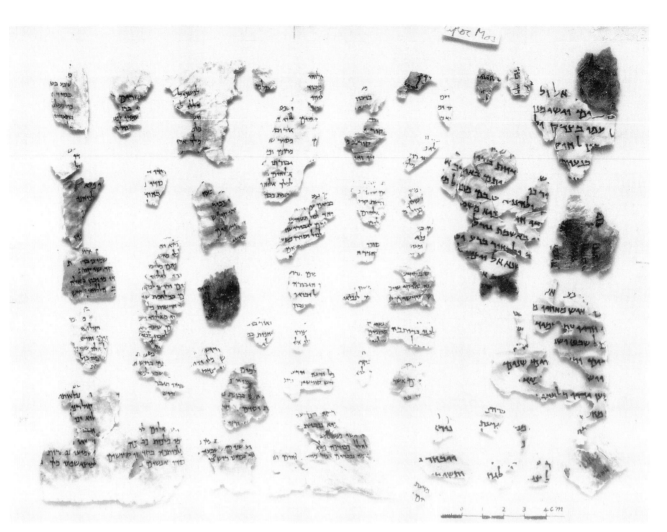

PLATE 470

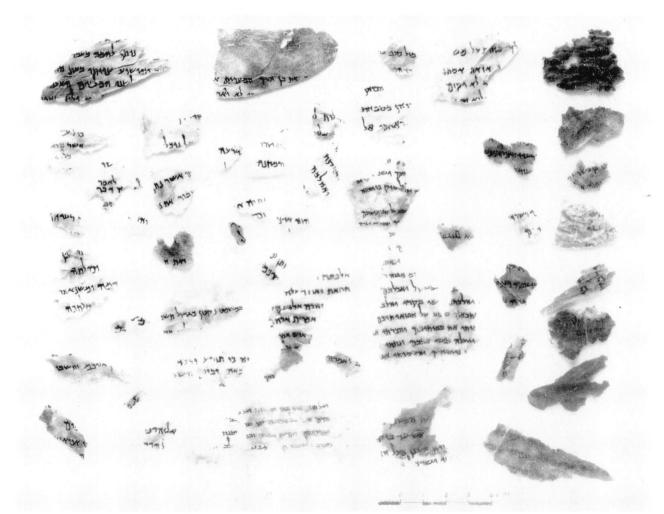

PLATE 471

Plate 472

Plate 473

PLATE 474

PLATE 475

PLATE 476

PLATE 478

PLATE 477

PLATE 480

PLATE 479

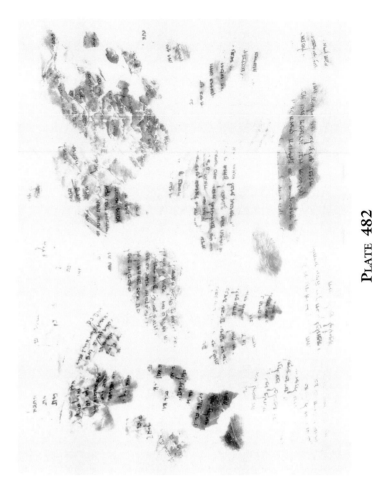

PLATE 482

PLATE 481

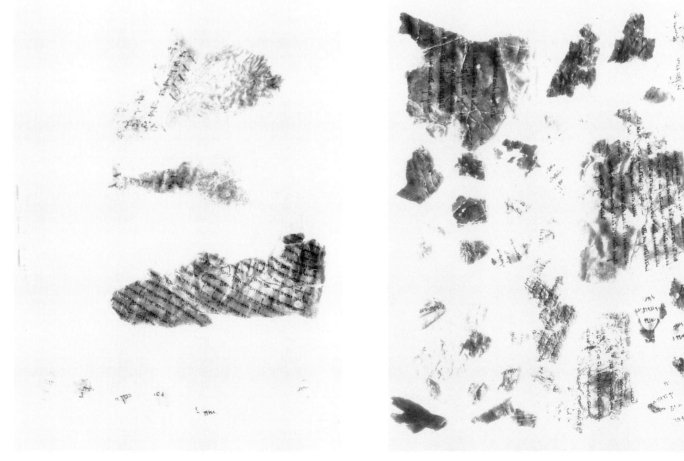

PLATE 483

PLATE 484

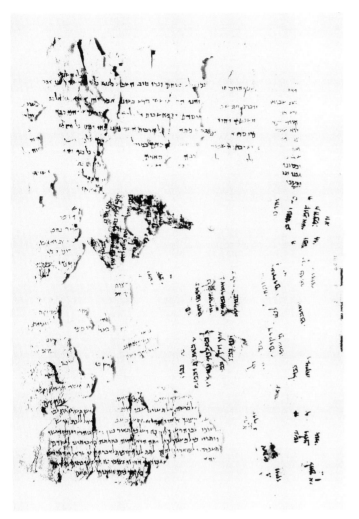

PLATE 486

PLATE 488

PLATE 485

PLATE 487

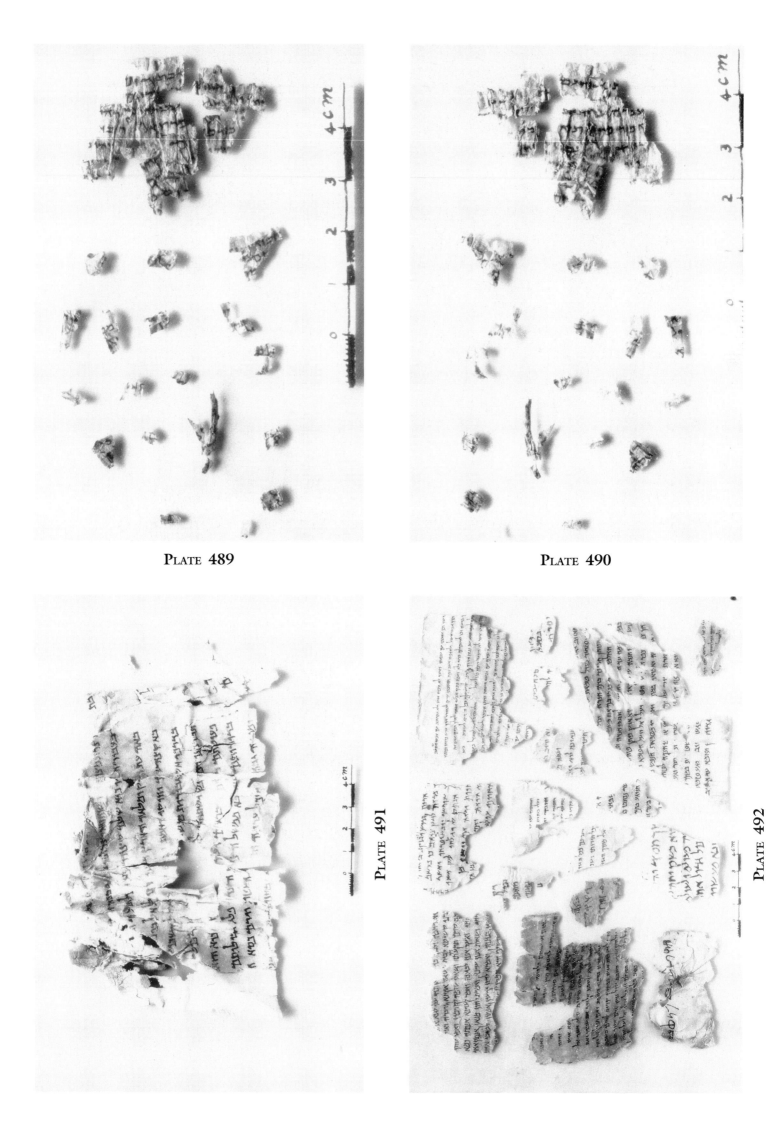

PLATE 489

PLATE 490

PLATE 491

PLATE 492

PLATE 493

PLATE 494

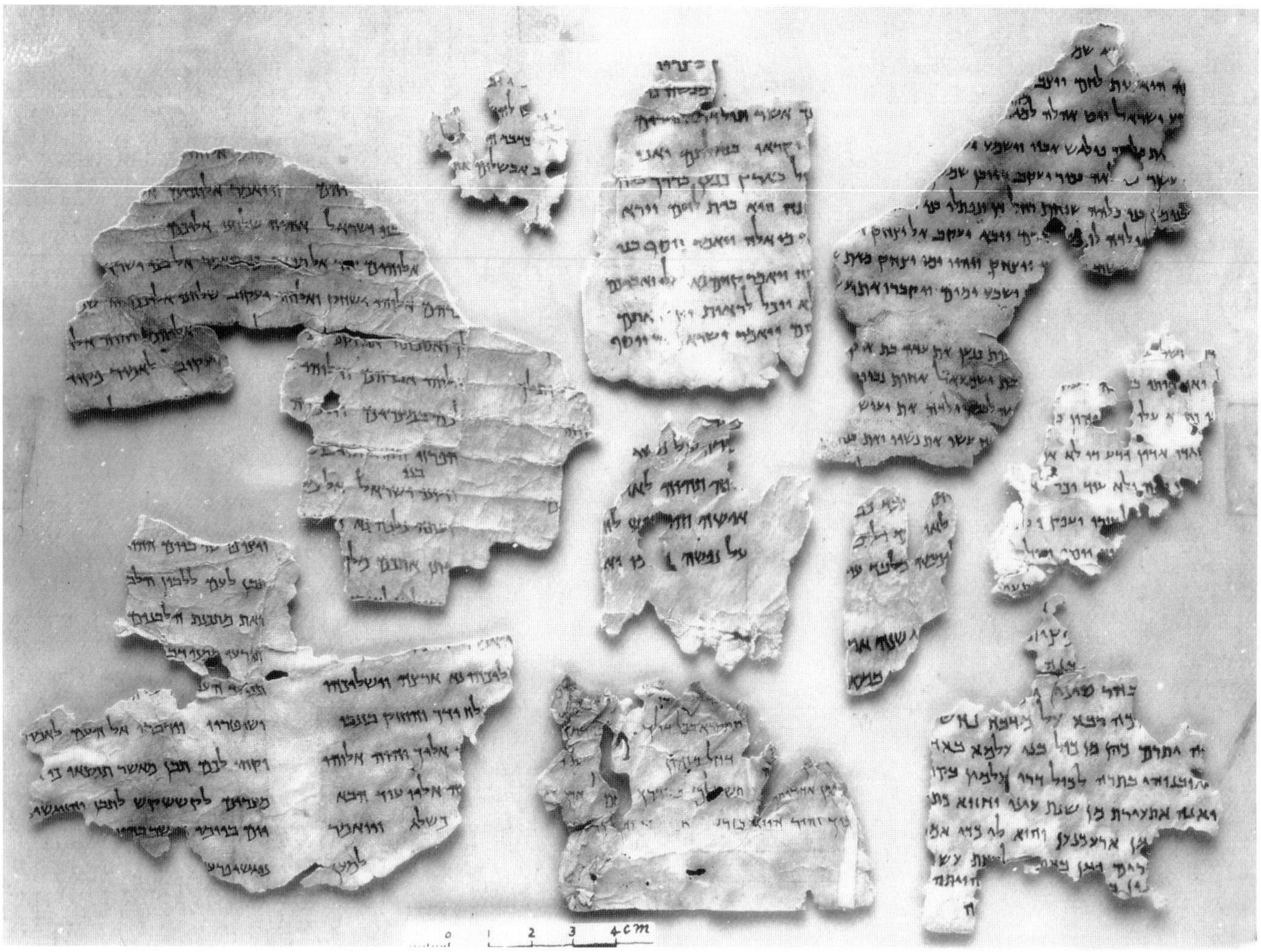

PLATE 495

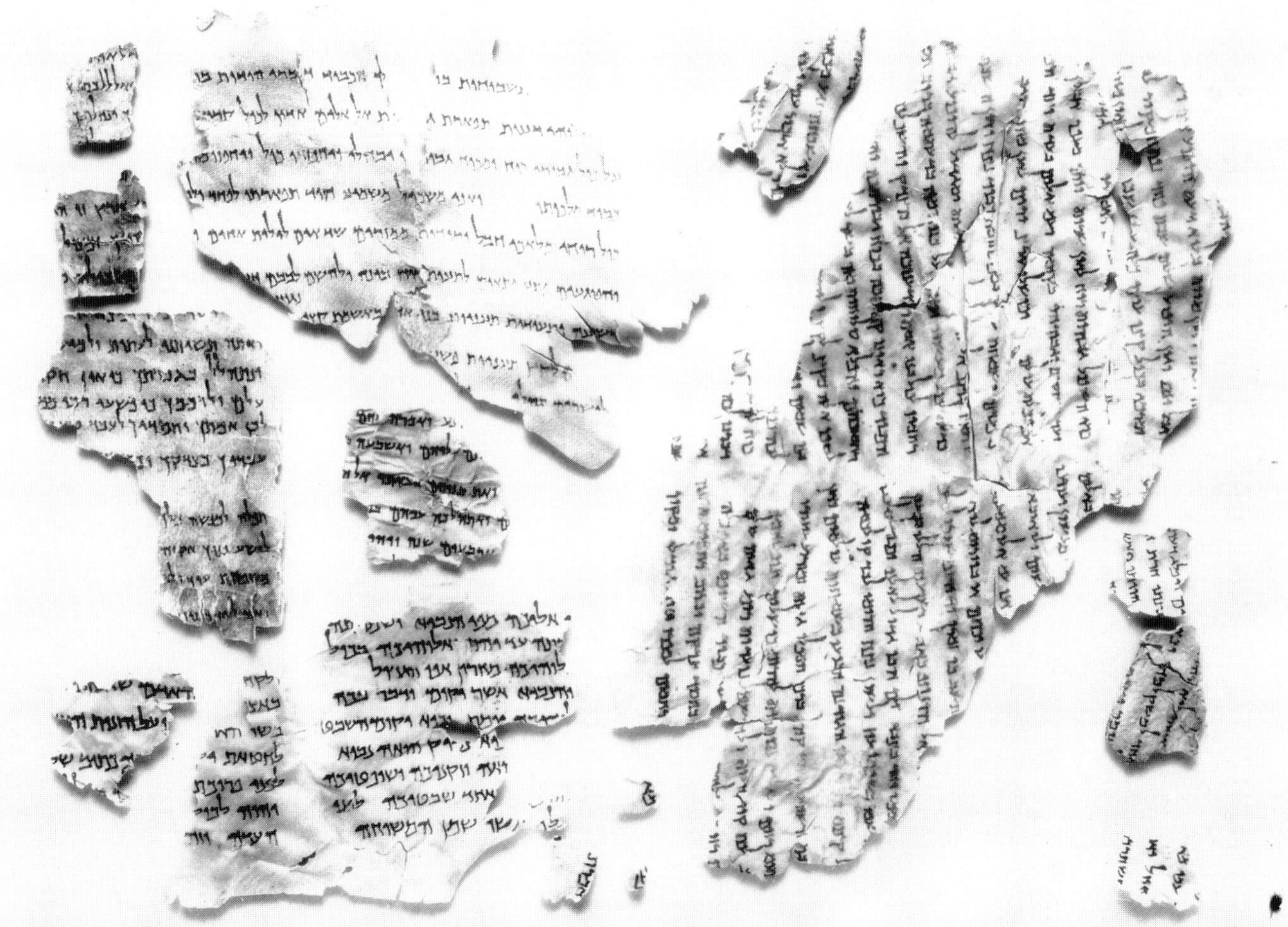

PLATE 496

PLATE 497

PLATE 498

PLATE 499

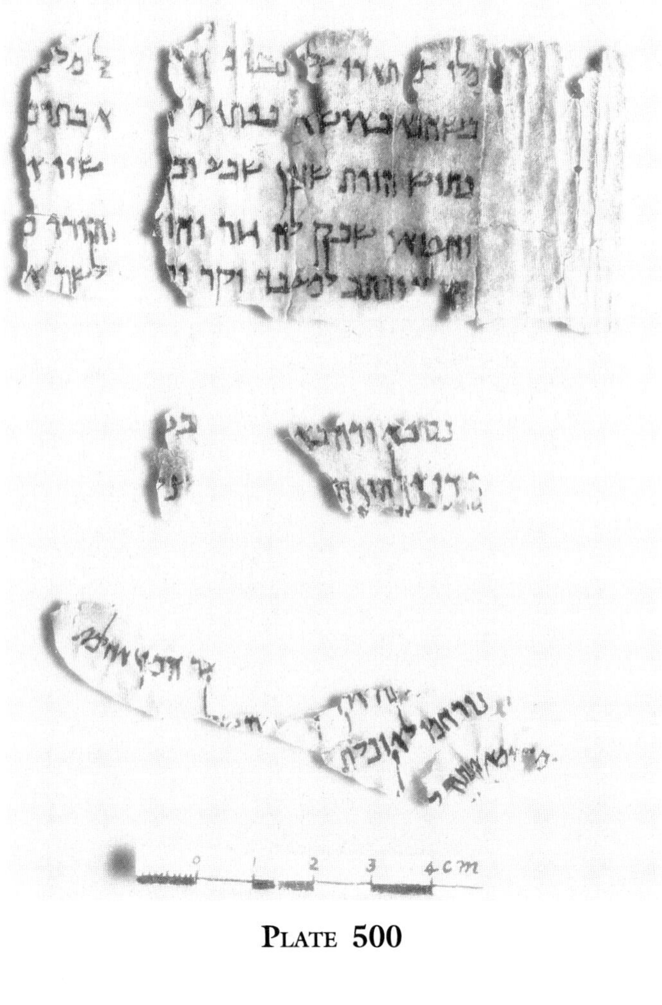

PLATE 501

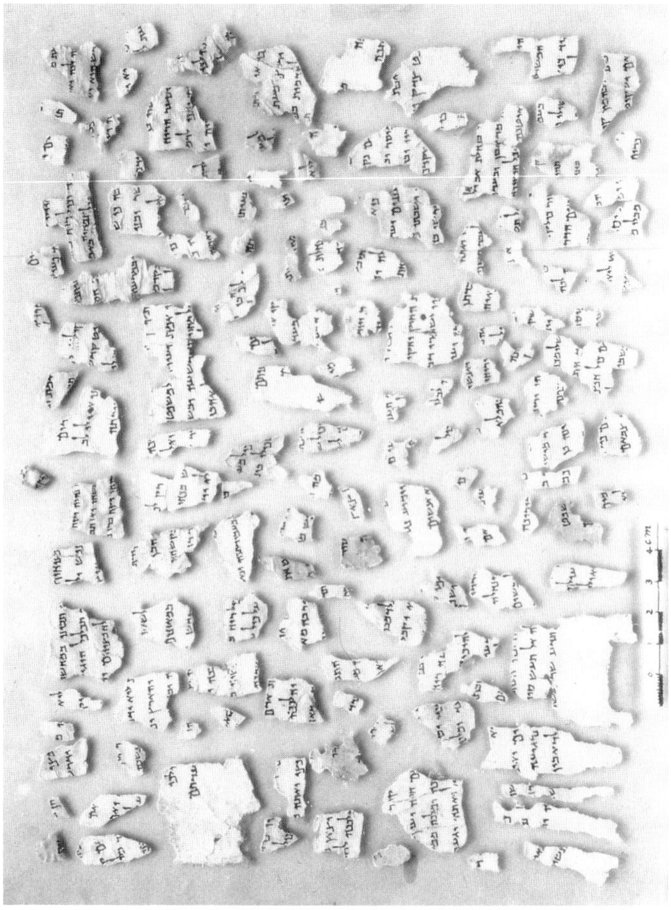

PLATE 503

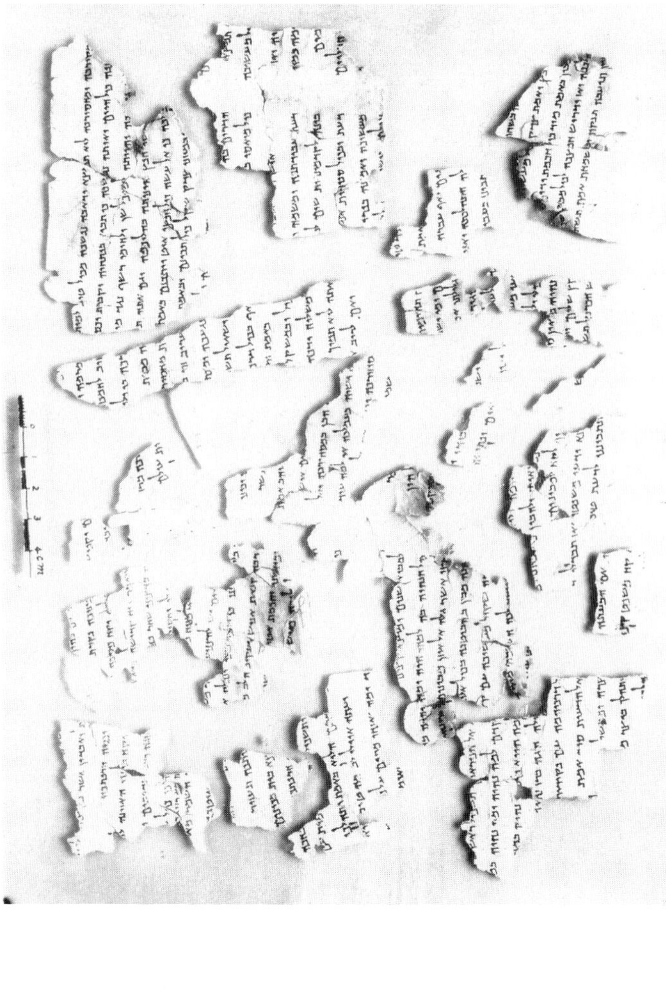

PLATE 500

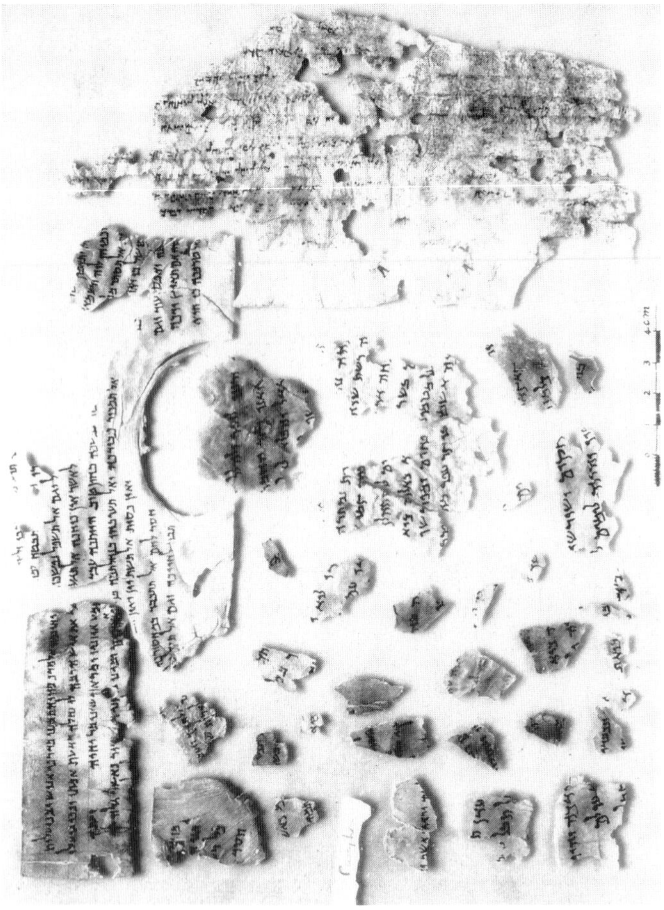

PLATE 502

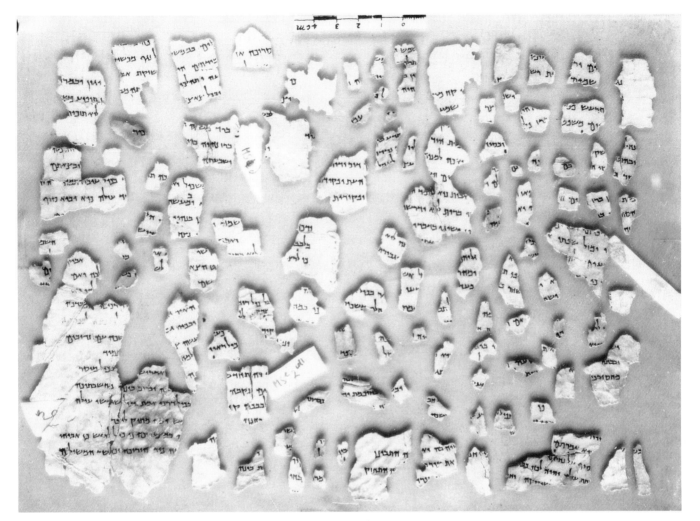

PLATE 504

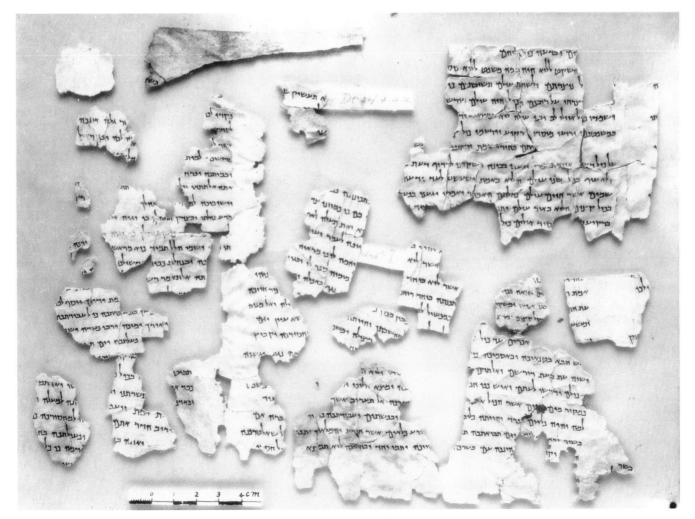

PLATE 505

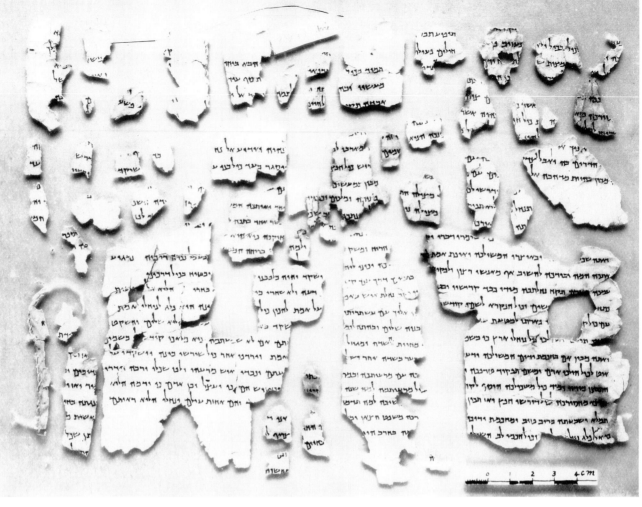

PLATE 506

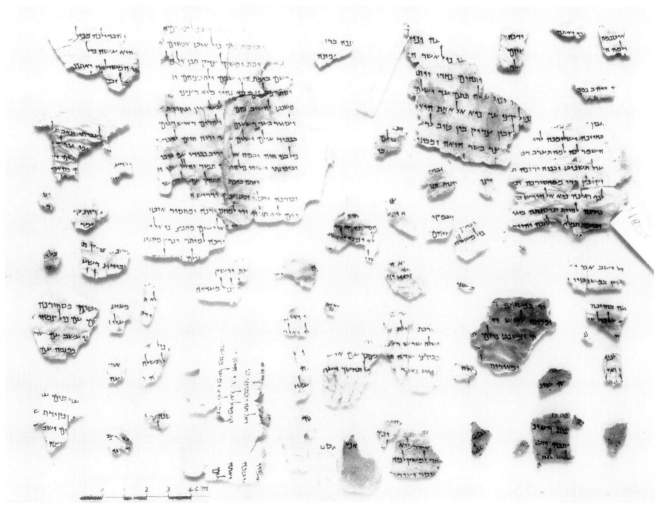

PLATE 507

PLATE 508

PLATE 509

PLATE 510

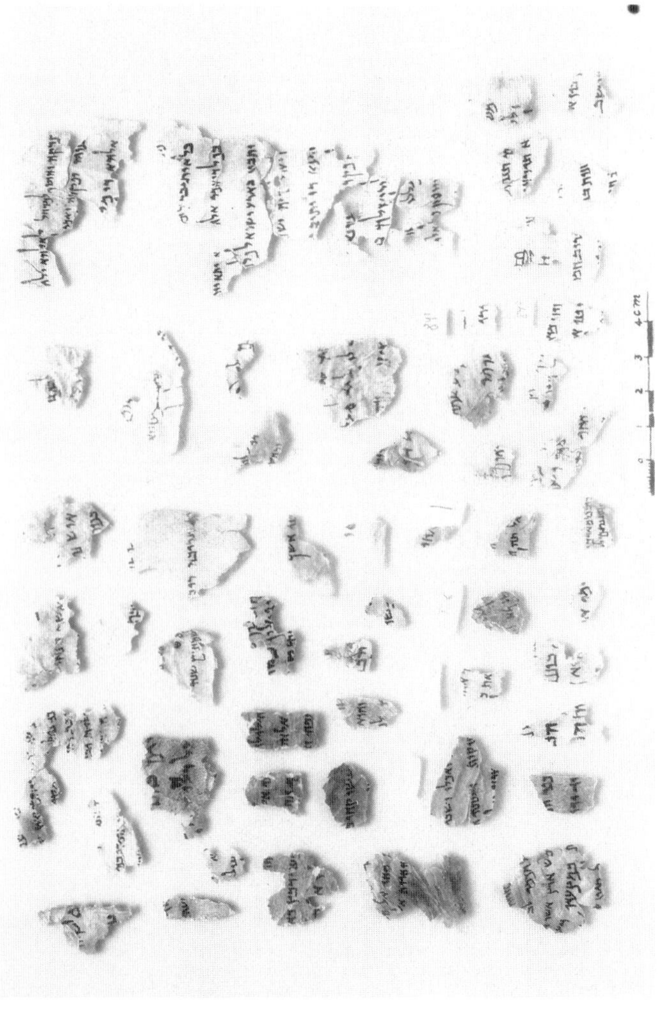

PLATE 511

PLATE 512

PLATE 529

PLATE 530

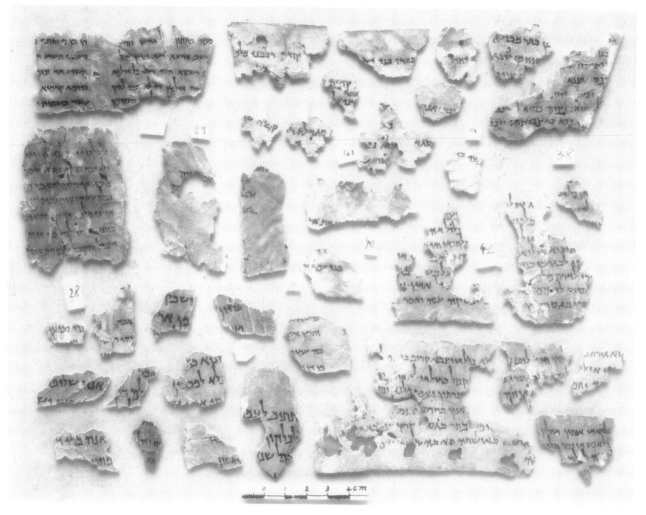

PLATE 531

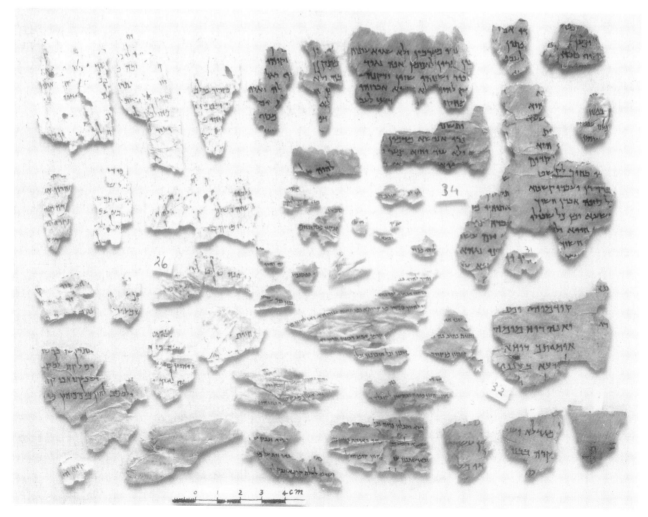

PLATE 532

PLATE 534

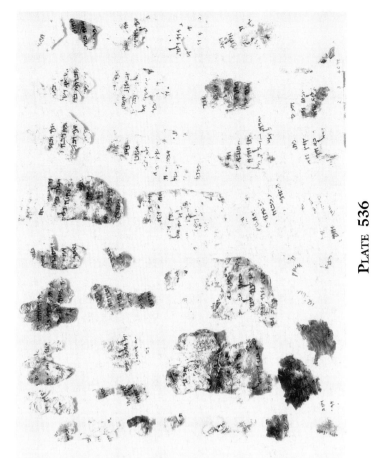

PLATE 536

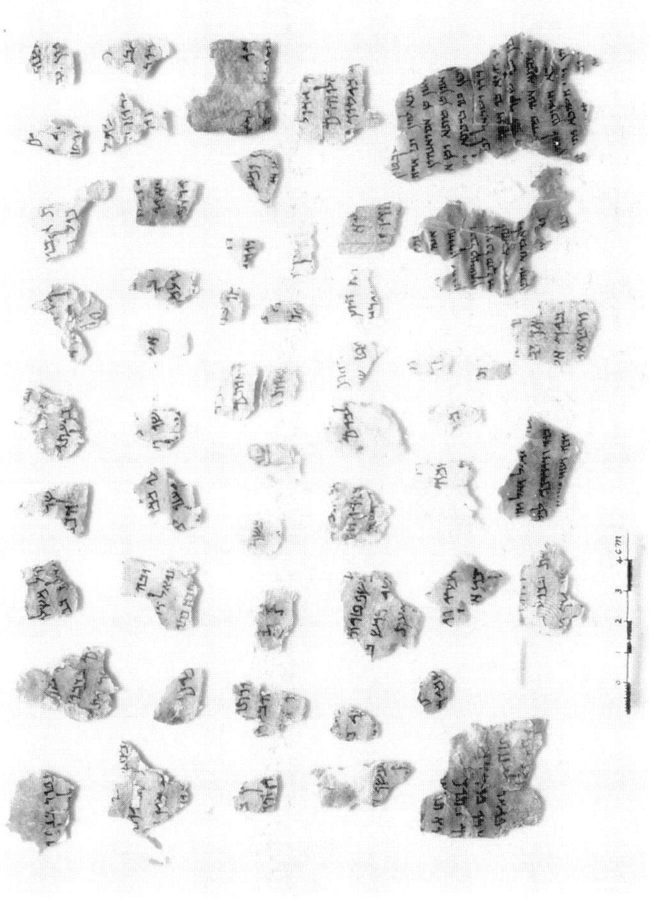

PLATE 533

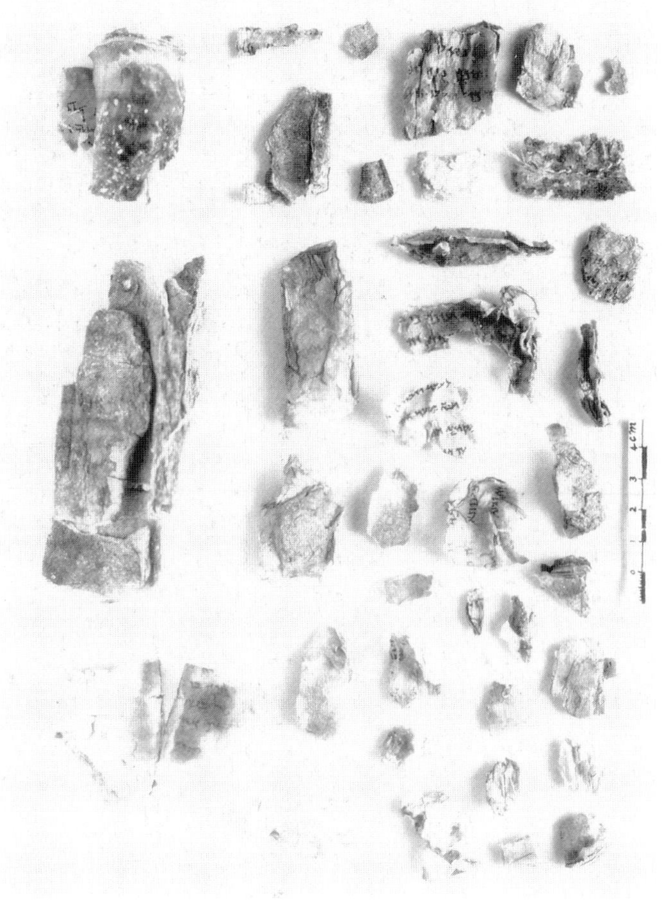

PLATE 535

PLATE 538

PLATE 540

PLATE 537

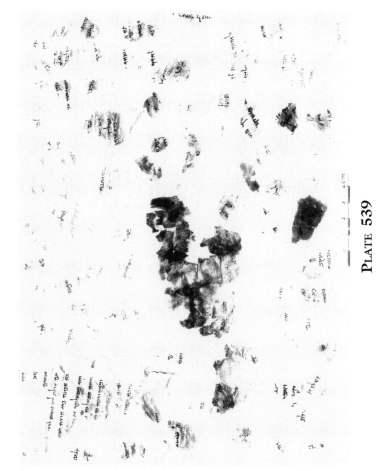

PLATE 539

PLATE 541

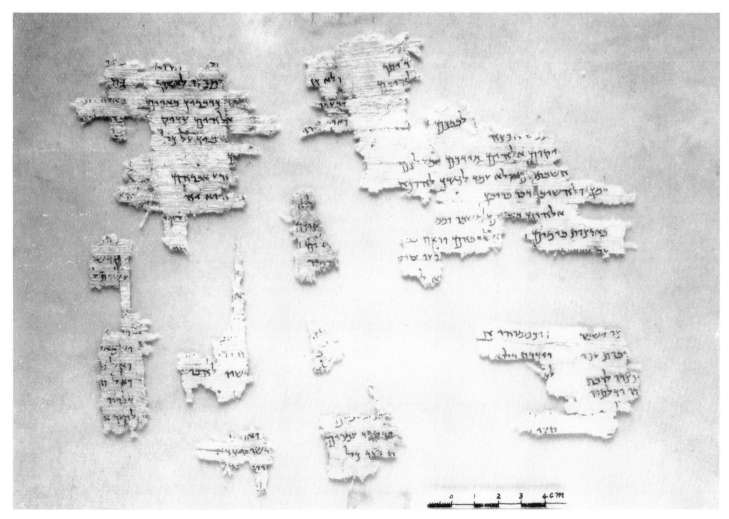

PLATE 542

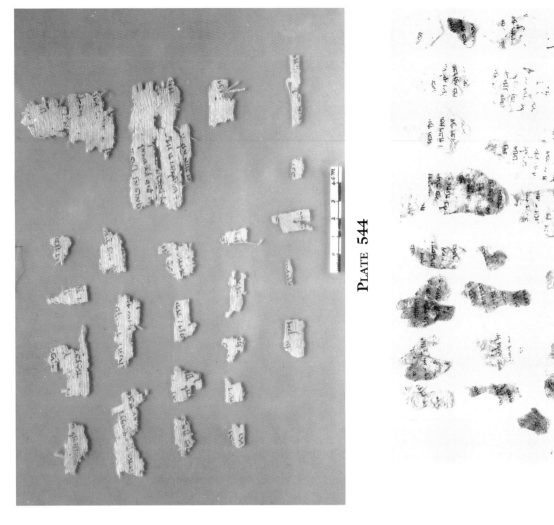

PLATE 544

PLATE 546

PLATE 543

PLATE 545

PLATE 547

FRAGMENTS DE QUMRAN

PLATE 548

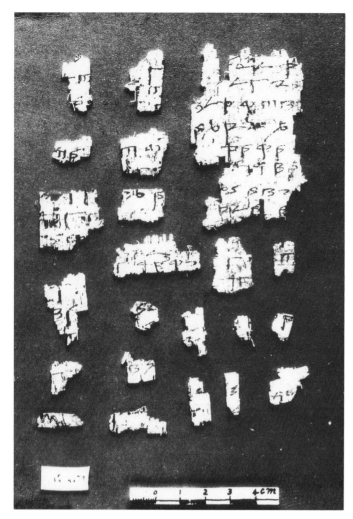

PLATE 549

PLATE 550

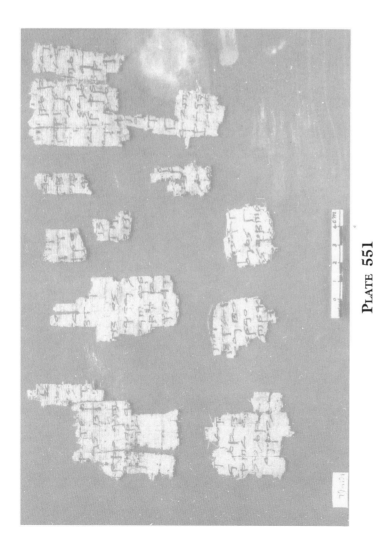

PLATE 551

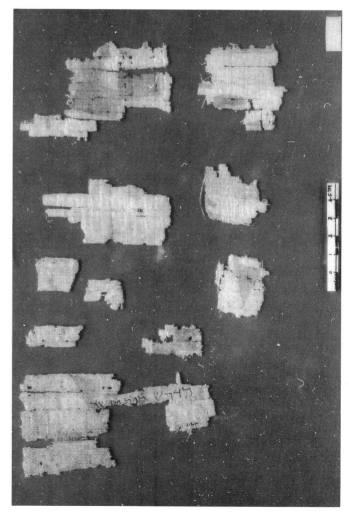

PLATE 552

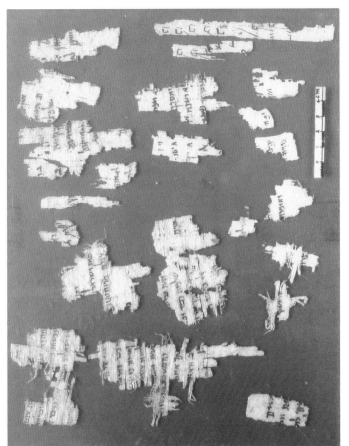

PLATE 554

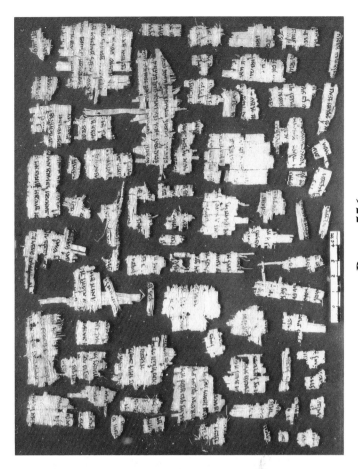

PLATE 556

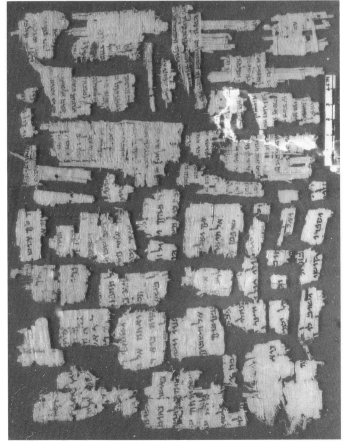

PLATE 553

PLATE 555

PLATE 558

PLATE 560

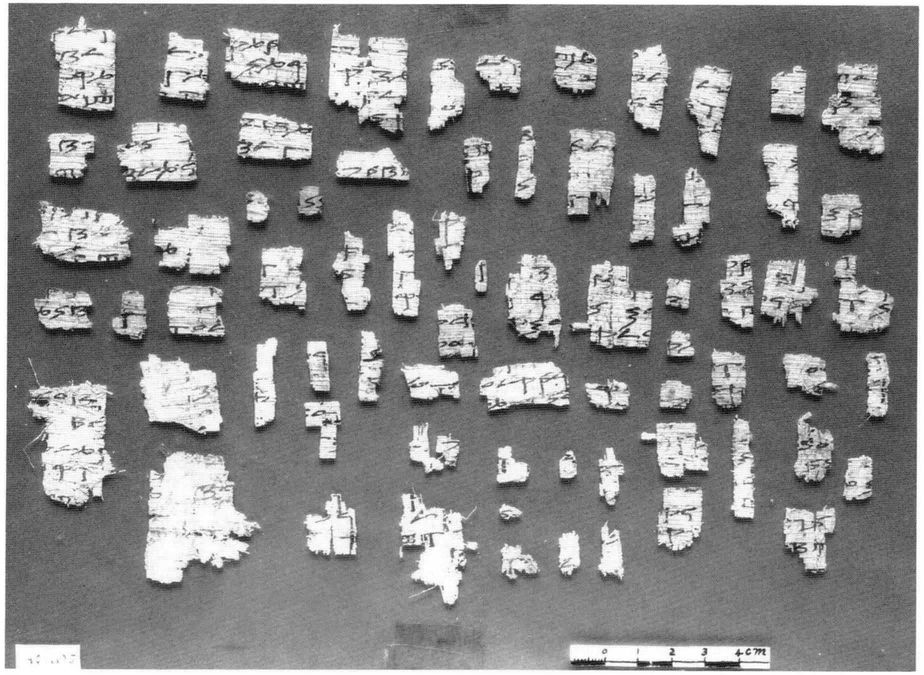

PLATE 557

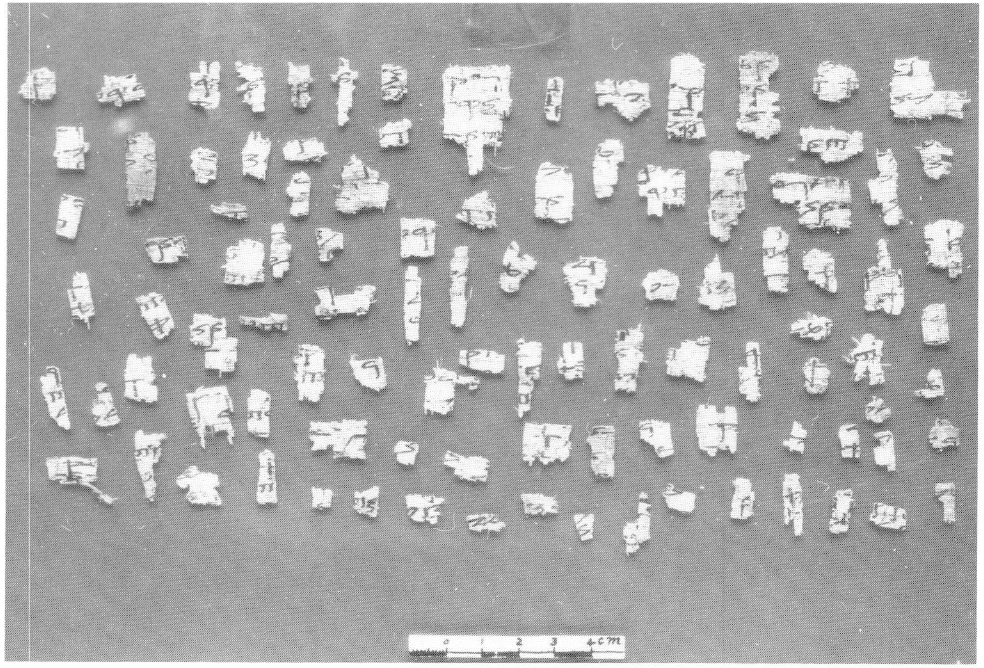

PLATE 559

PLATE 562

PLATE 564

PLATE 561

PLATE 563

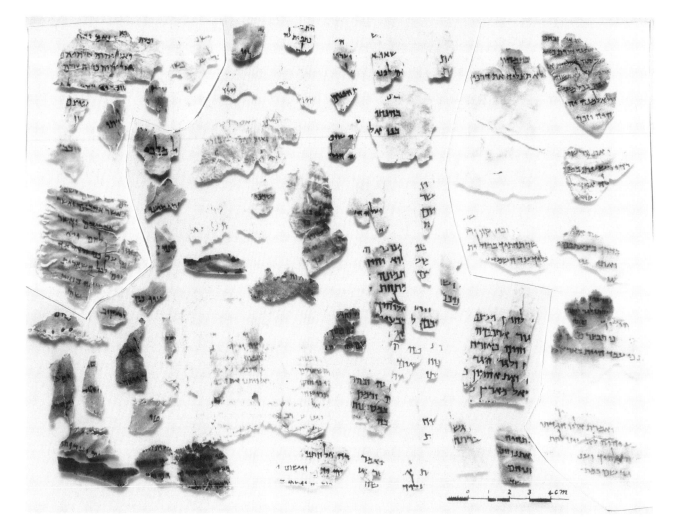

PLATE 565

PLATE 566

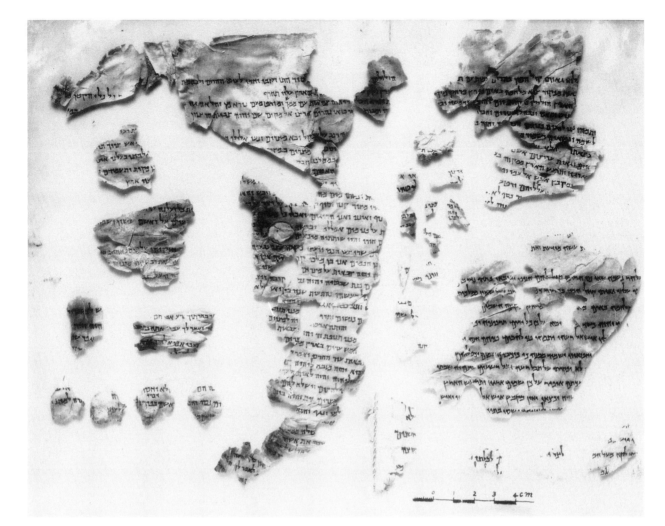

PLATE 567

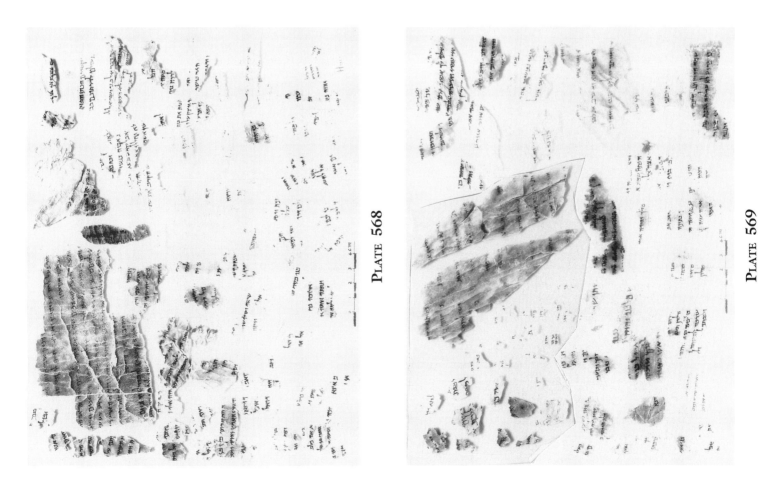

PLATE 568

PLATE 569

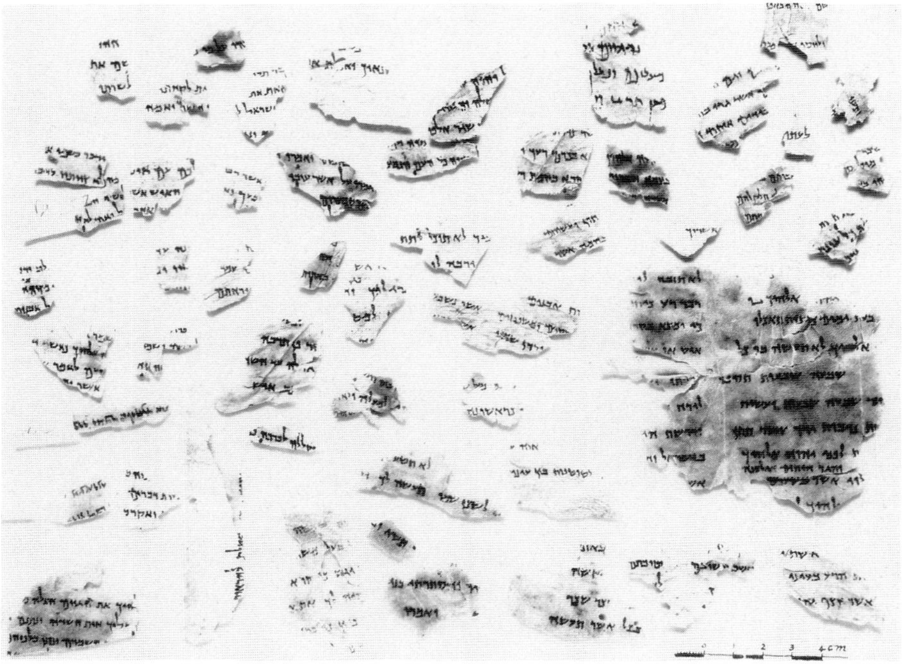

PLATE 571

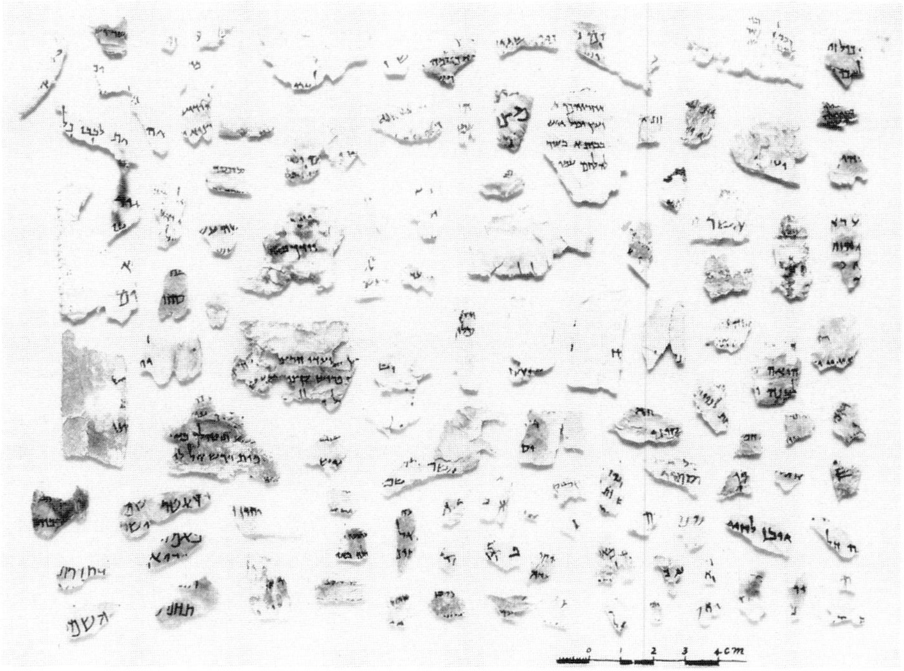

PLATE 573

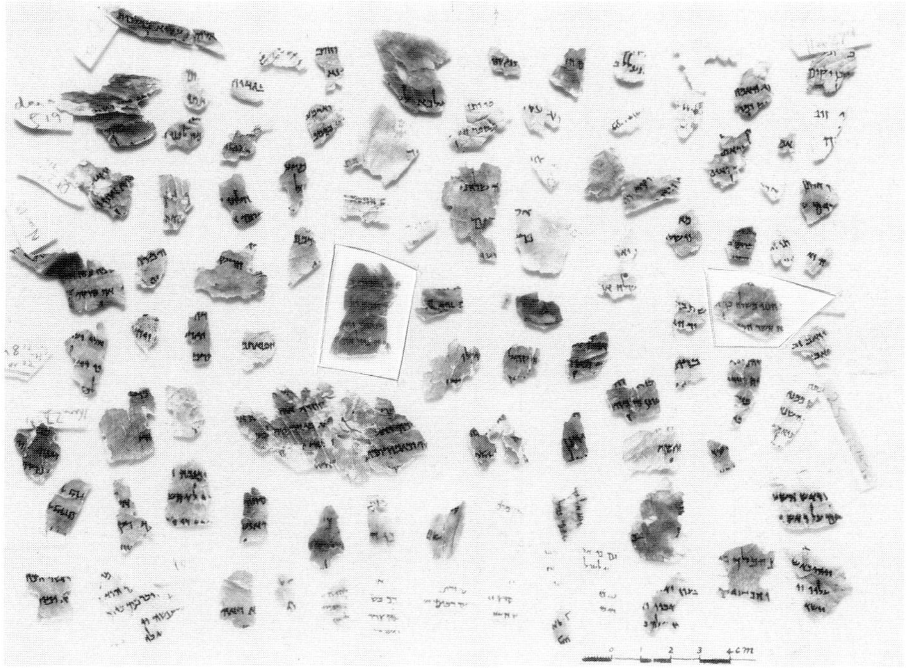

PLATE 570

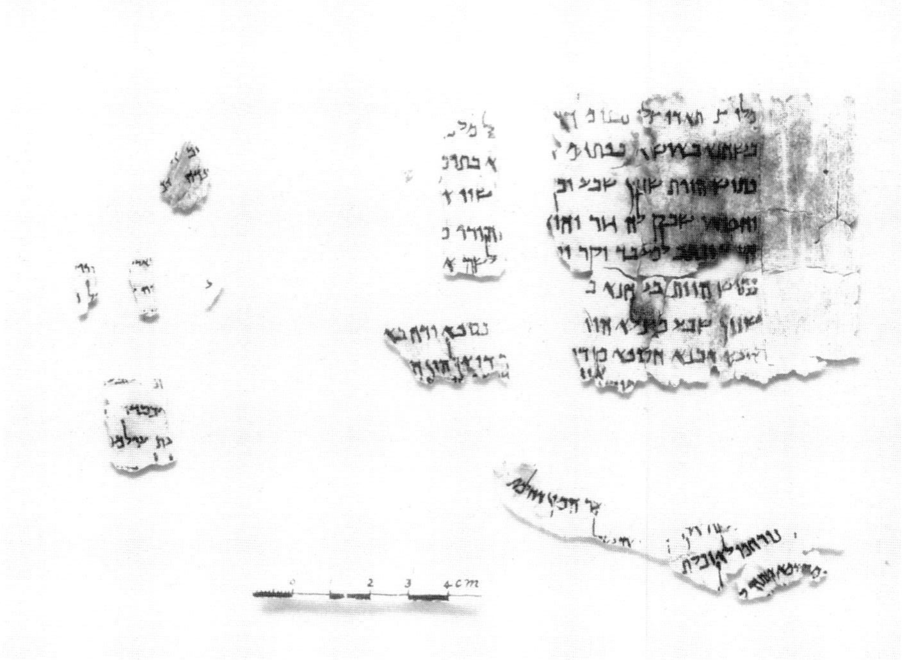

PLATE 572

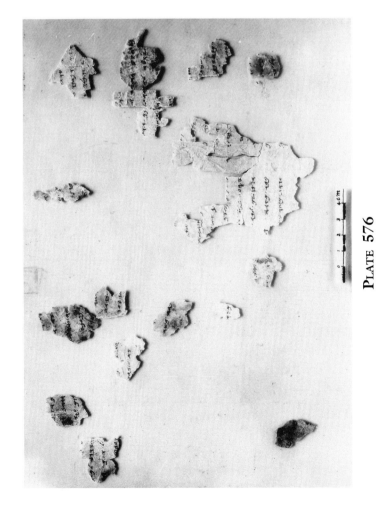

PLATE 574

PLATE 575

PLATE 576

PLATE 577

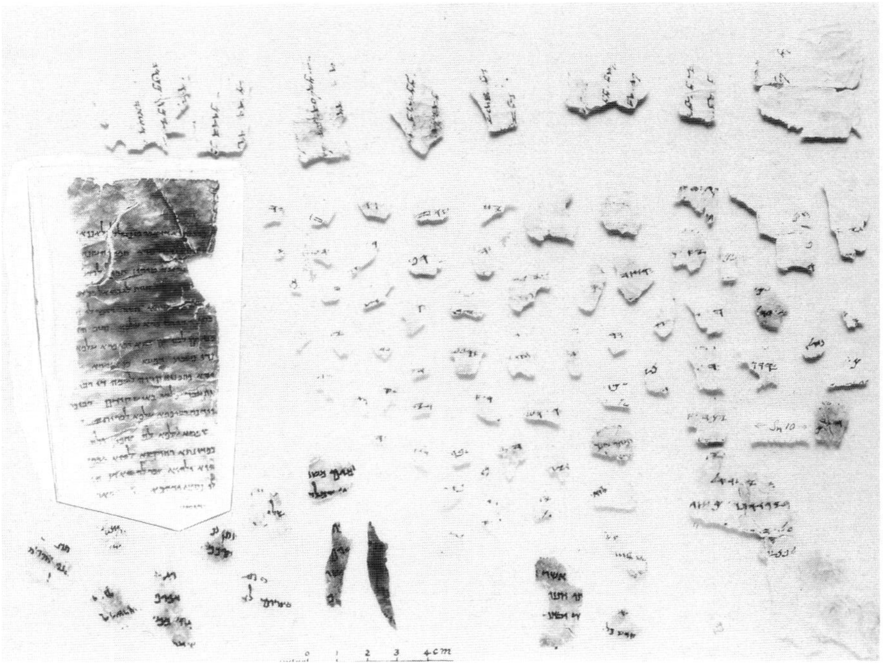

PLATE 578

PLATE 579

PLATE 580

PLATE 581

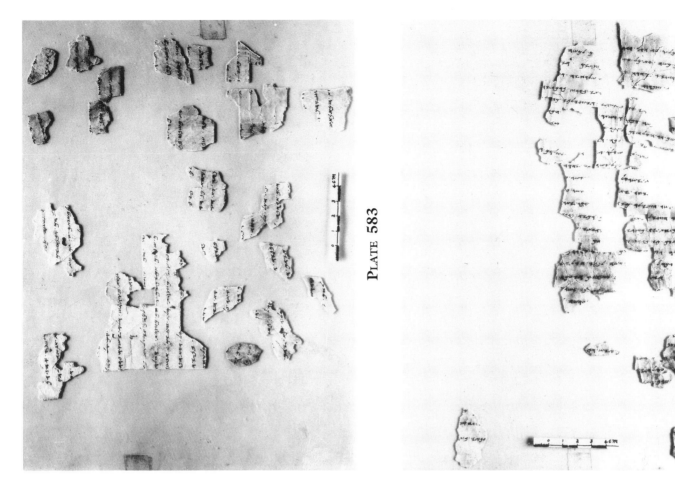

PLATE 583

PLATE 585

PLATE 582

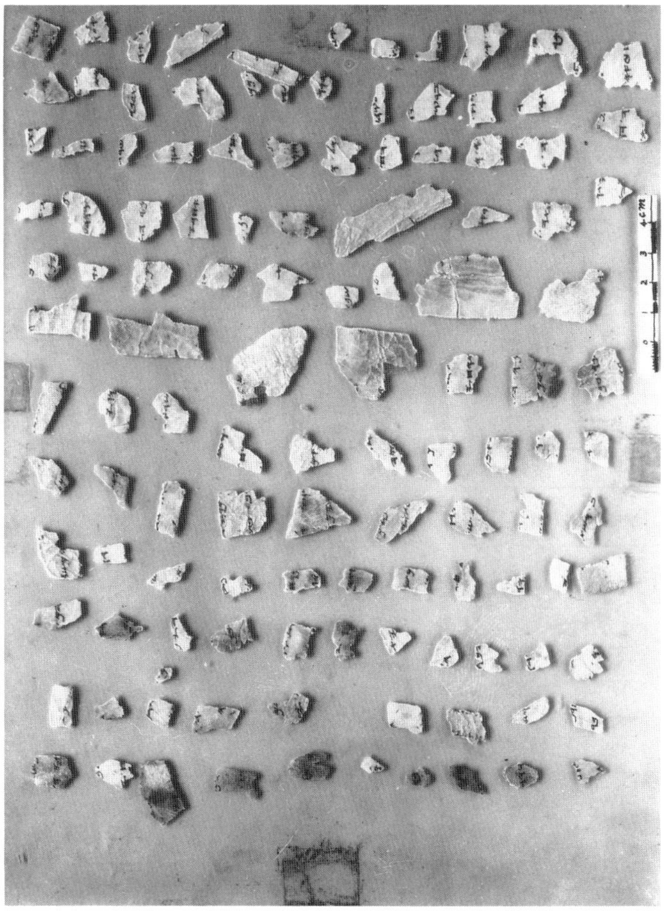

PLATE 584

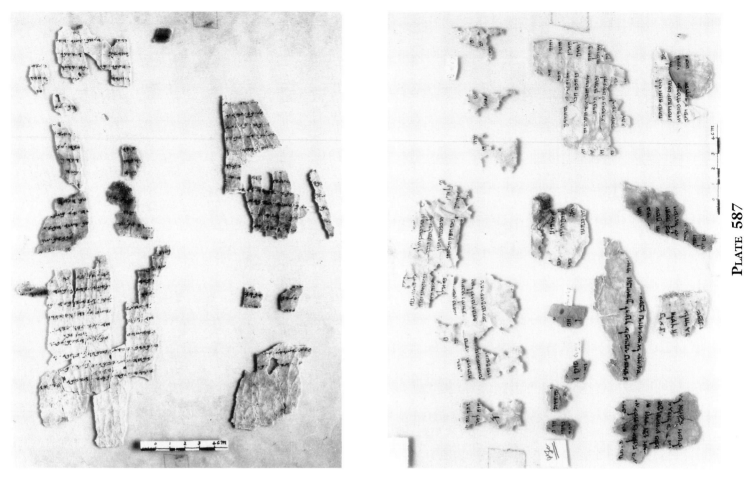

PLATE 586

PLATE 587

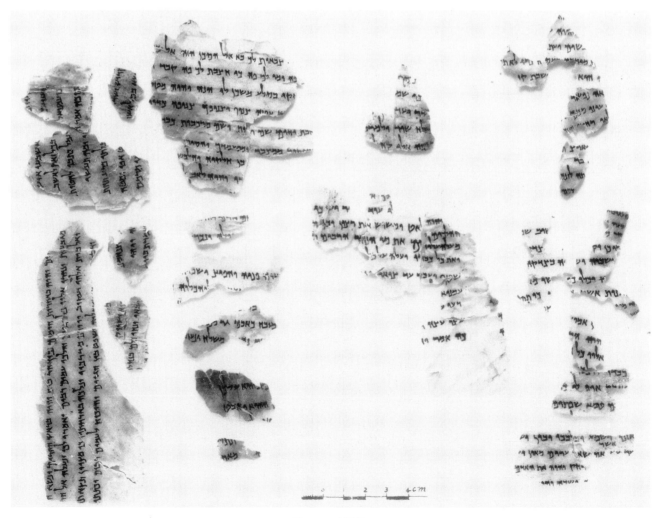

PLATE 588

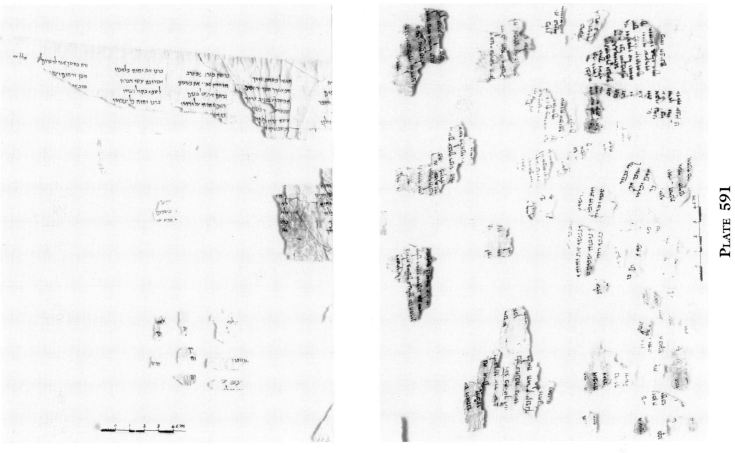

PLATE 591

PLATE 590

PLATE 589

PLATE 593

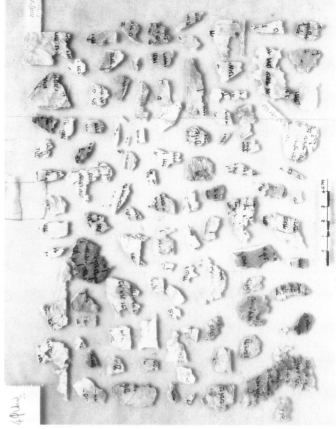

PLATE 595

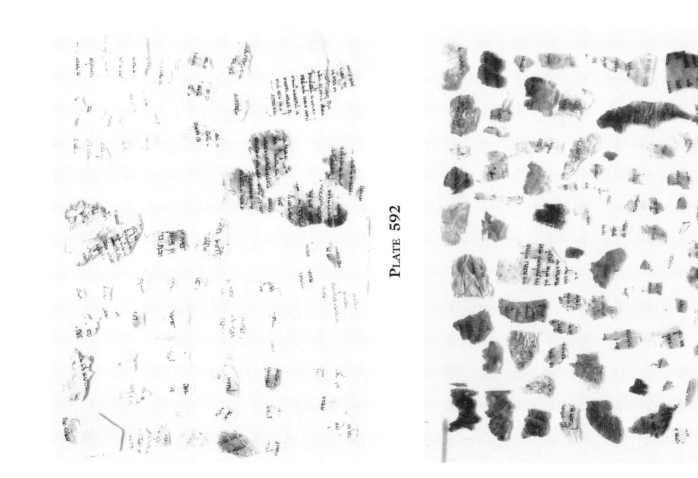

PLATE 592

PLATE 594

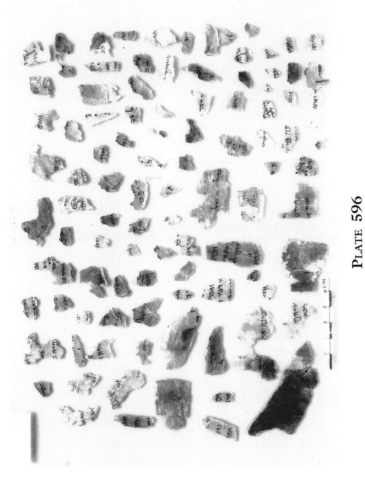

PLATE 597

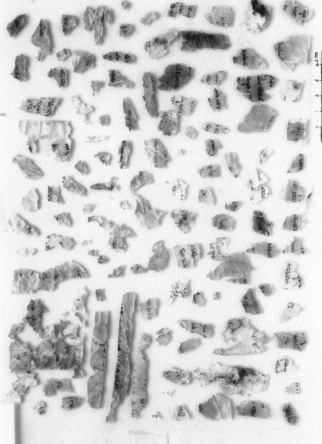

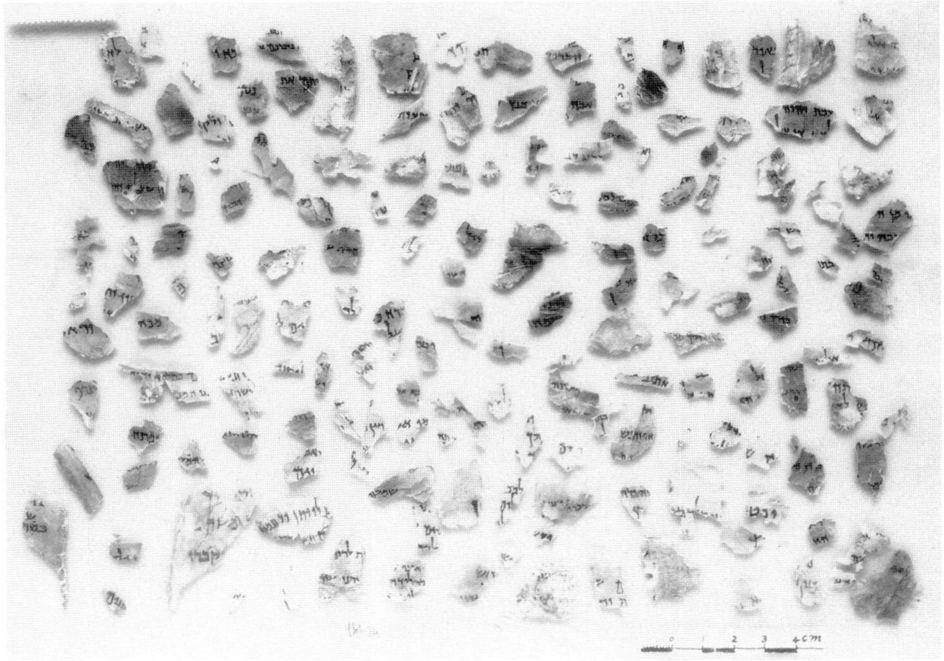

PLATE 599

PLATE 596

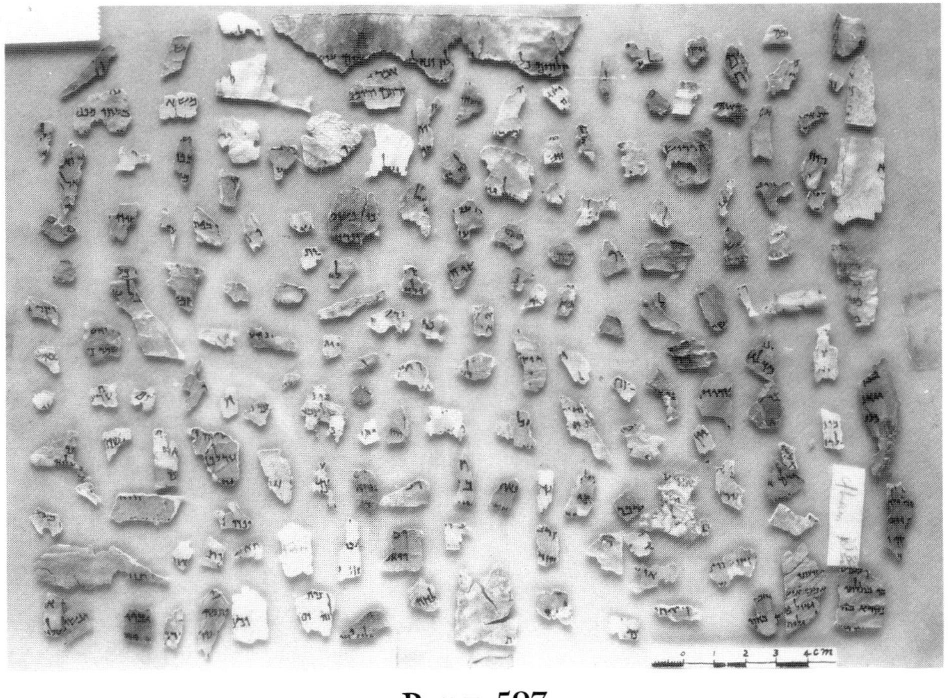

PLATE 598

PLATE 601

PLATE 603

PLATE 600

PLATE 602

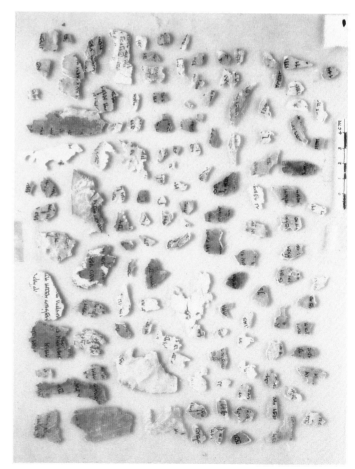

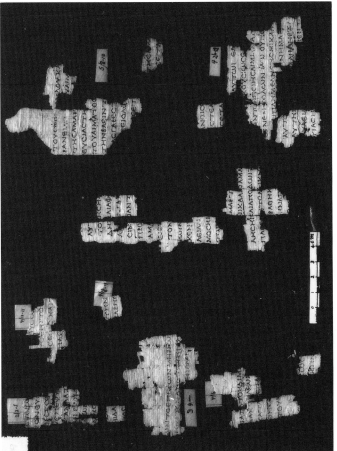

PLATE 604

PLATE 605

PLATE 606

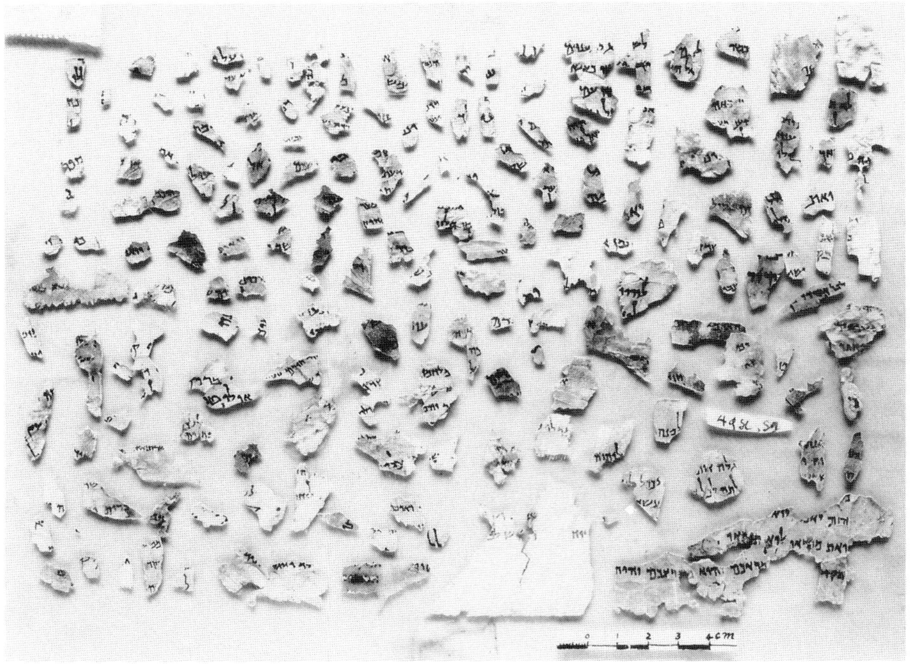

PLATE 607

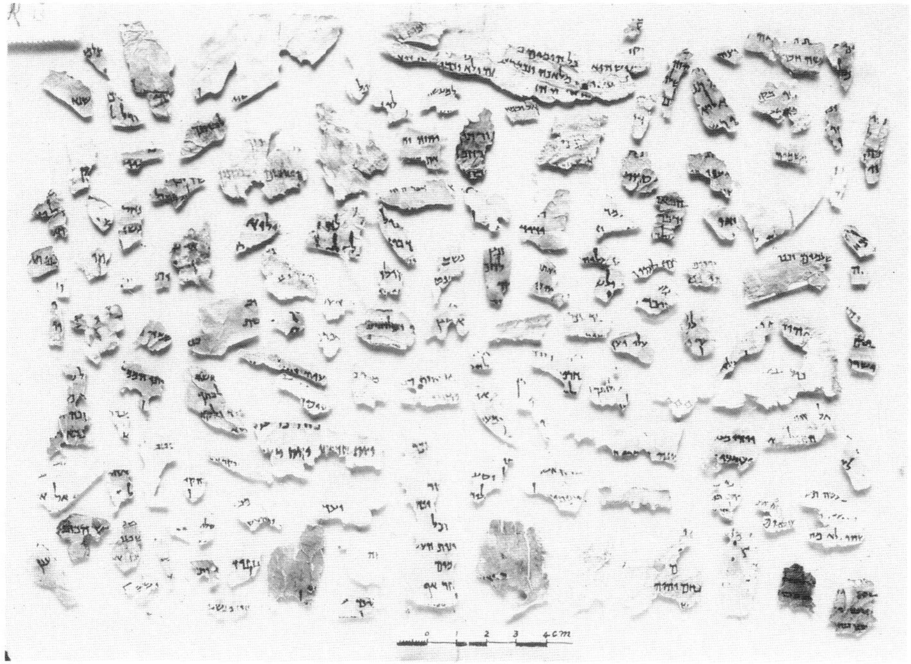

PLATE 609

PLATE 611

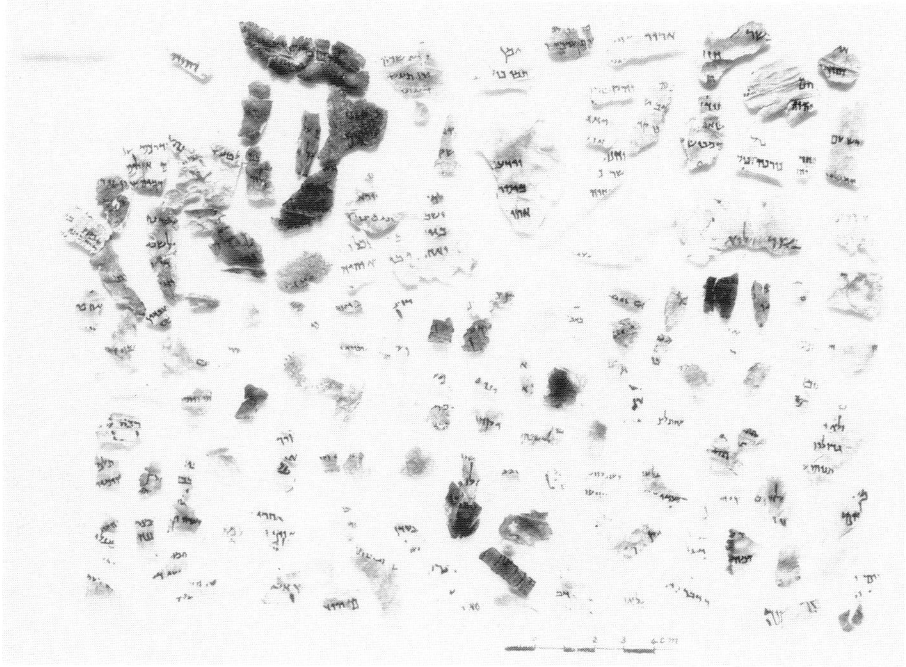

PLATE 608

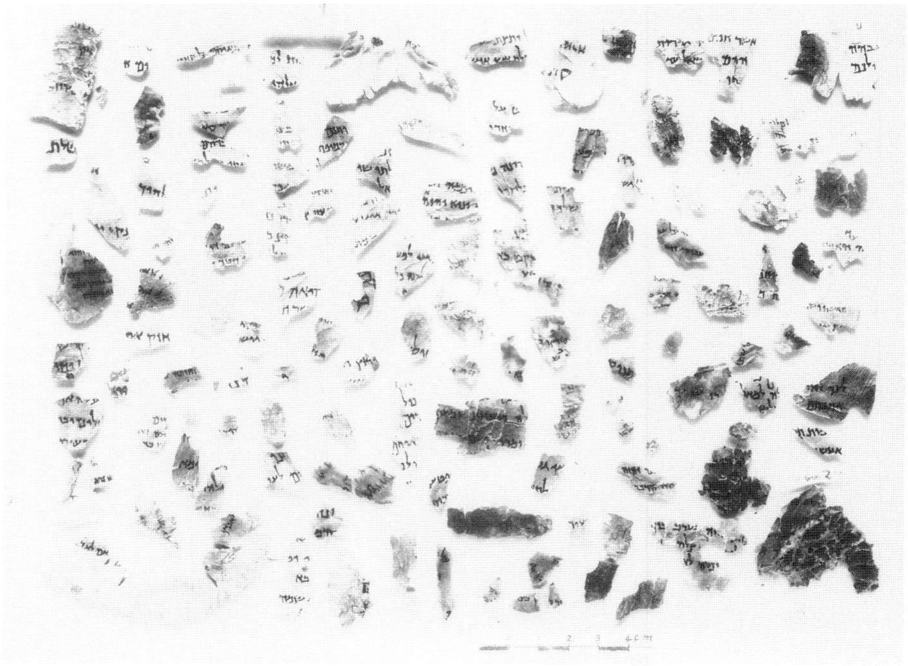

PLATE 610

PLATE 613

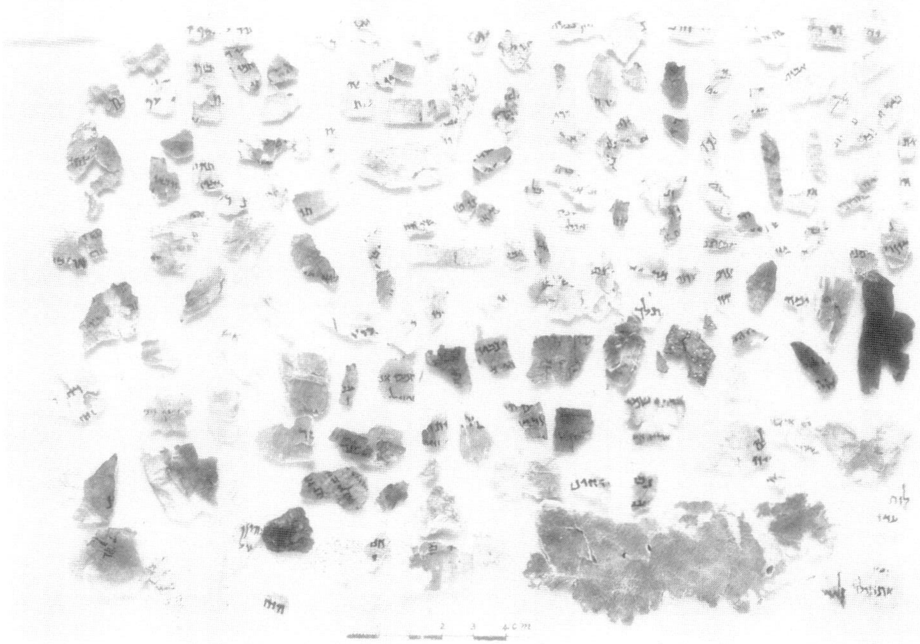

PLATE 615

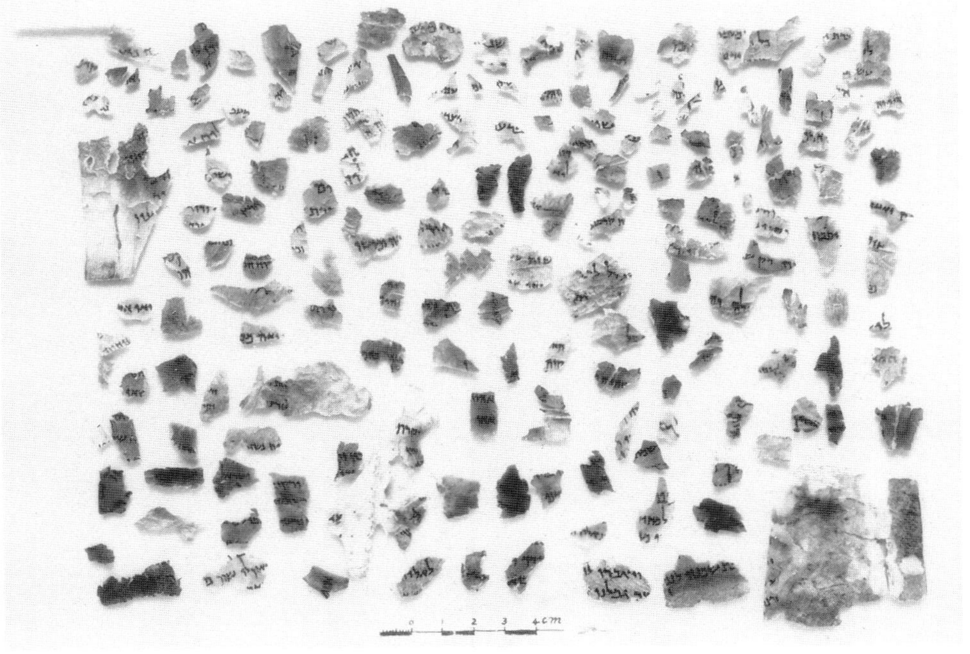

PLATE 612

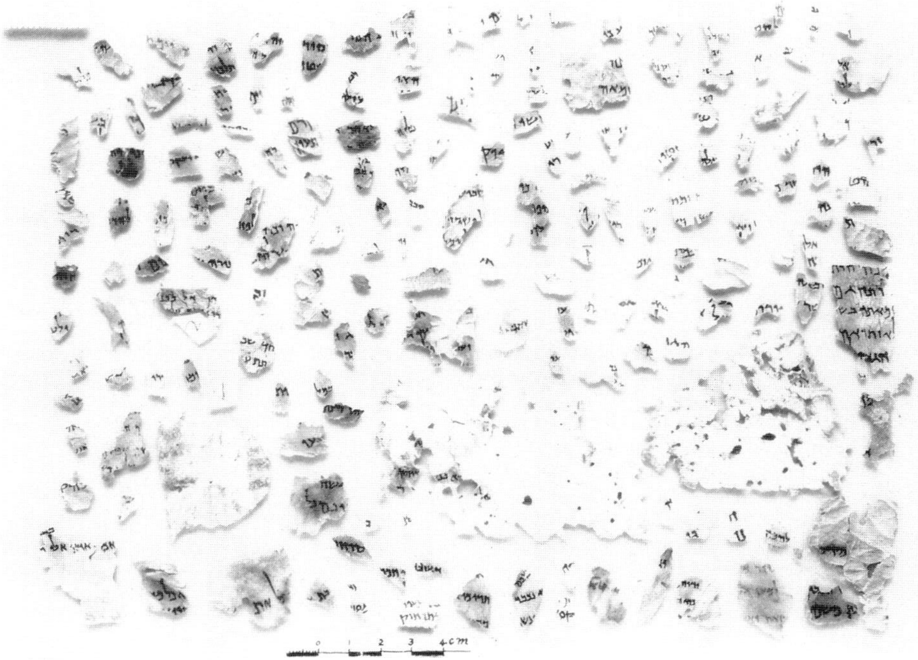

PLATE 614

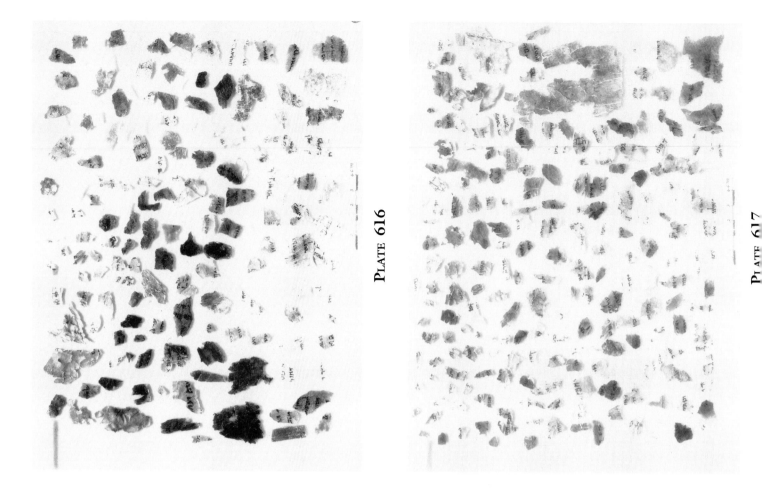

PLATE 616

PLATE 617

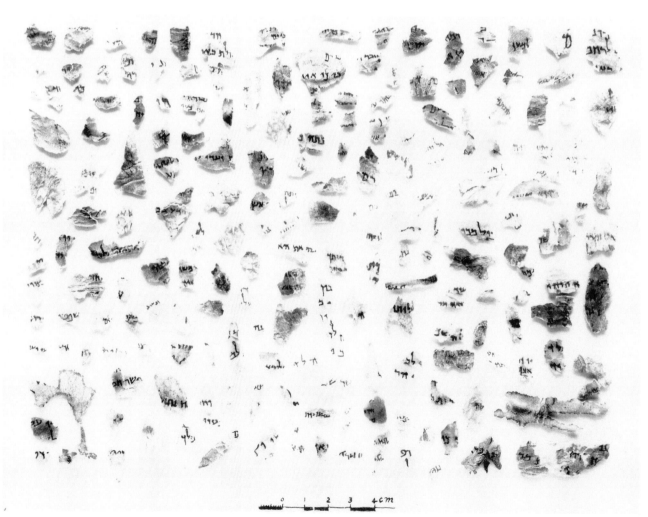

PLATE 618

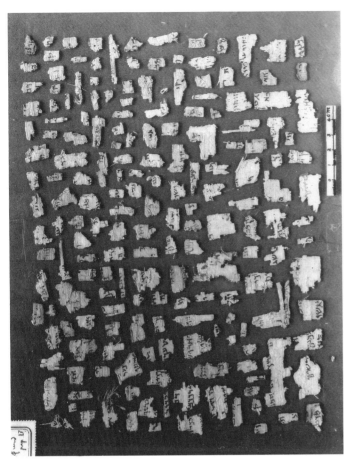

PLATE 634

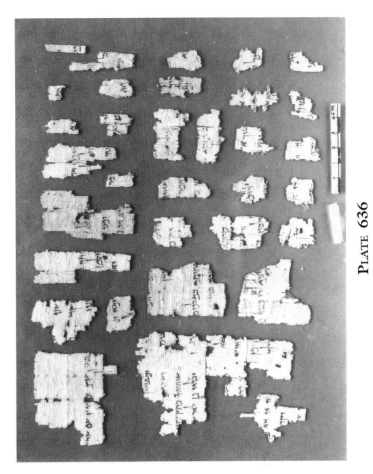

PLATE 636

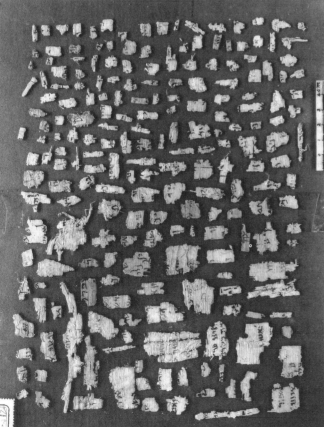

PLATE 633

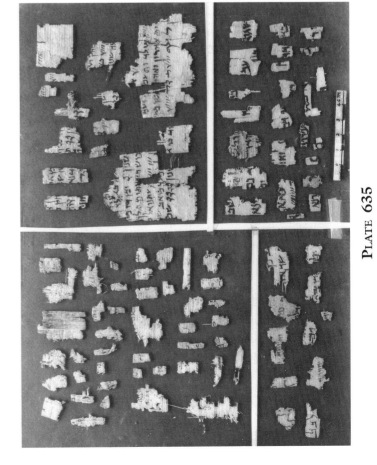

PLATE 635

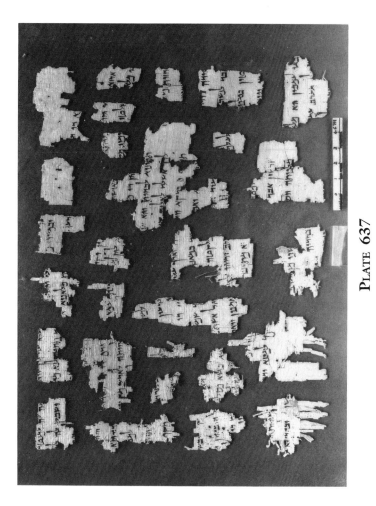

PLATE 637

PLATE 638

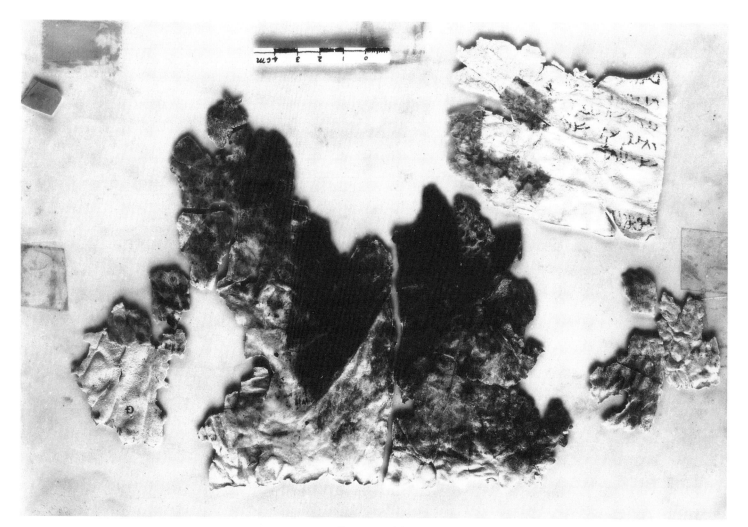

PLATE 639

PLATE 640

PLATE 641

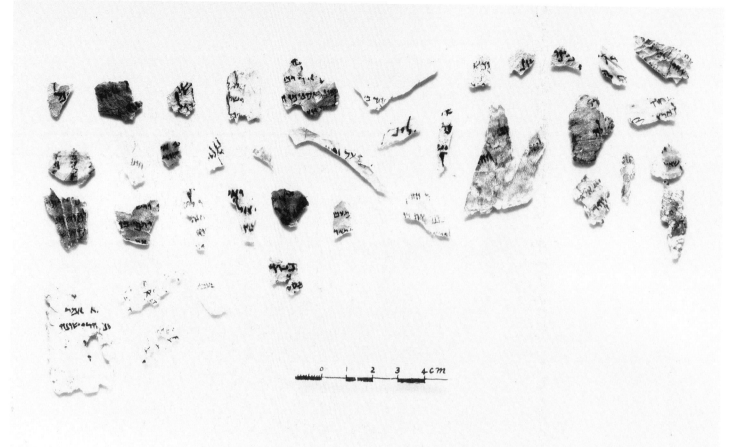

PLATE 642

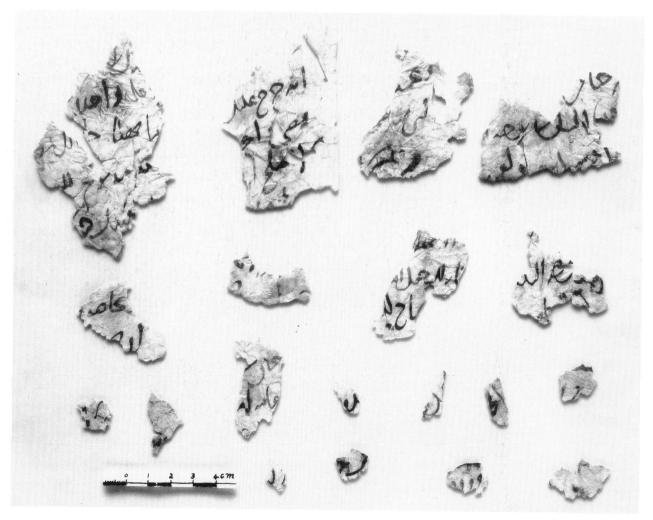

PLATE 643

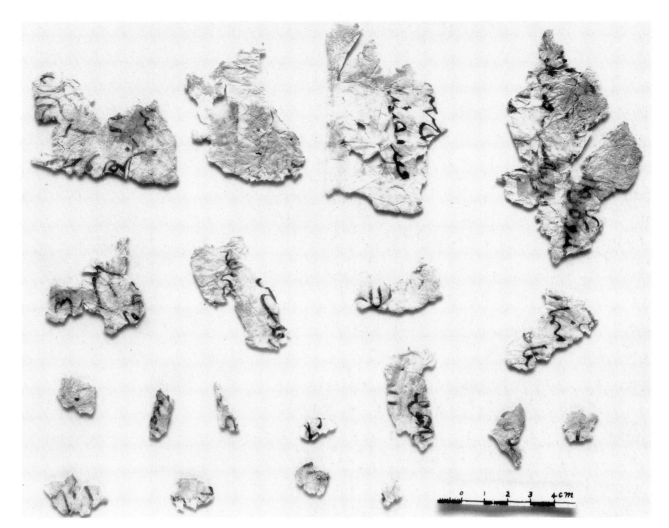

PLATE 644

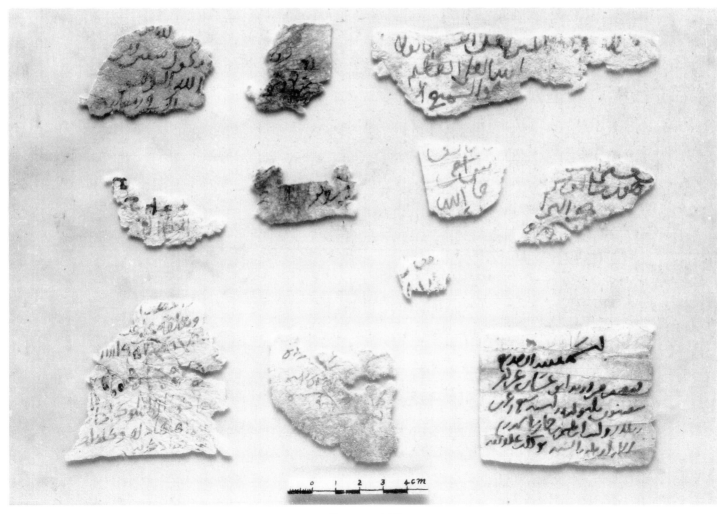

PLATE 645

PLATE 646

PLATE 647

PLATE 648

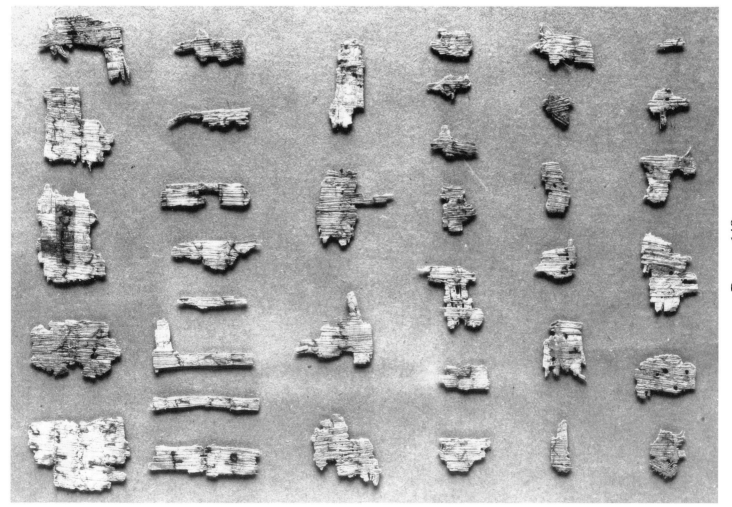

PLATE 649

PLATE 650

PLATE 651

PLATE 652

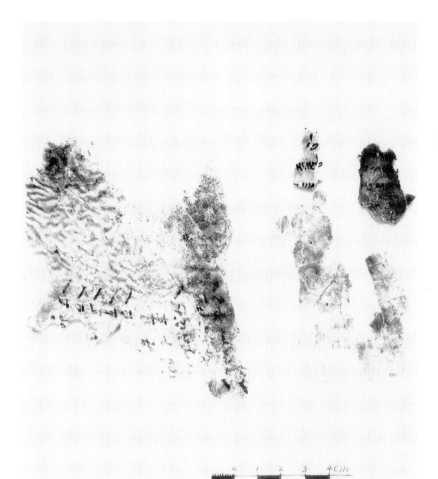

PLATE 653

PLATE 654

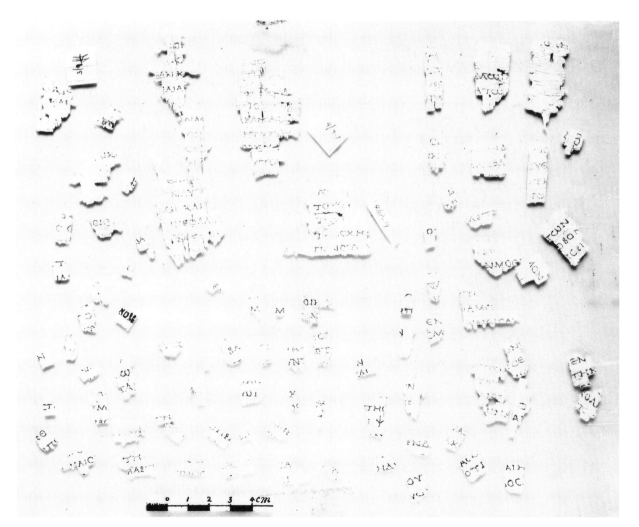

PLATE 655

PLATE 656

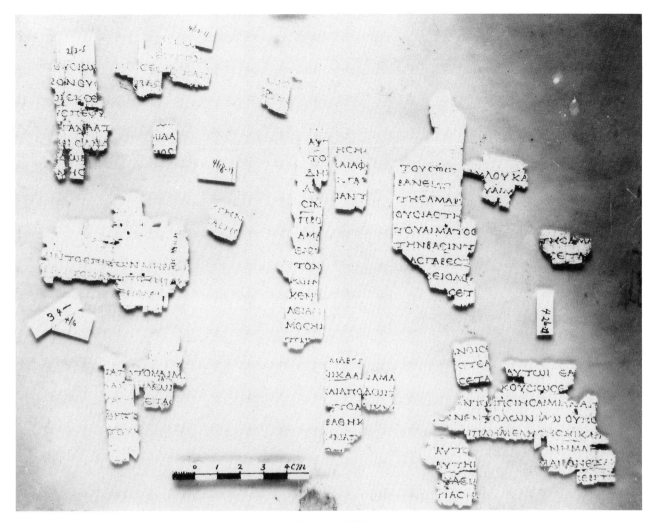

PLATE 657

PLATE 658

PLATE 659

PLATE 660

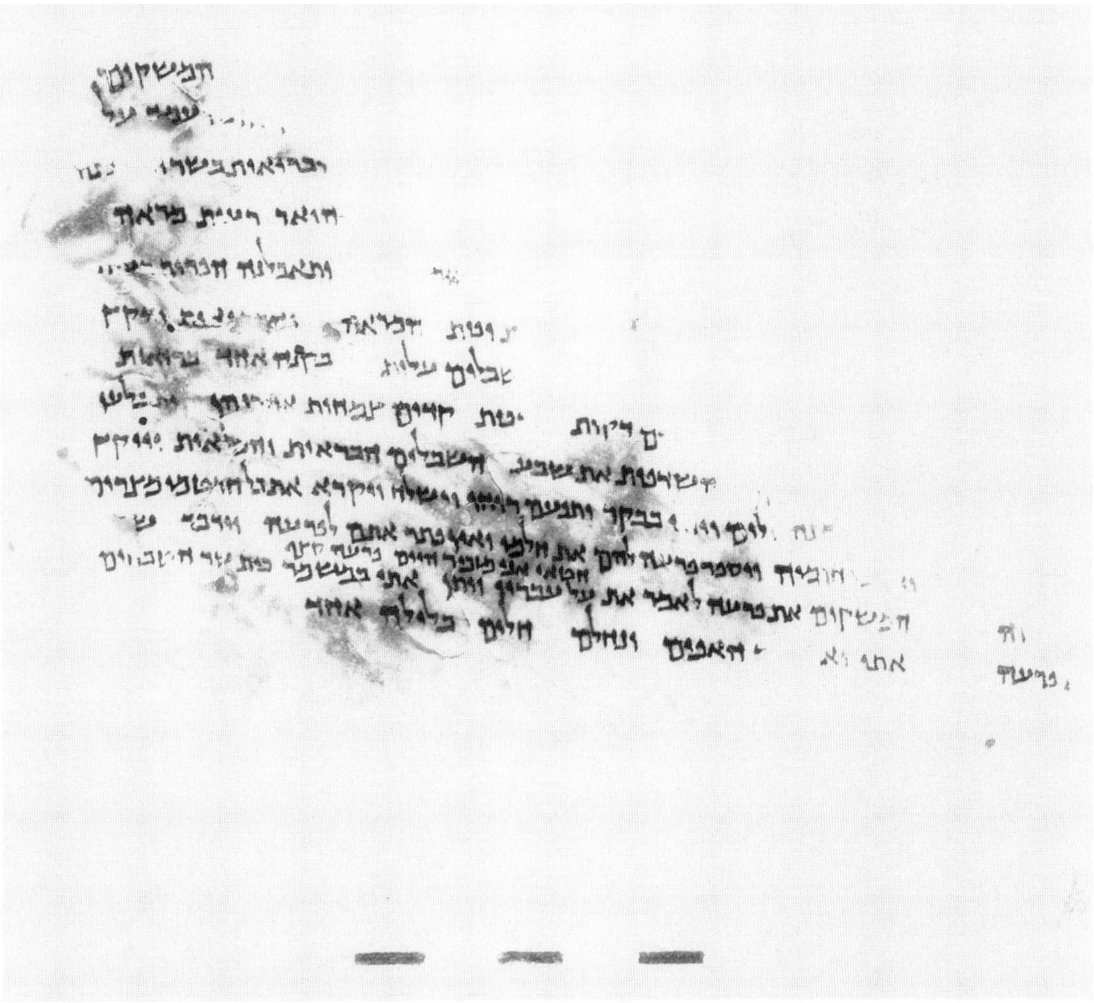

Plate 661

Plate 662

PLATE 663

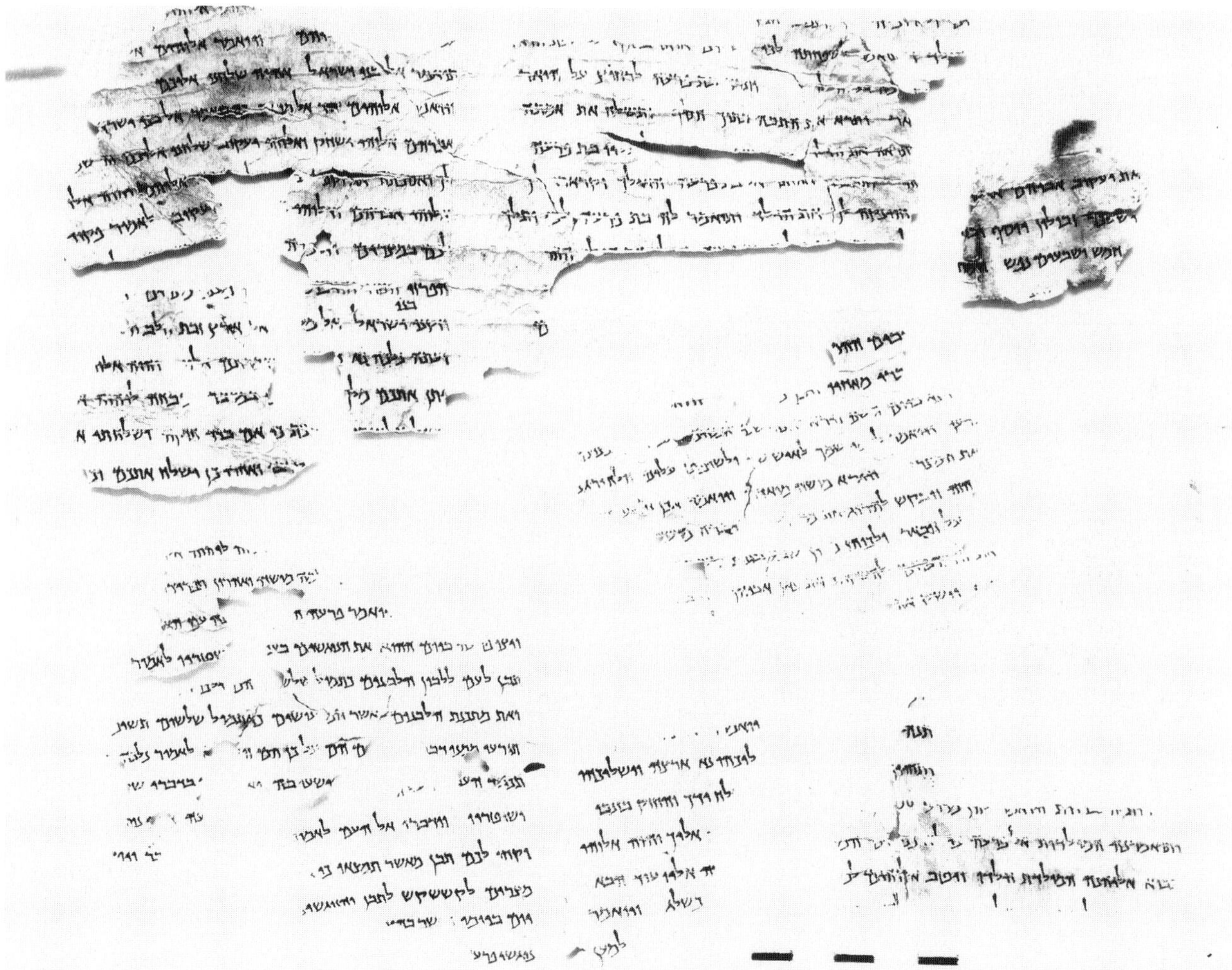

PLATE 664

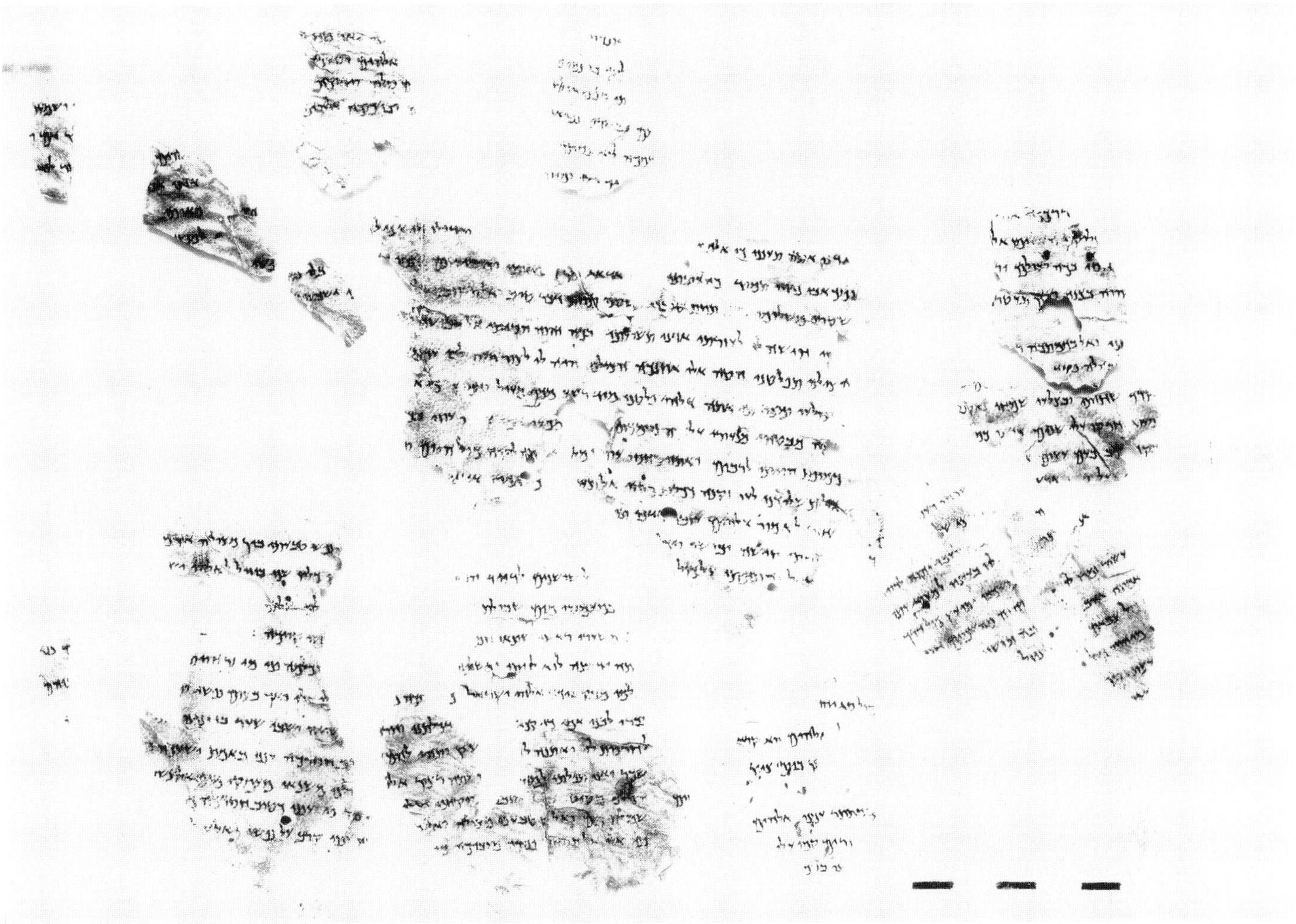

PLATE 673

PLATE 674

PLATE 675

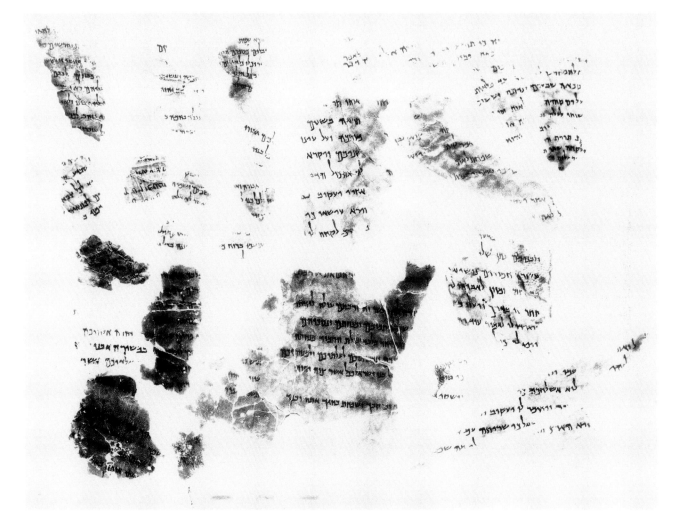

PLATE 676

PLATE 689

PLATE 690

PLATE 691

PLATE 692

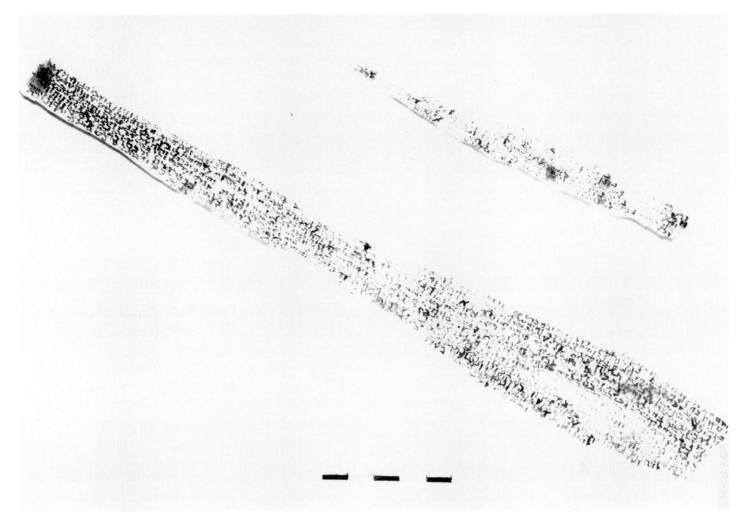

PLATE 693

PLATE 694

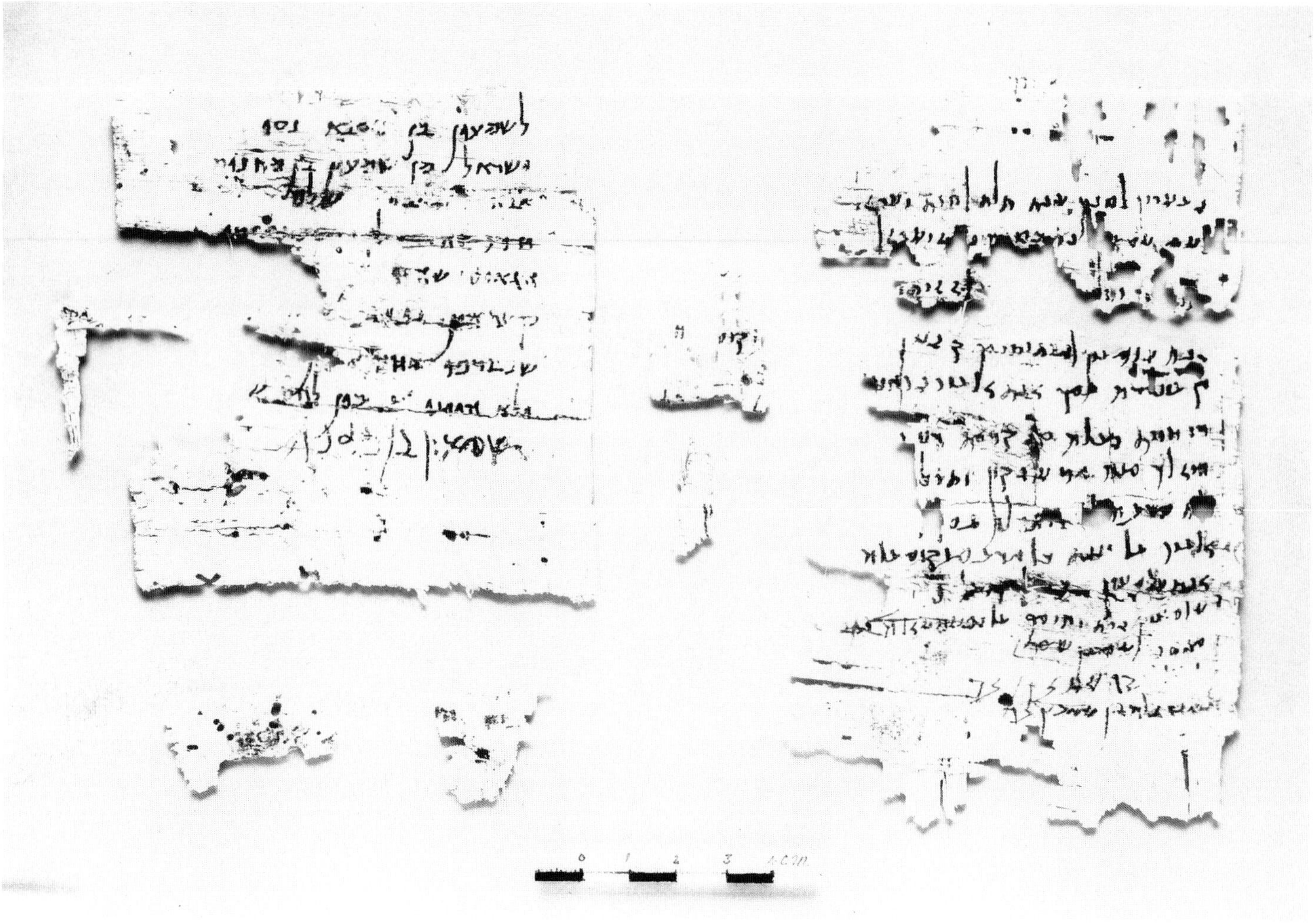

PLATE 695

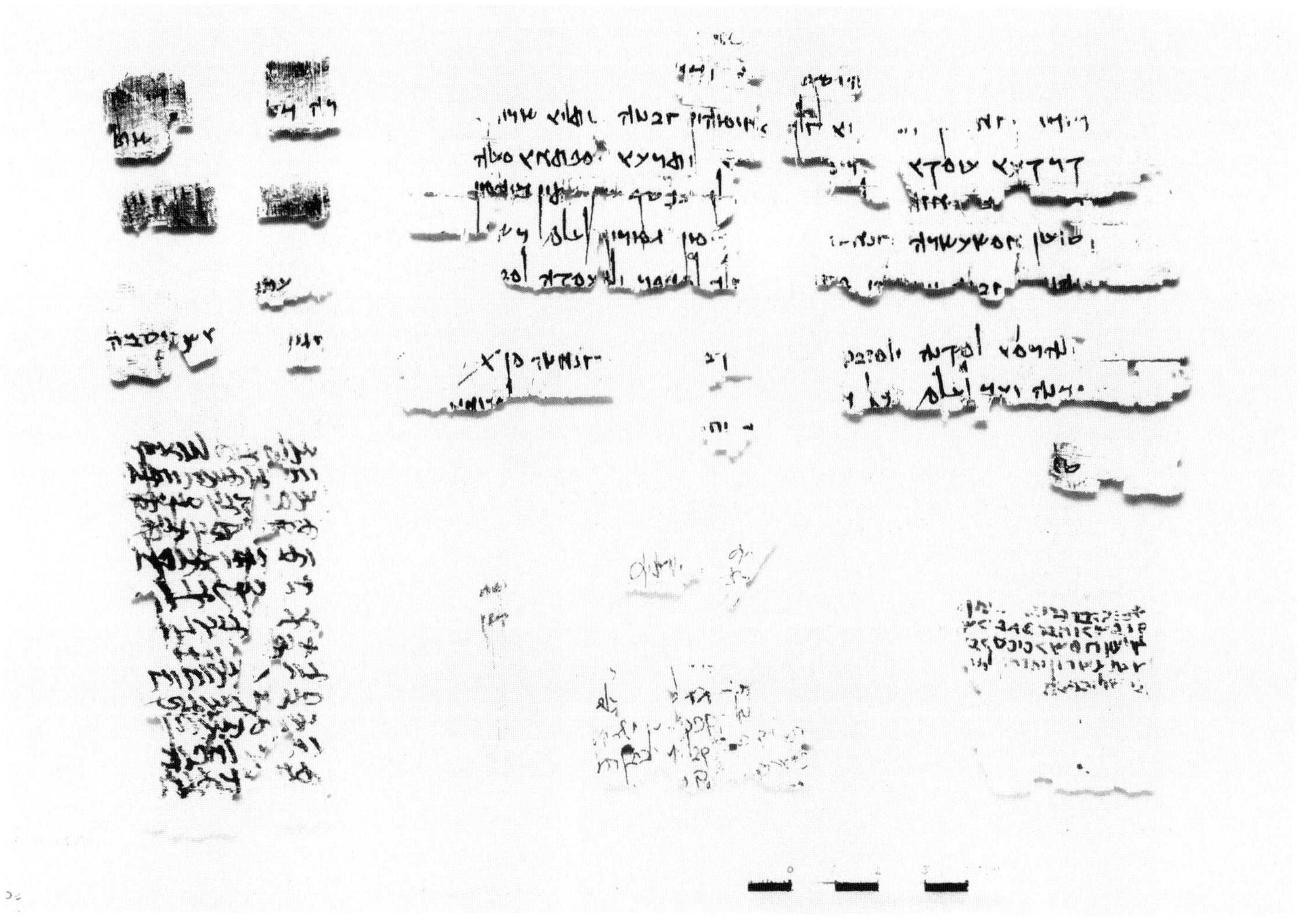

PLATE 696

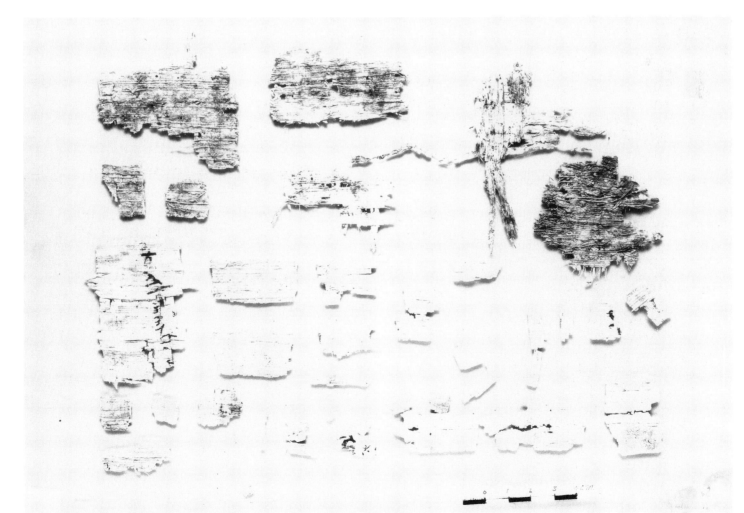

PLATE 697

PLATE 698

PLATE 699

PLATE 700

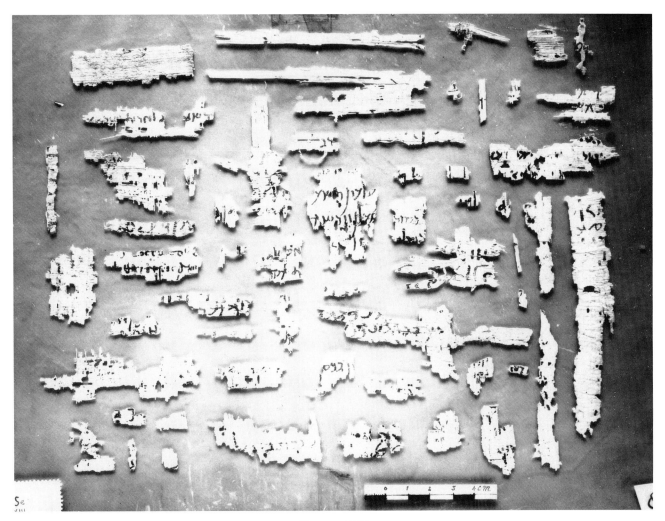

PLATE 701

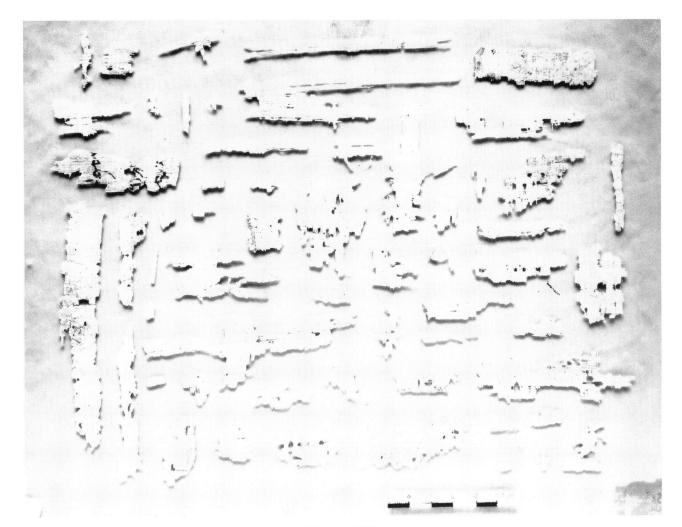

PLATE 702

PLATE 703

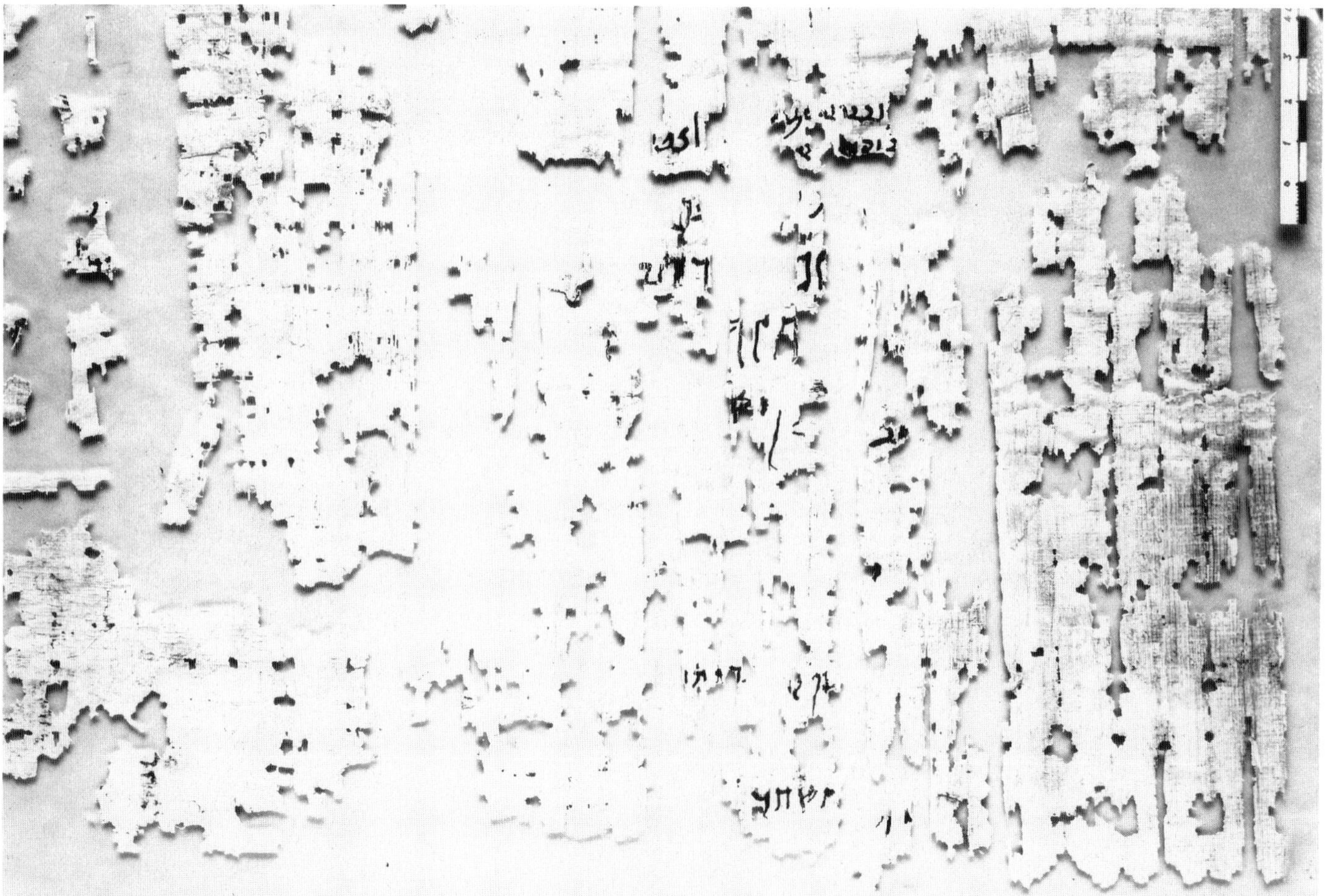

PLATE 704

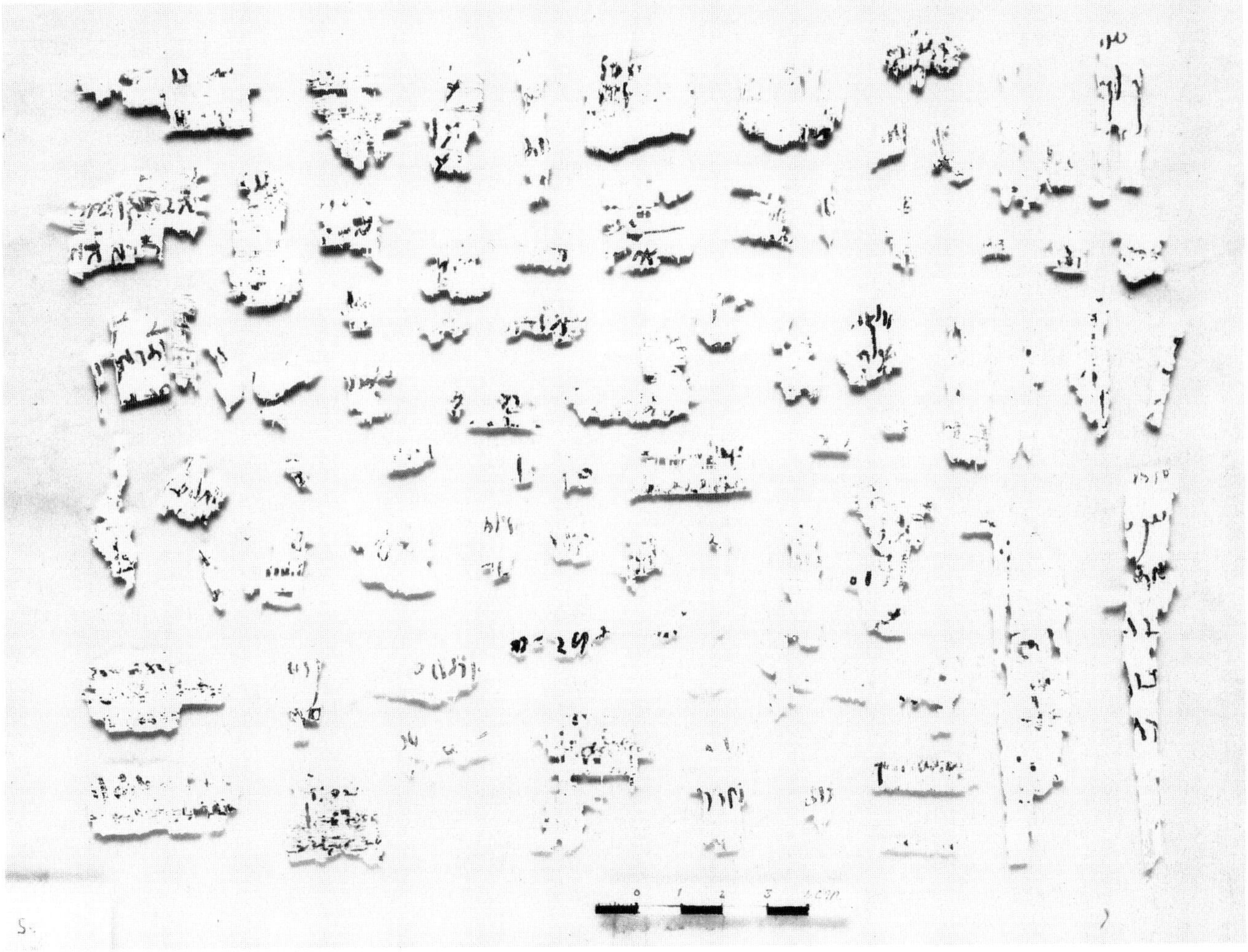

PLATE 705

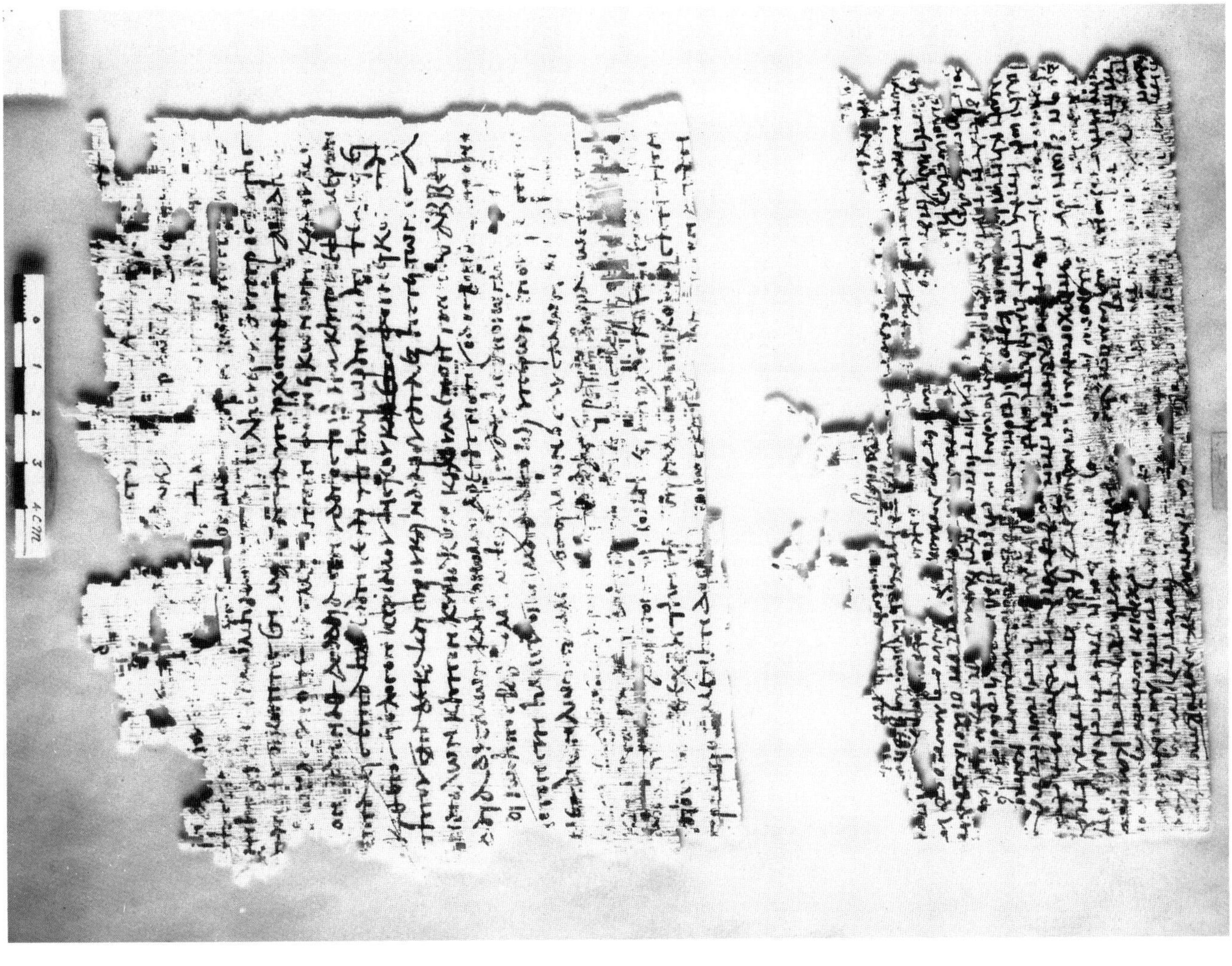

PLATE 706

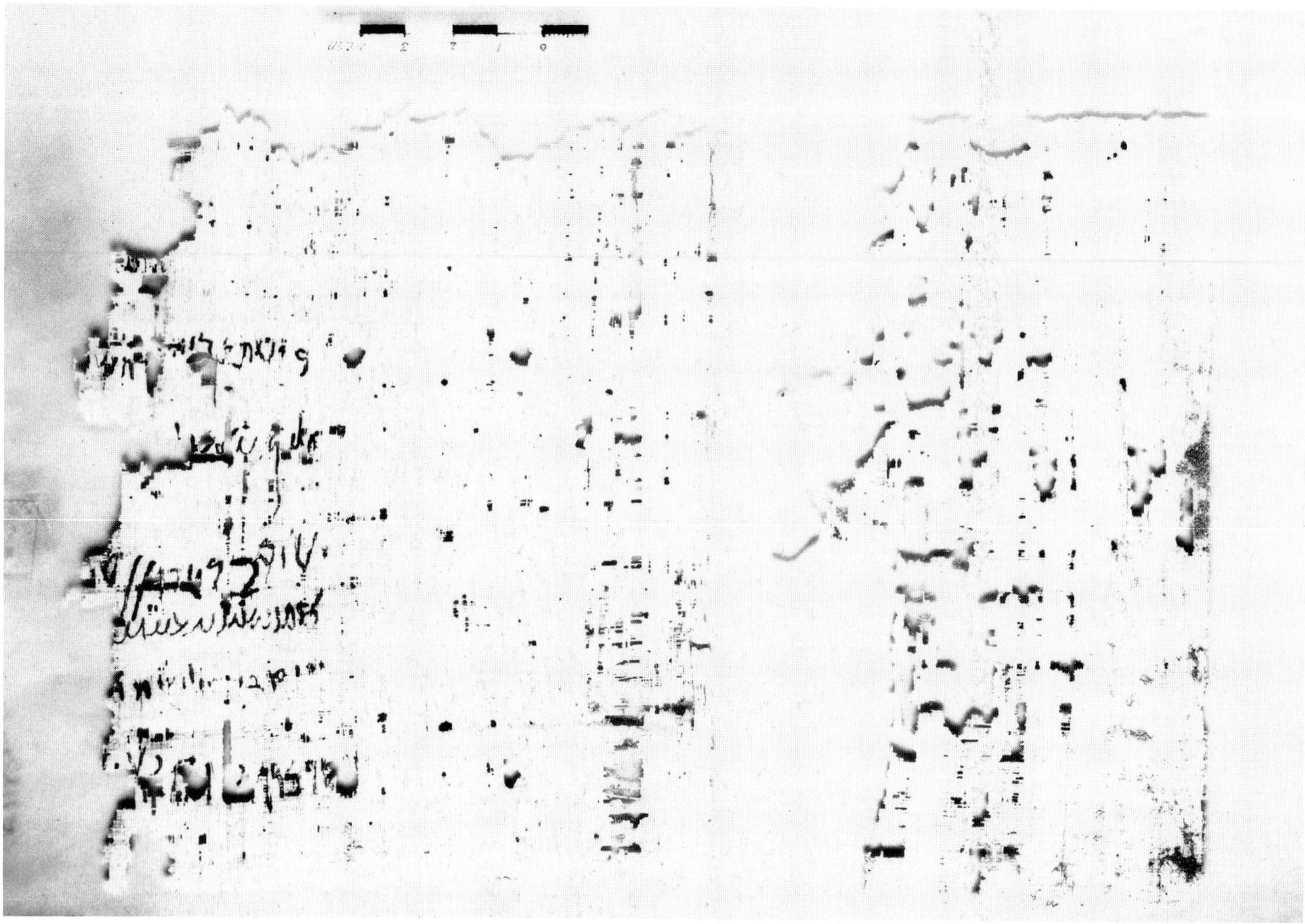

PLATE 707

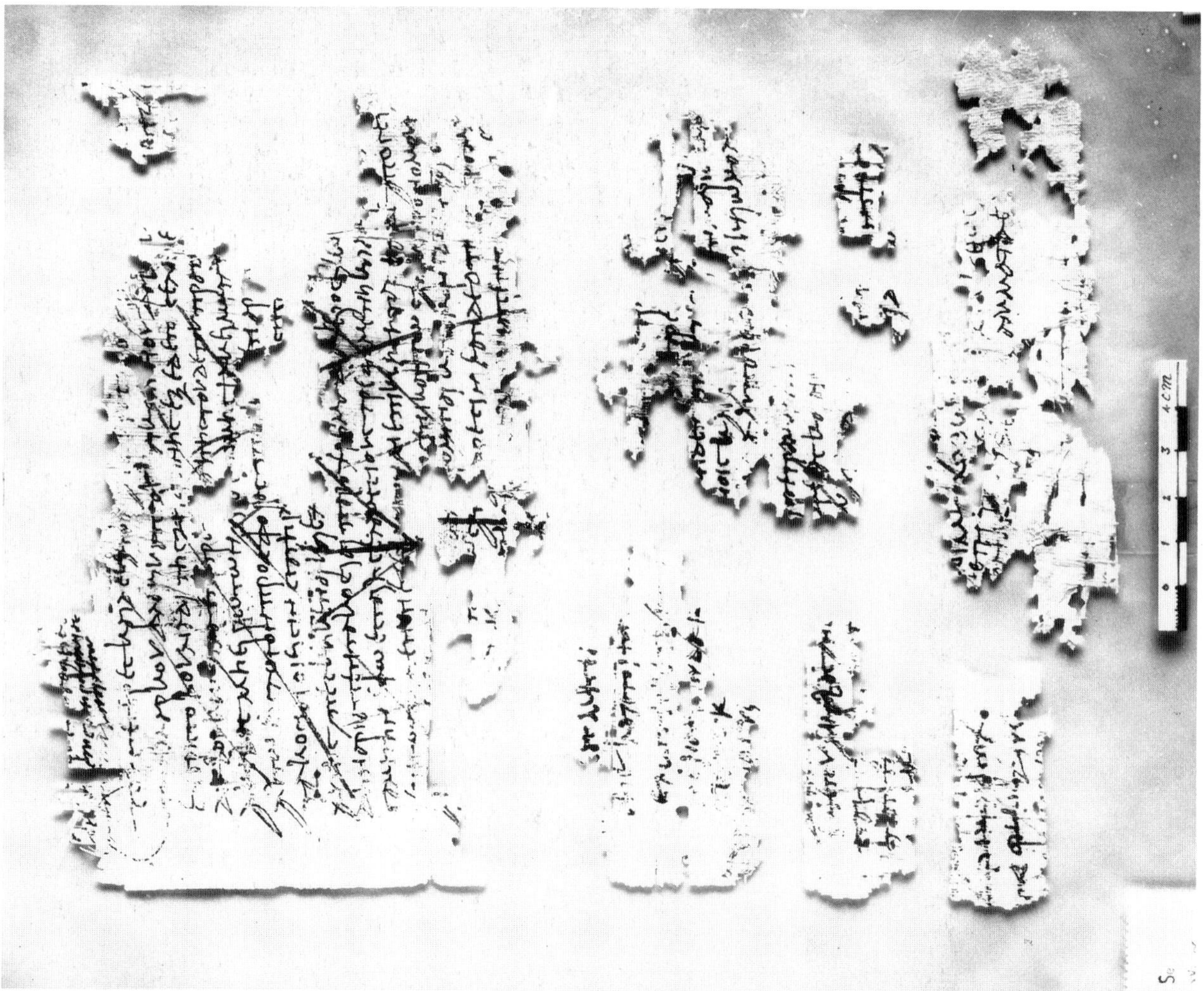

PLATE 708

PLATE 717

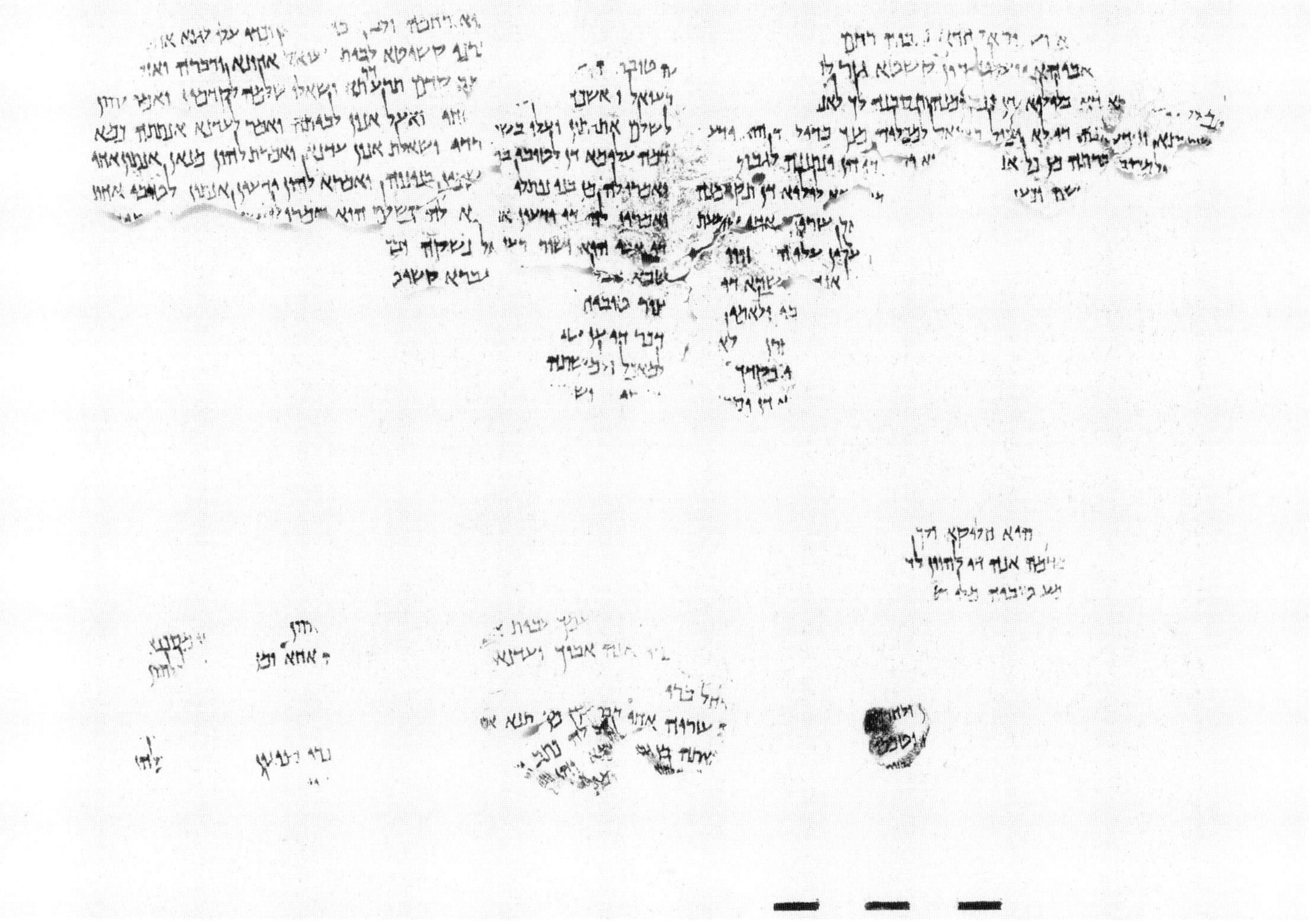

PLATE 718

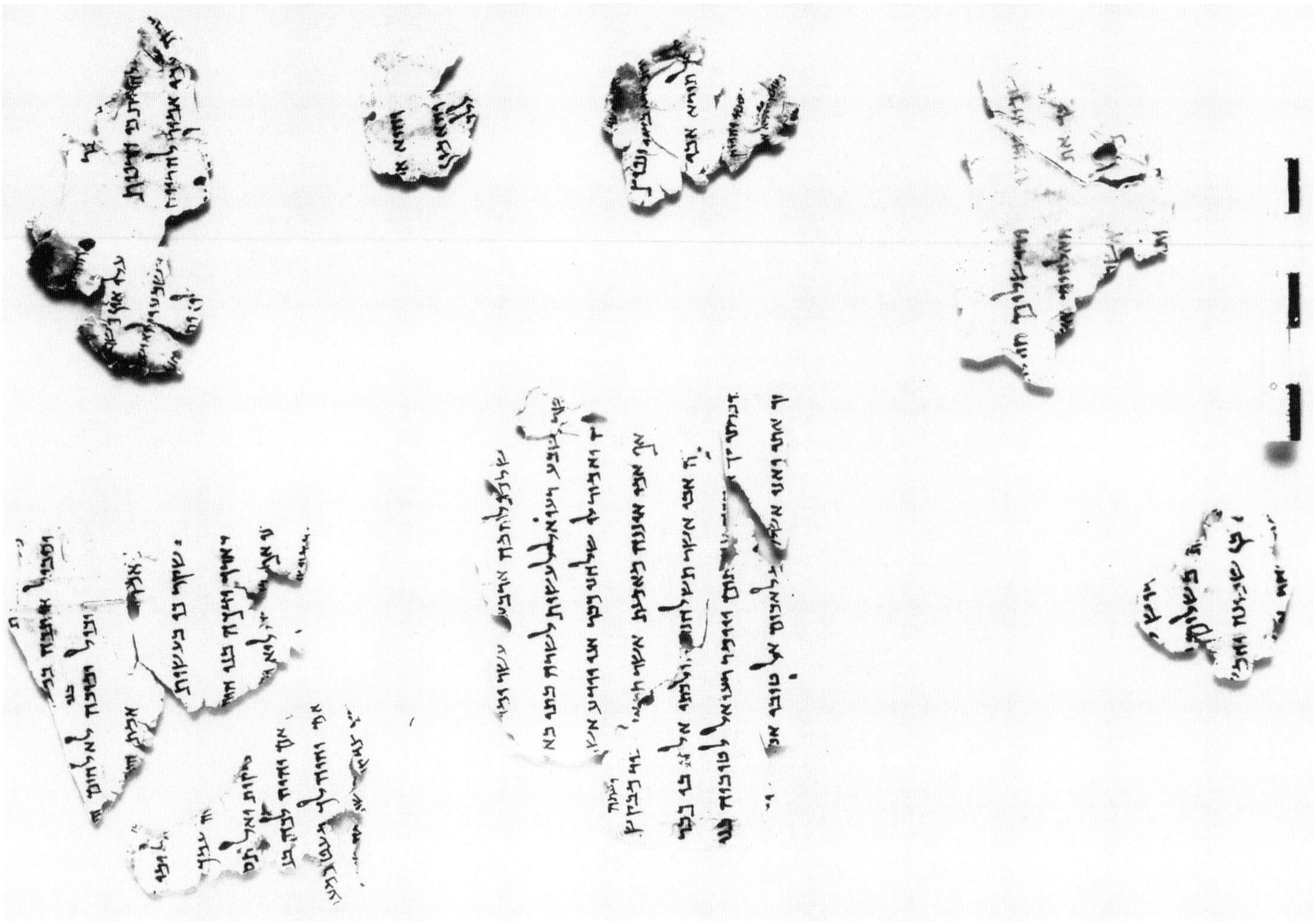

Plate 719

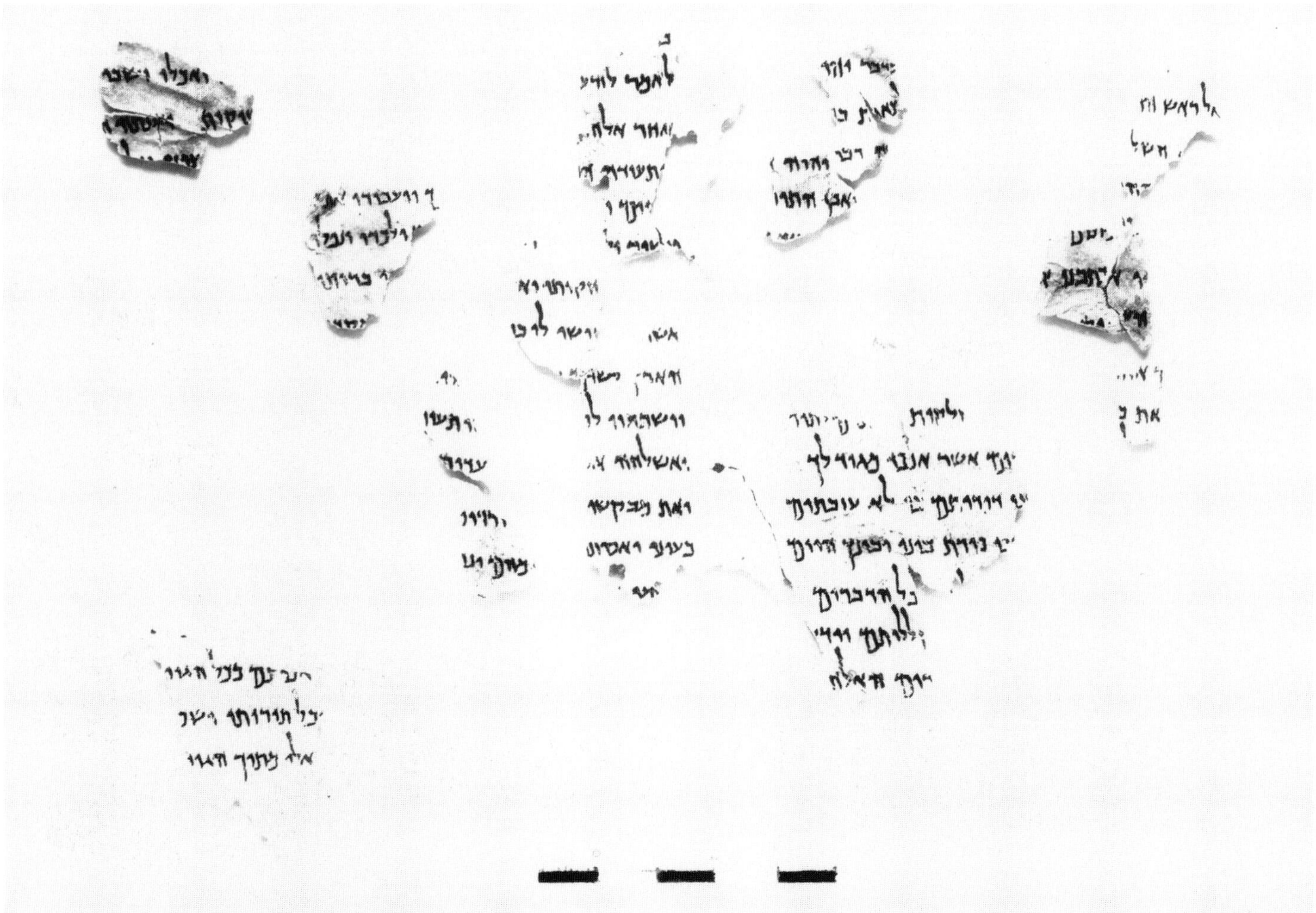

Plate 720

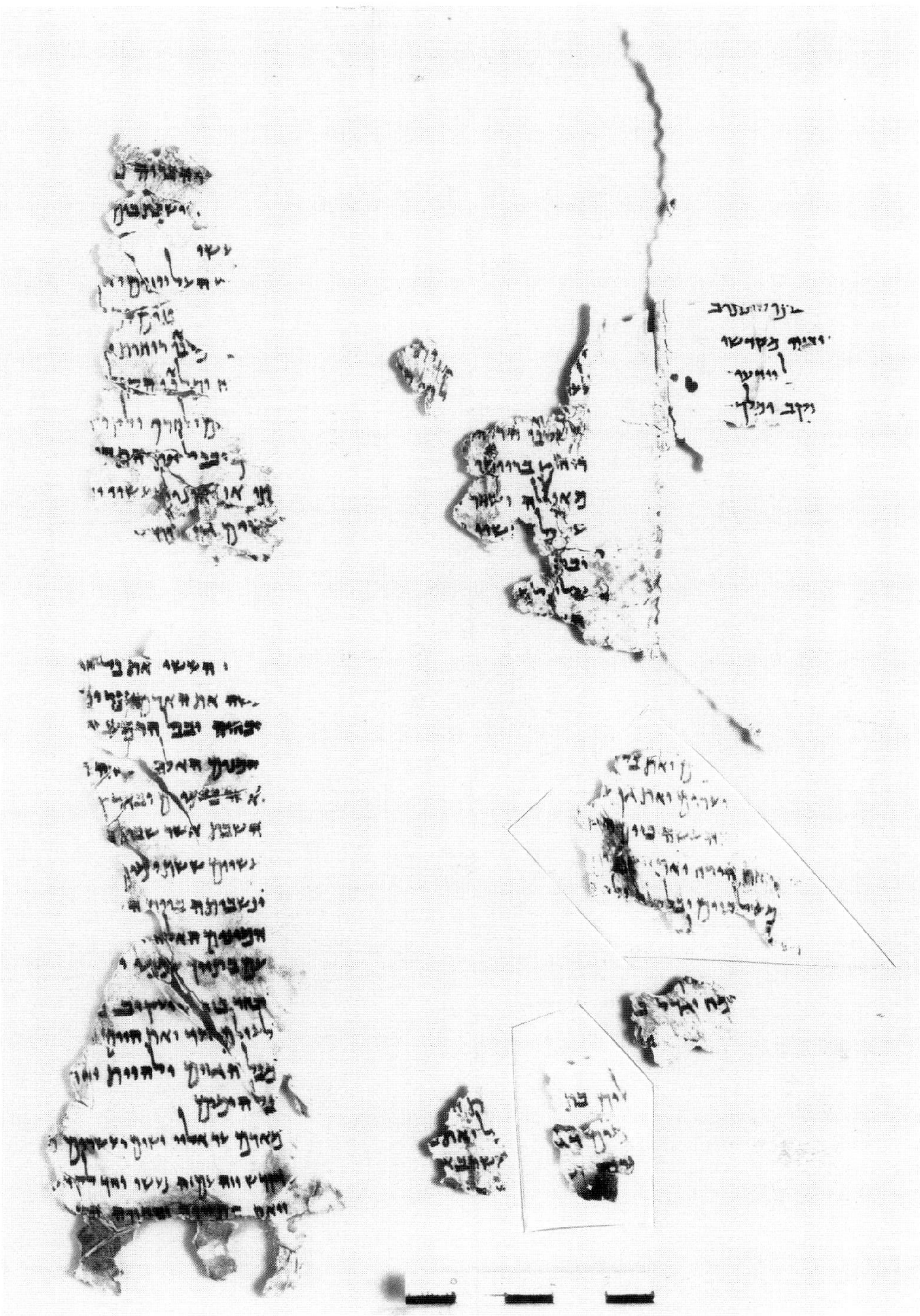

PLATE 721

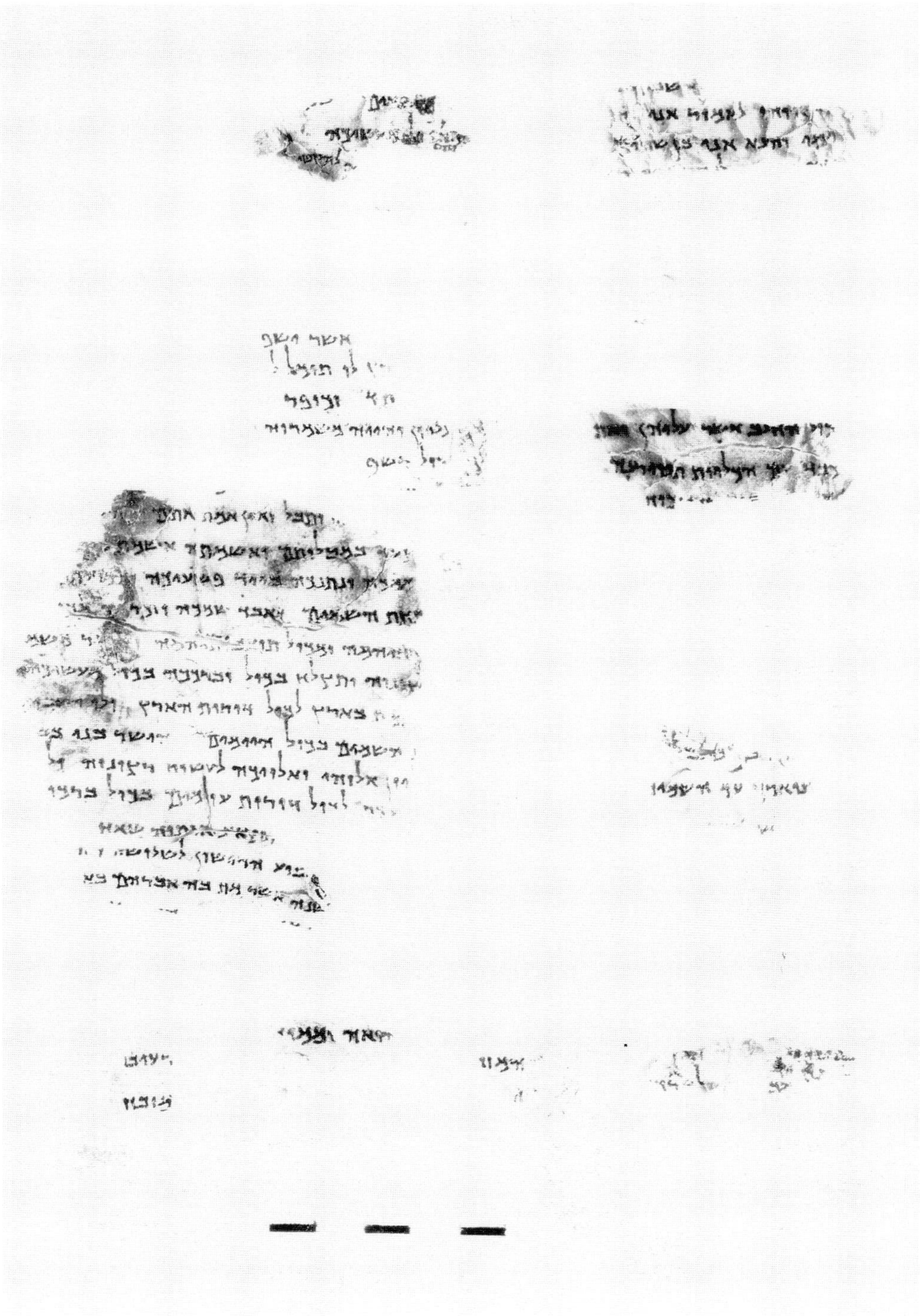

PLATE 722

PLATE 723

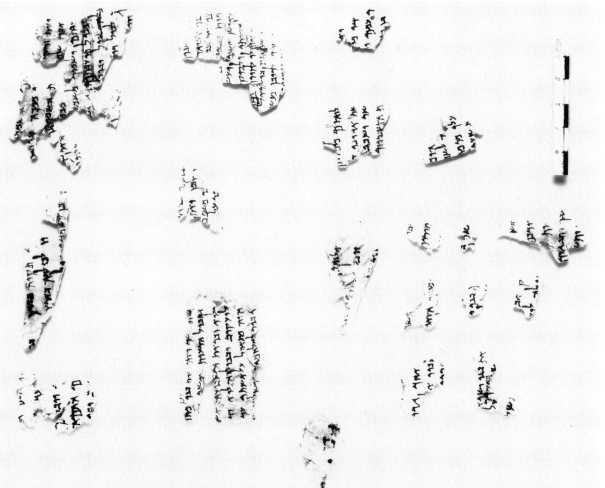

PLATE 724

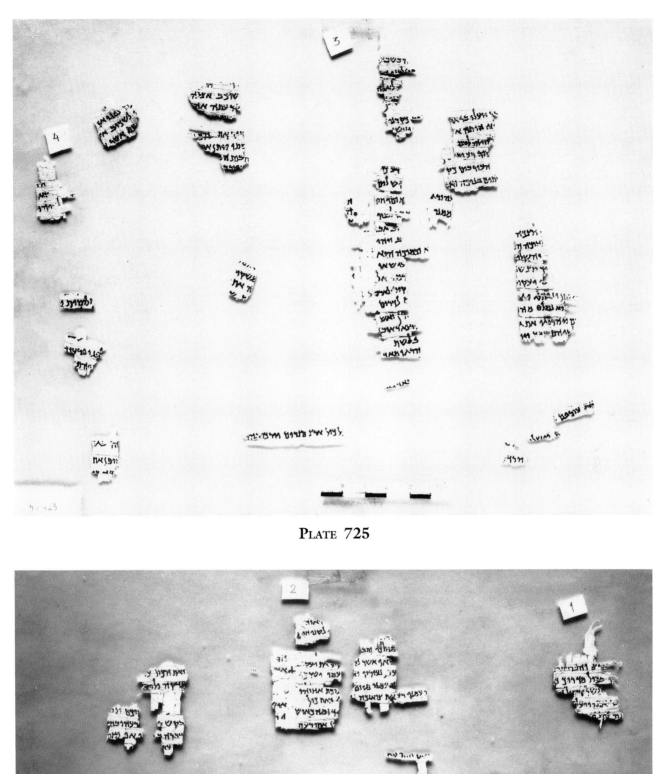

PLATE 725

PLATE 726

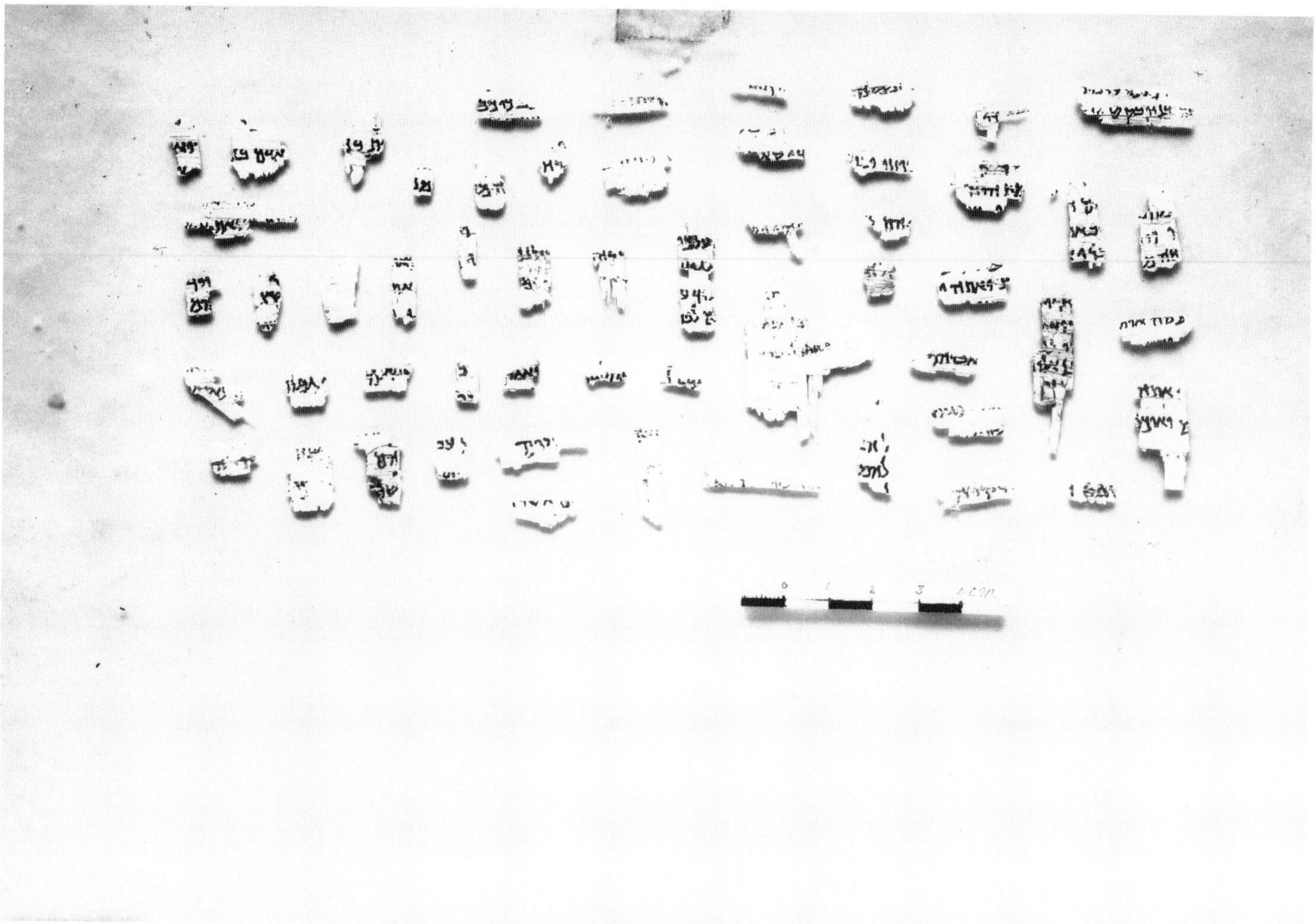

PLATE 727

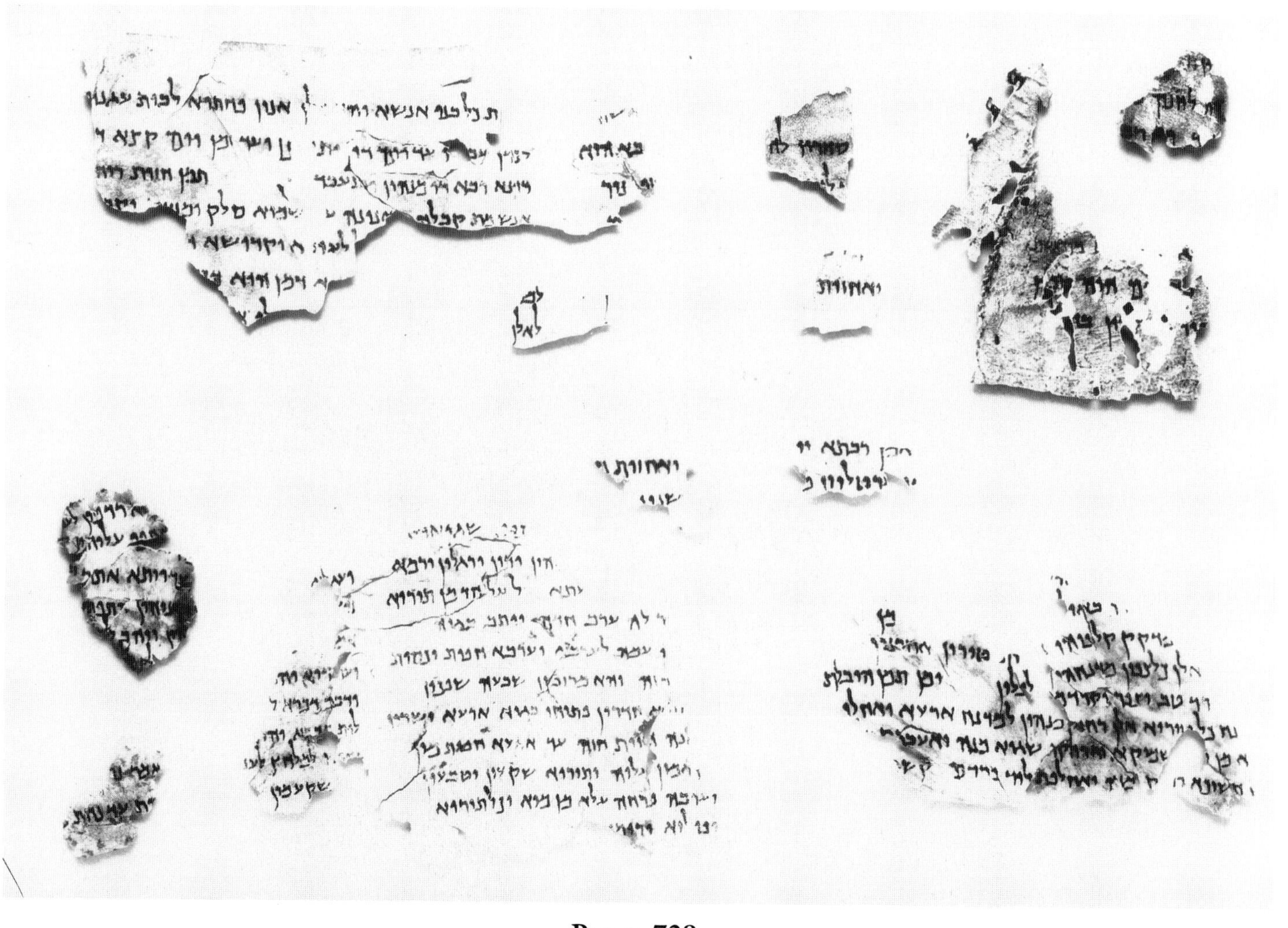

PLATE 728

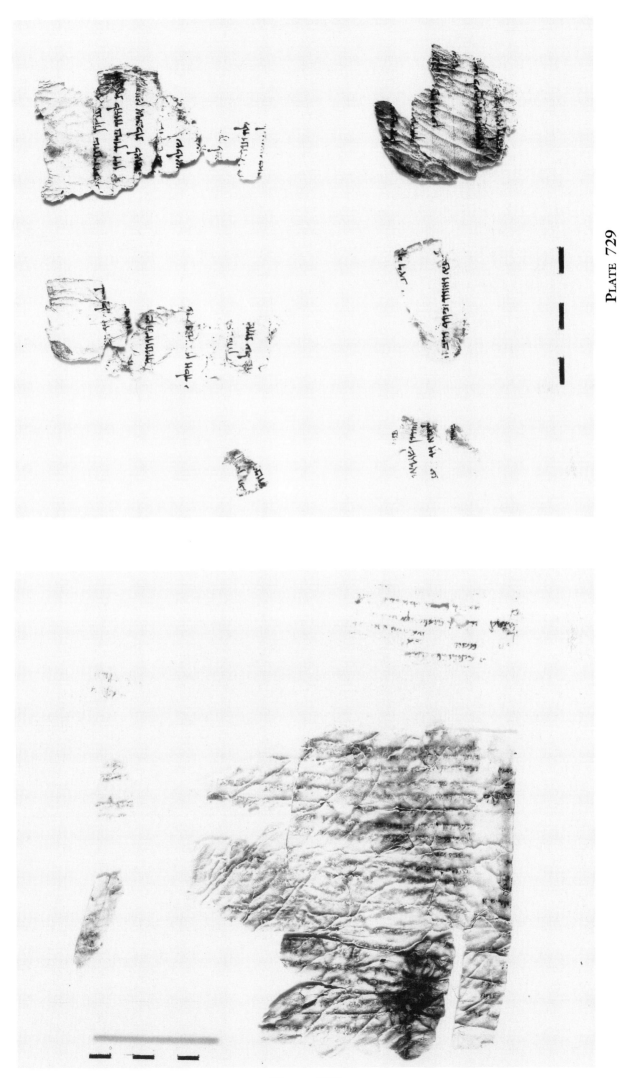

PLATE 729

PLATE 730

PLATE 731

PLATE 732

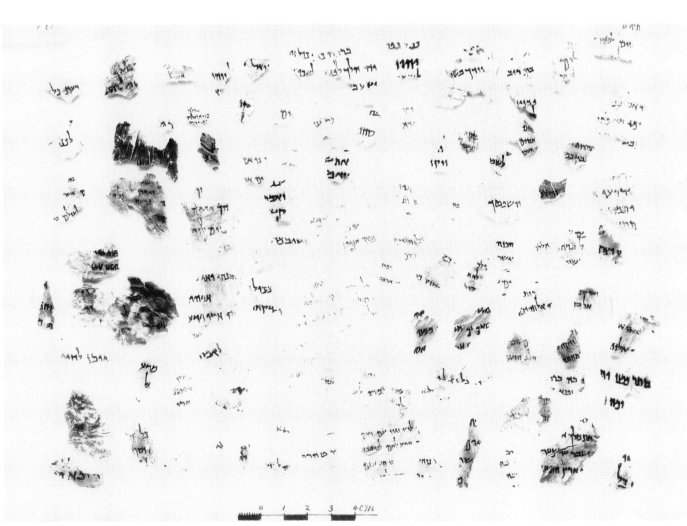

PLATE 746

PLATE 747

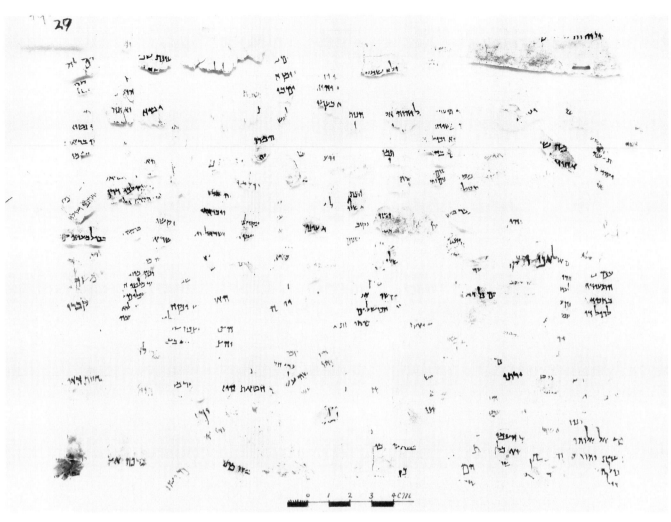

PLATE 748

PLATE 749

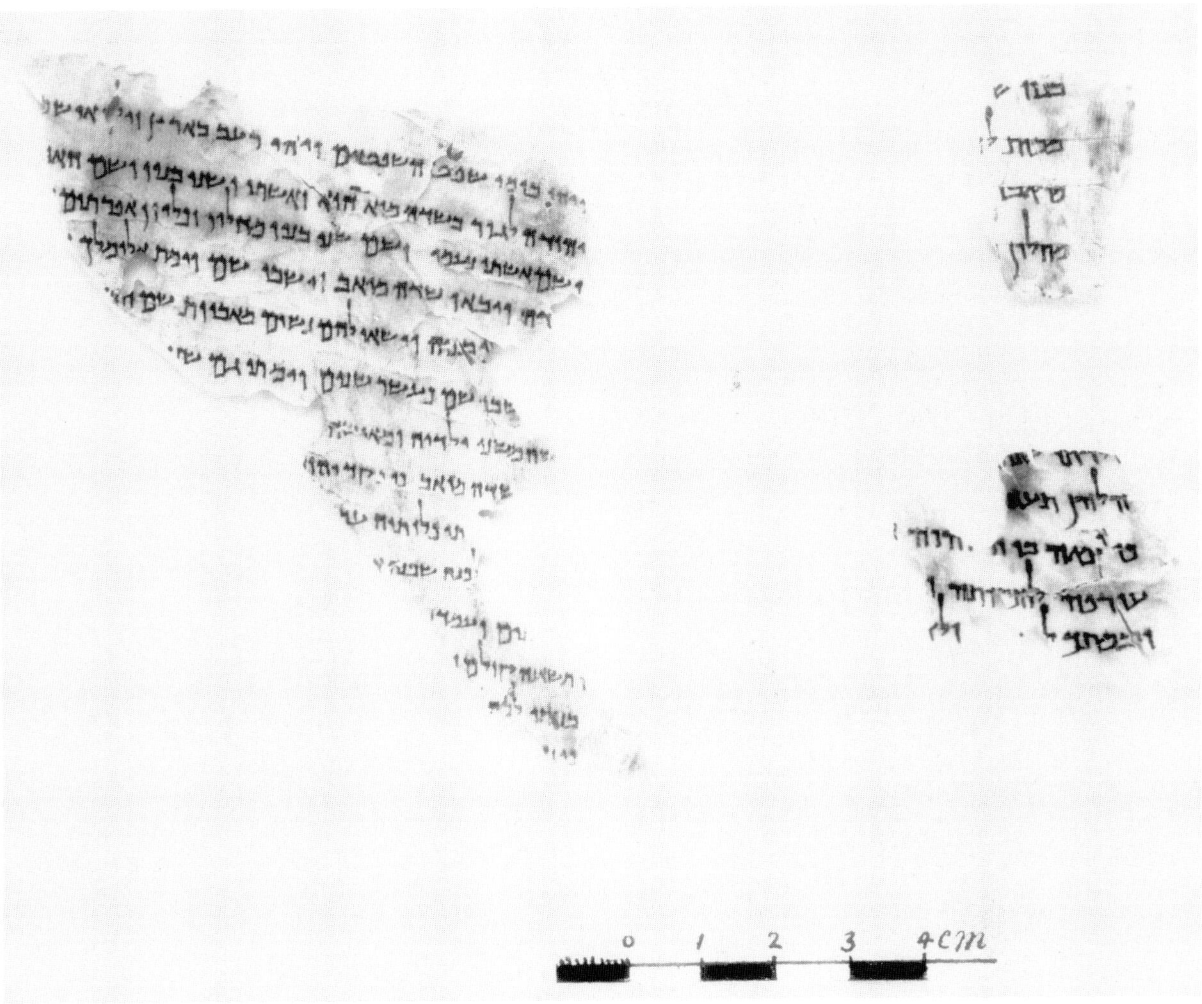

PLATE 766

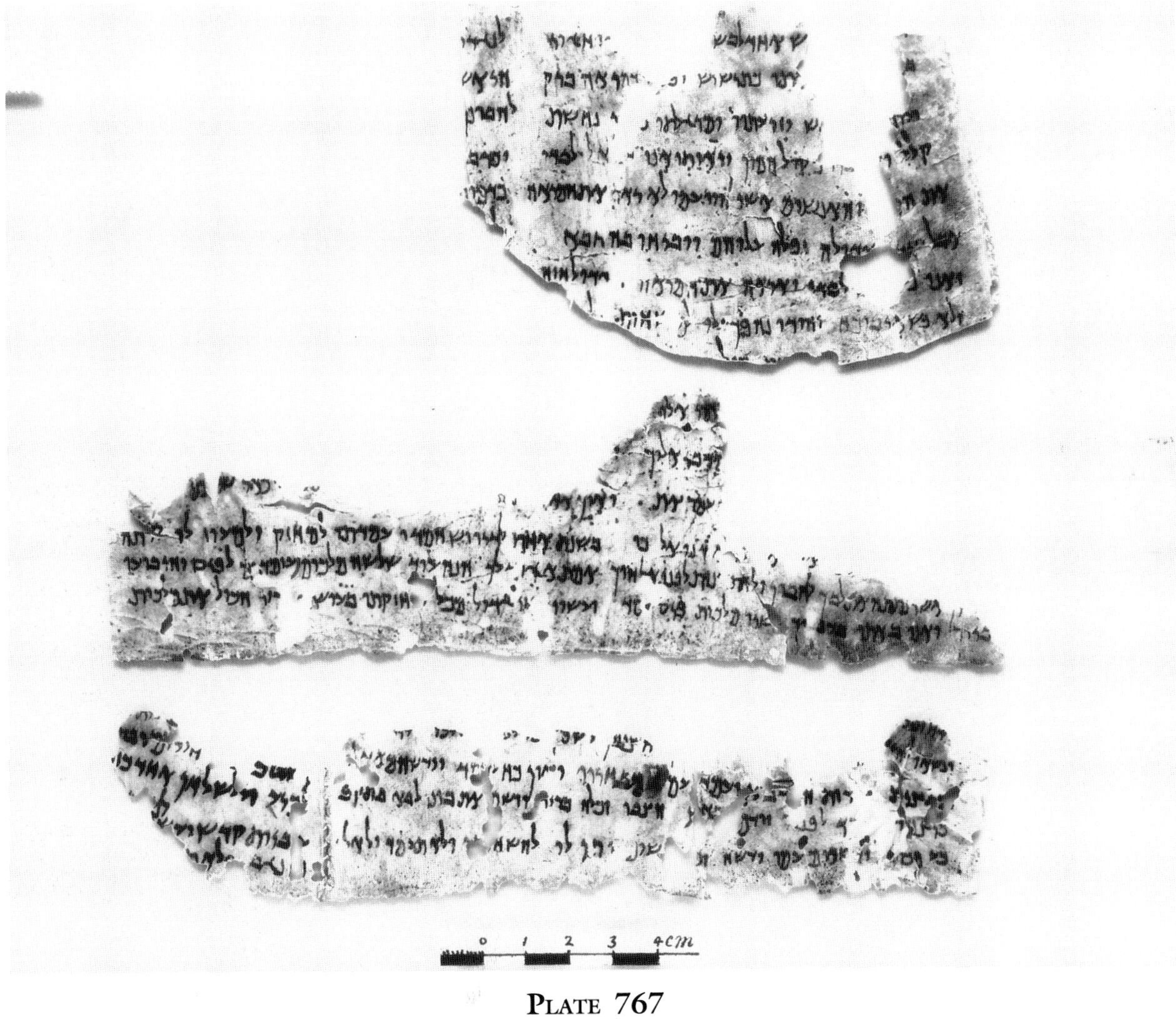

PLATE 767

PLATE 768

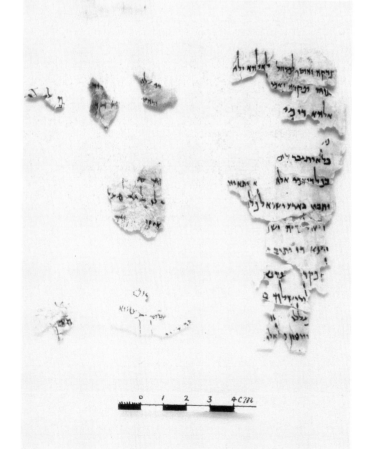

PLATE 769

PLATE 770

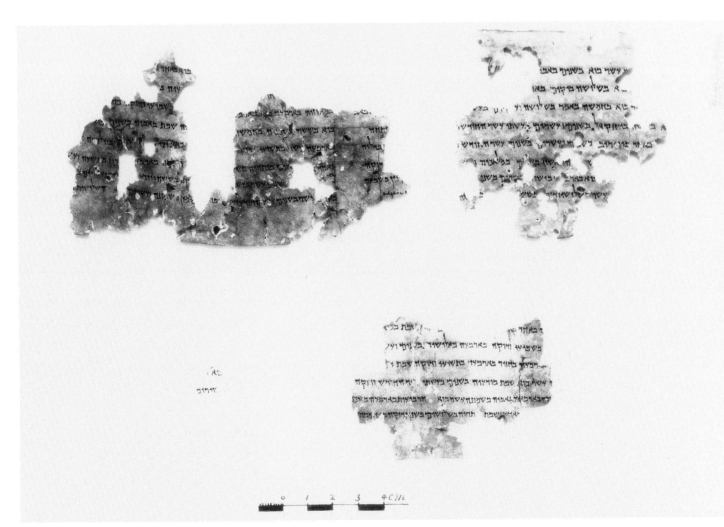

PLATE 771

PLATE 772

PLATE 773

PLATE 774

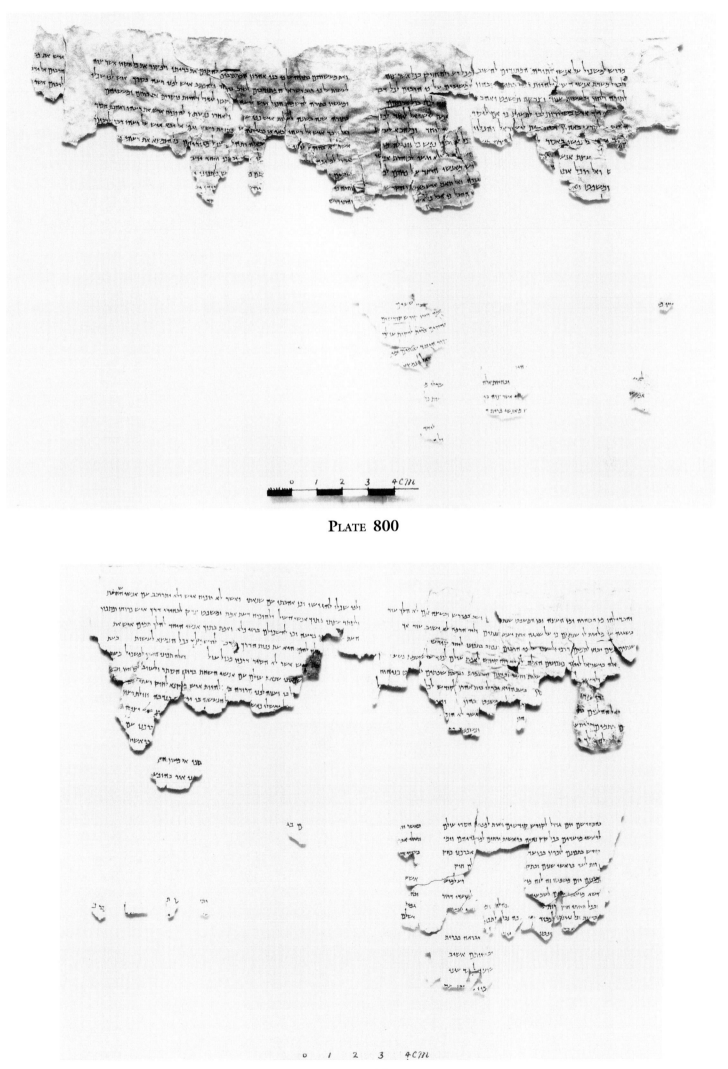

PLATE 800

PLATE 801

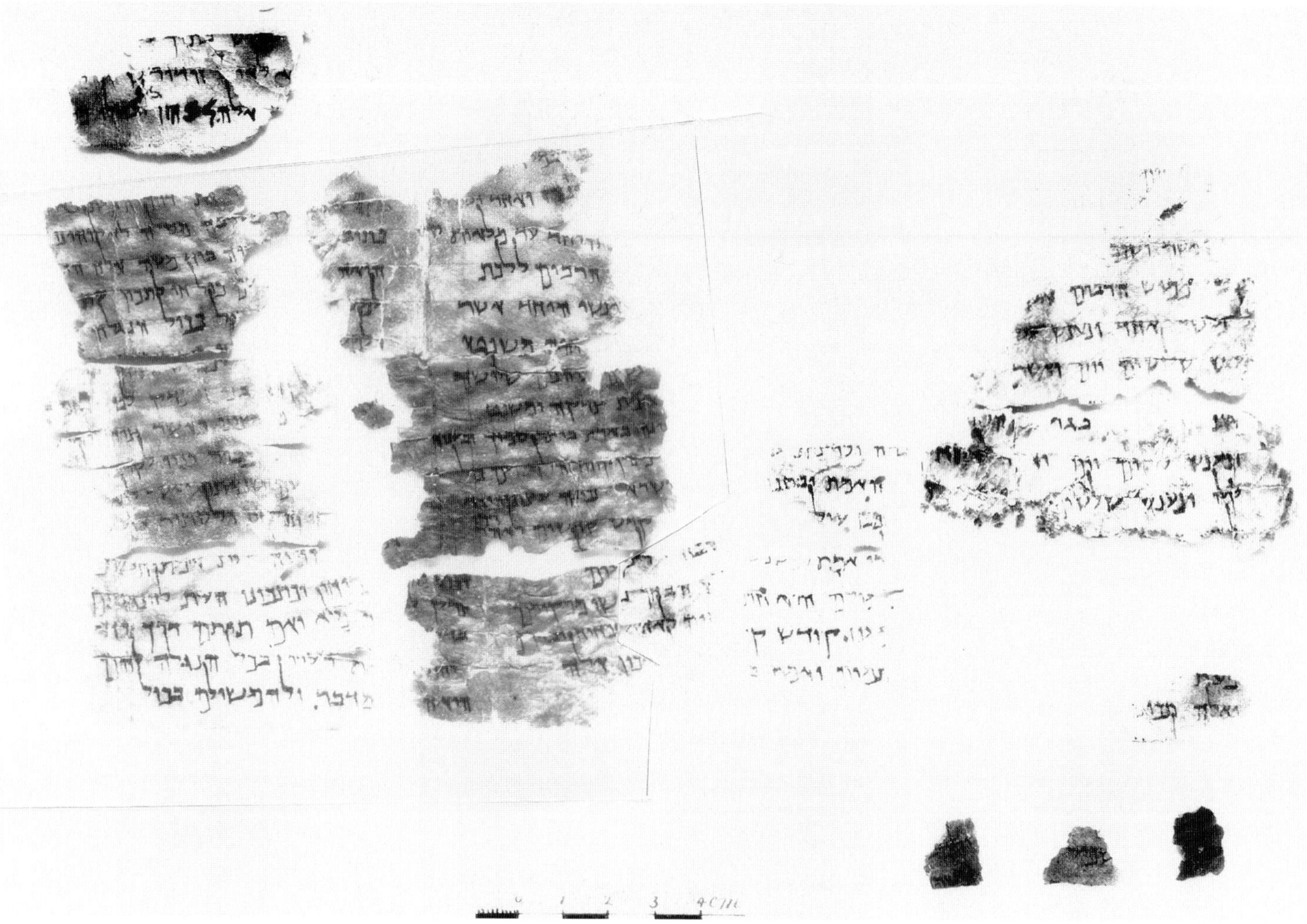

PLATE 802

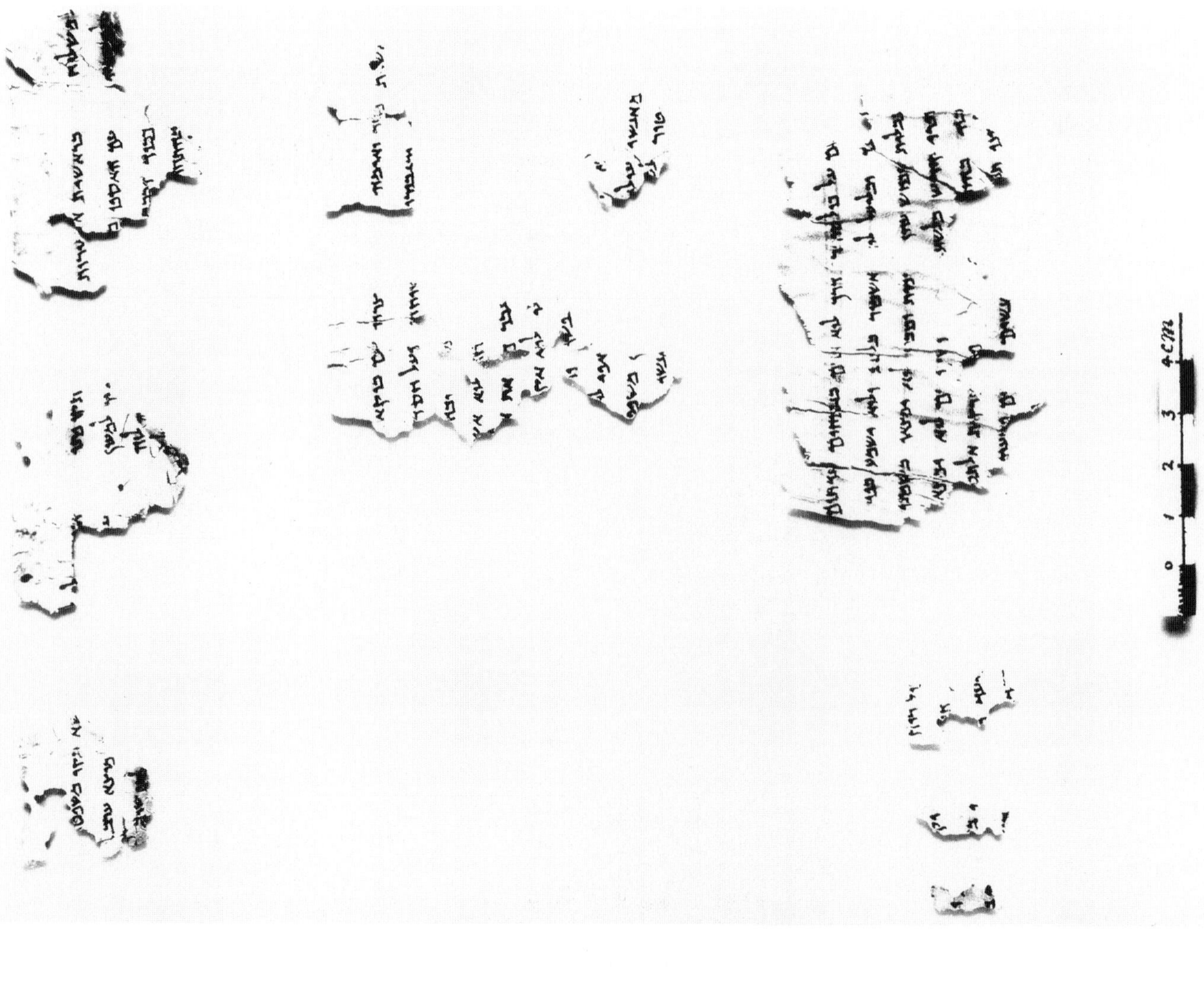

PLATE 803

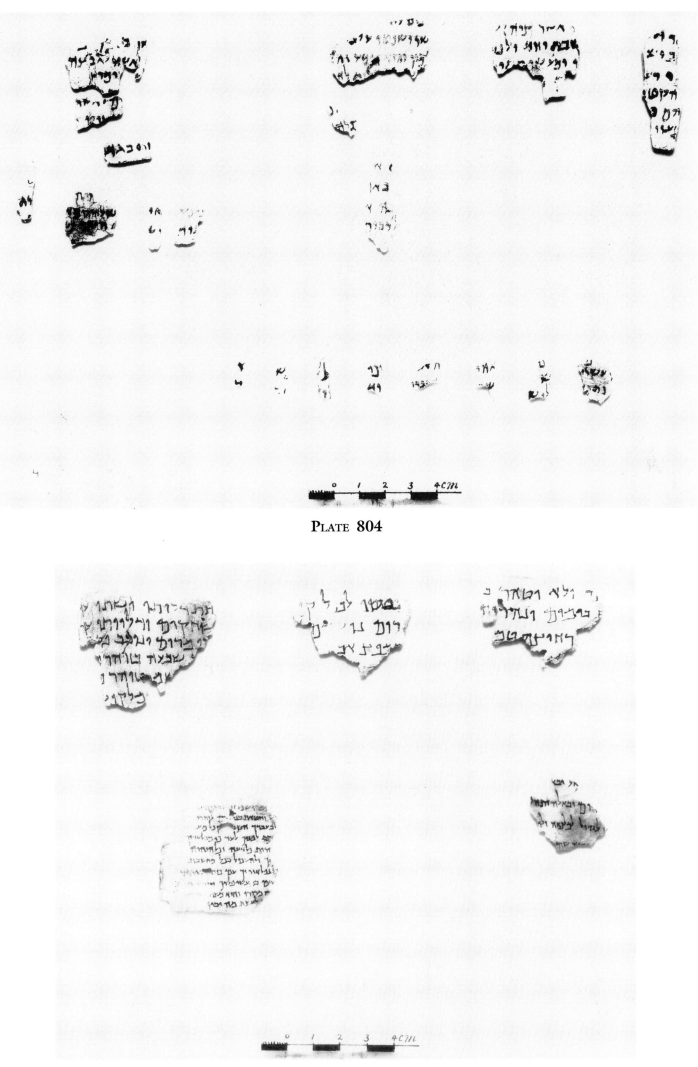

PLATE 804

PLATE 805

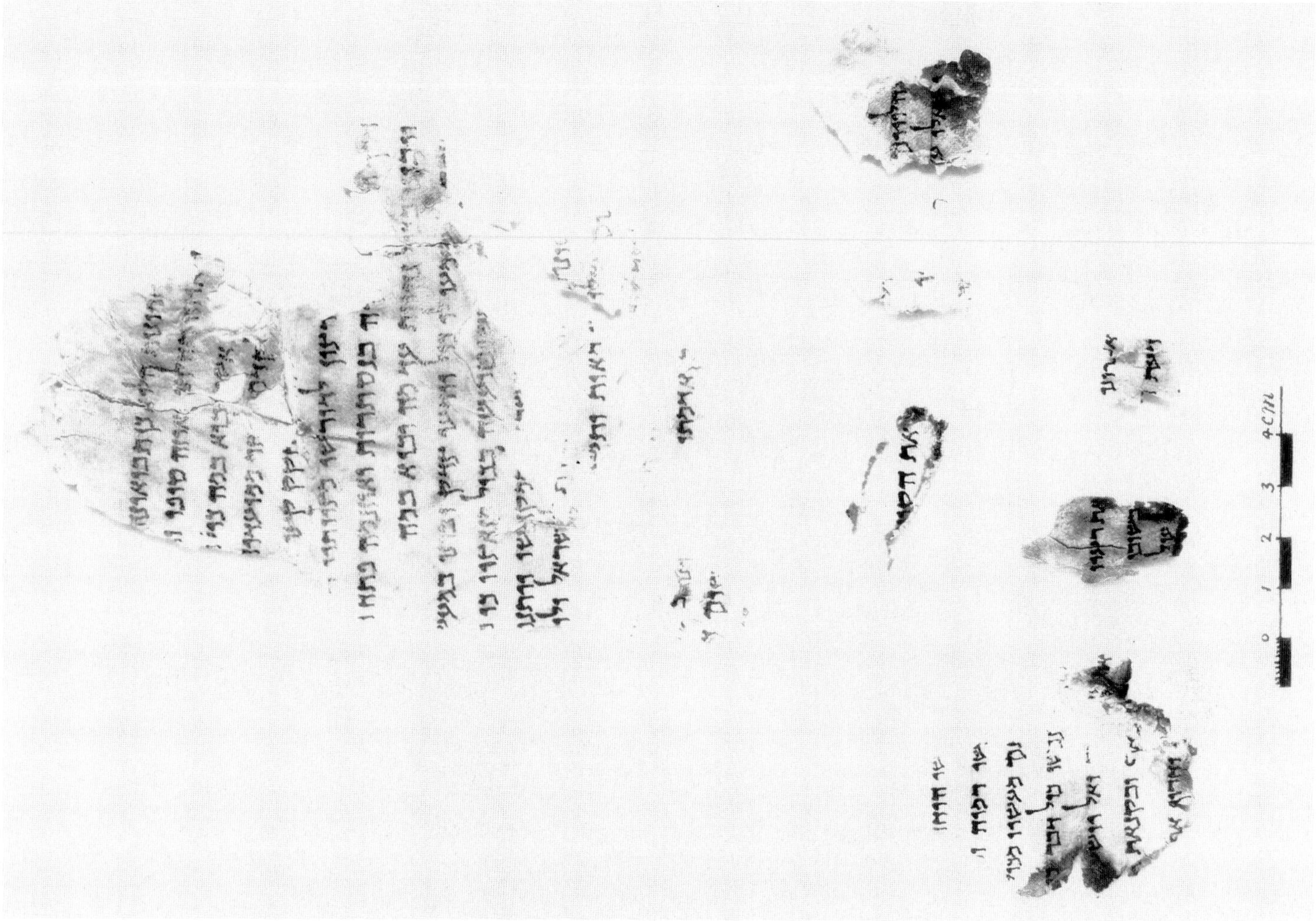

PLATE 806

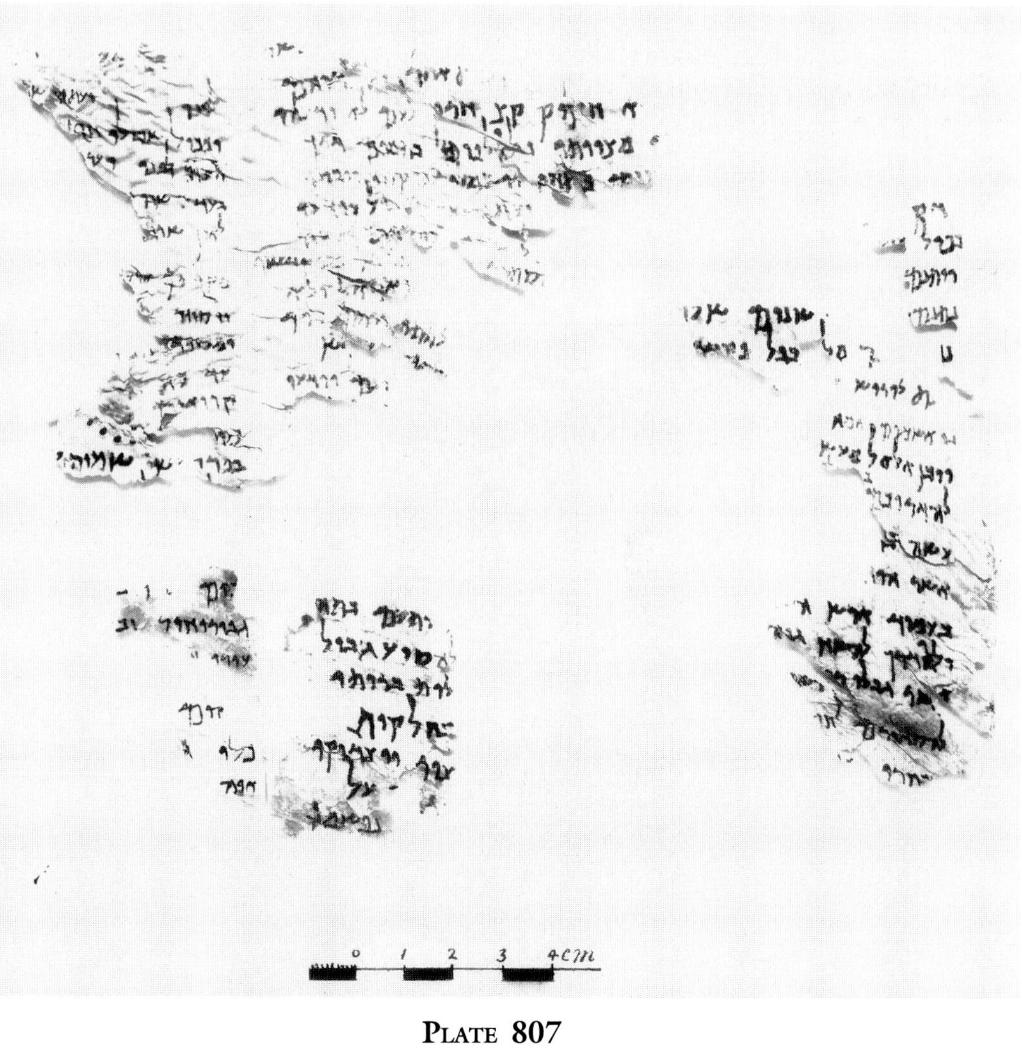

PLATE 807

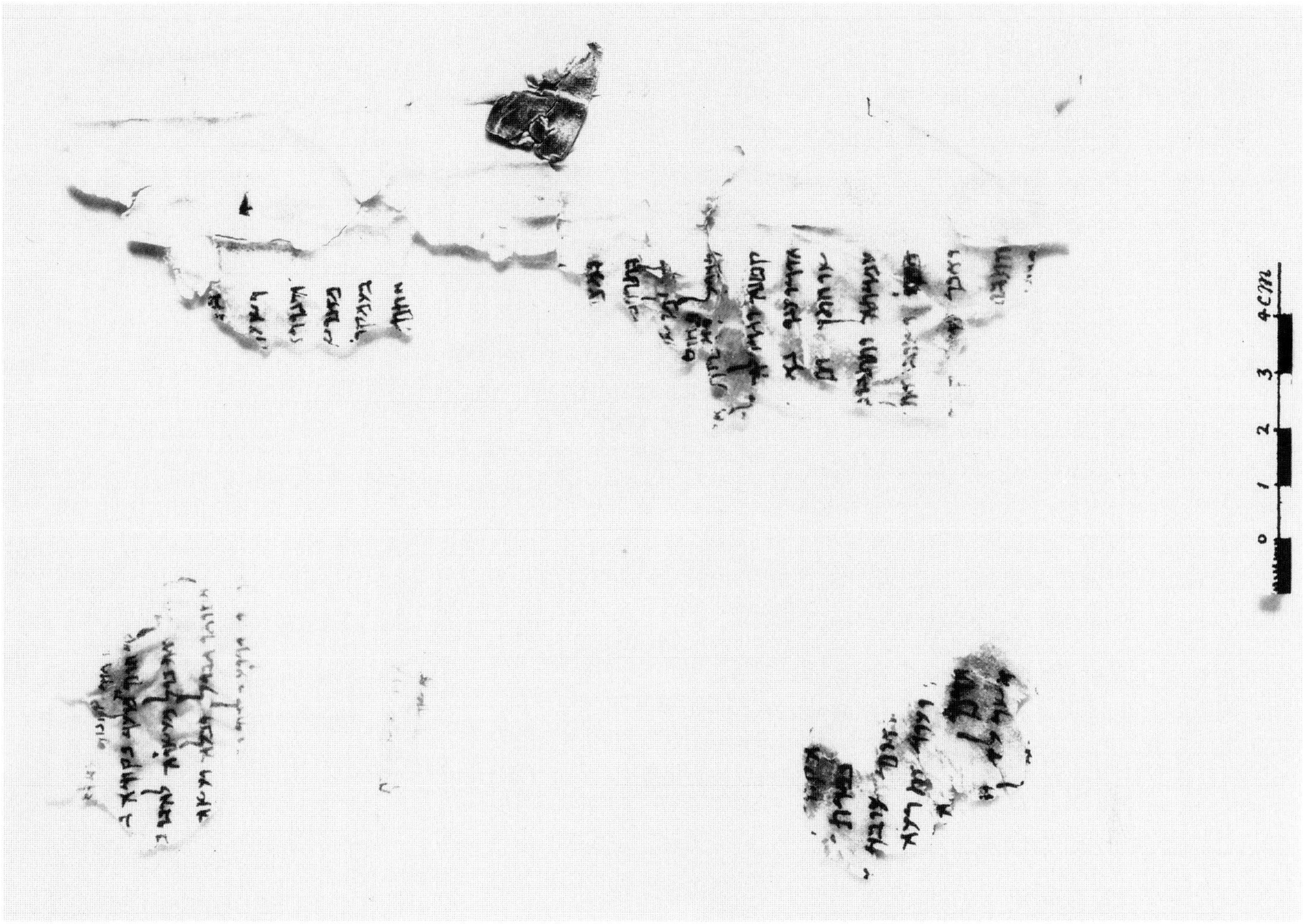

PLATE 808

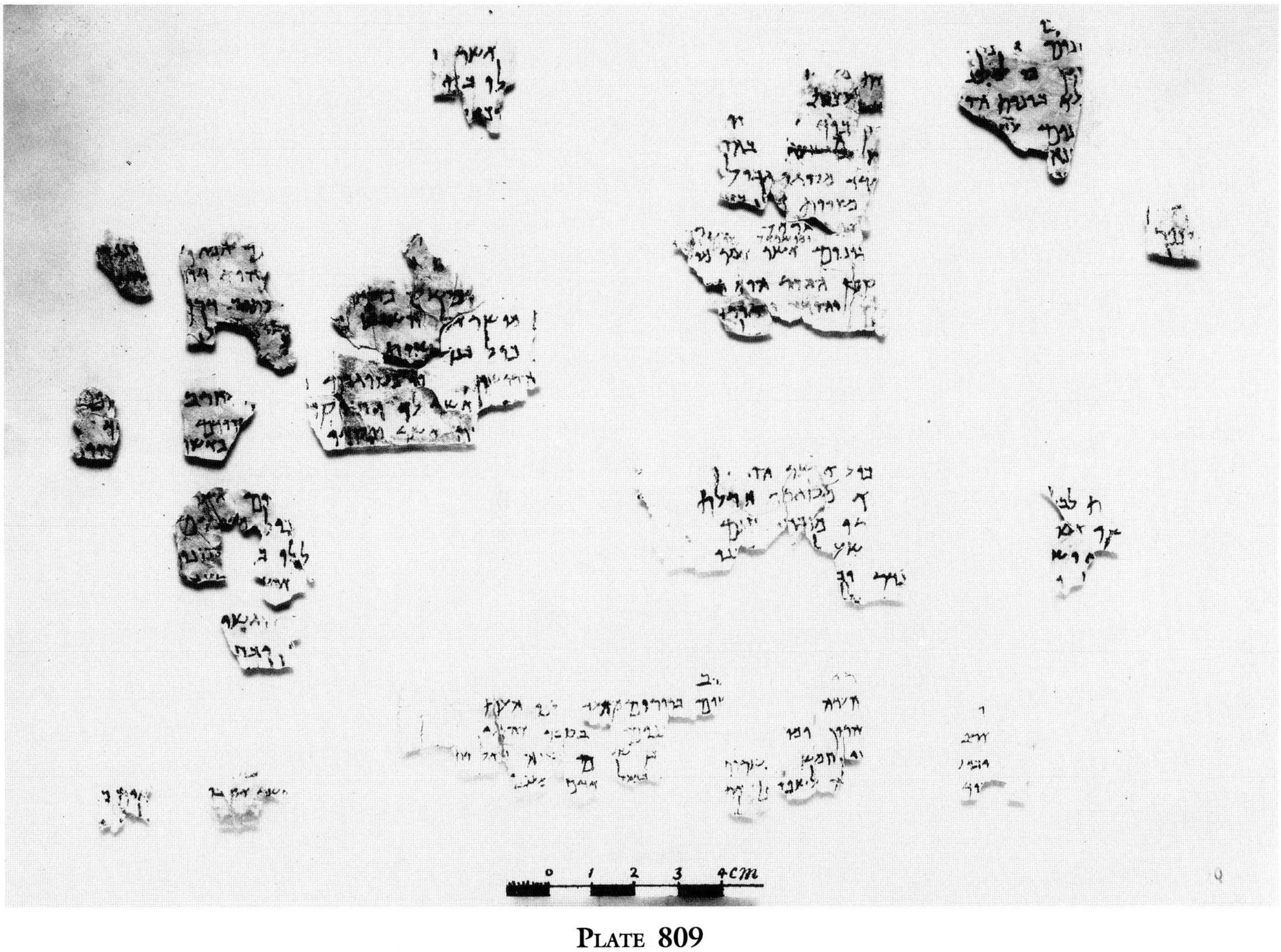

PLATE 809

PLATE 810

PLATE 811

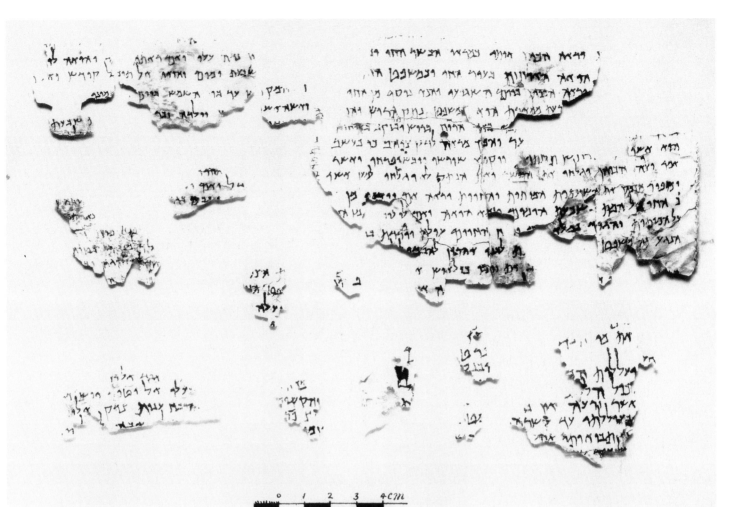

PLATE 812

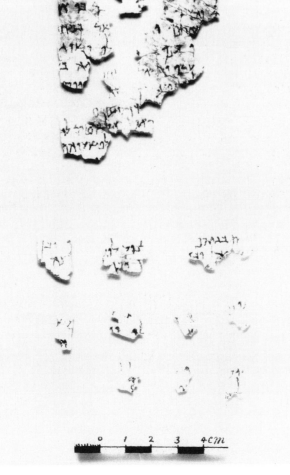

PLATE 813

PLATE 814

PLATE 815

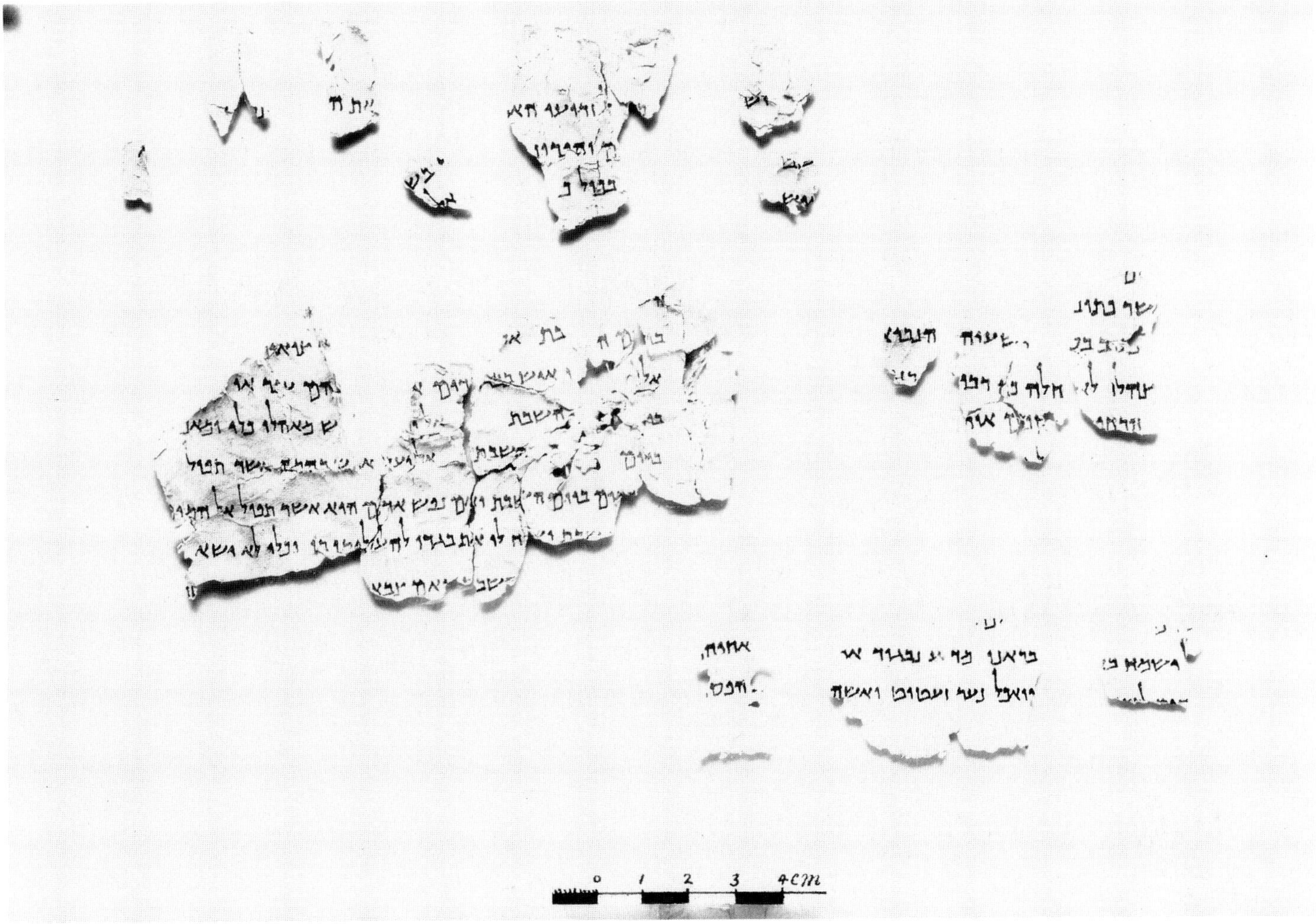

PLATE 832

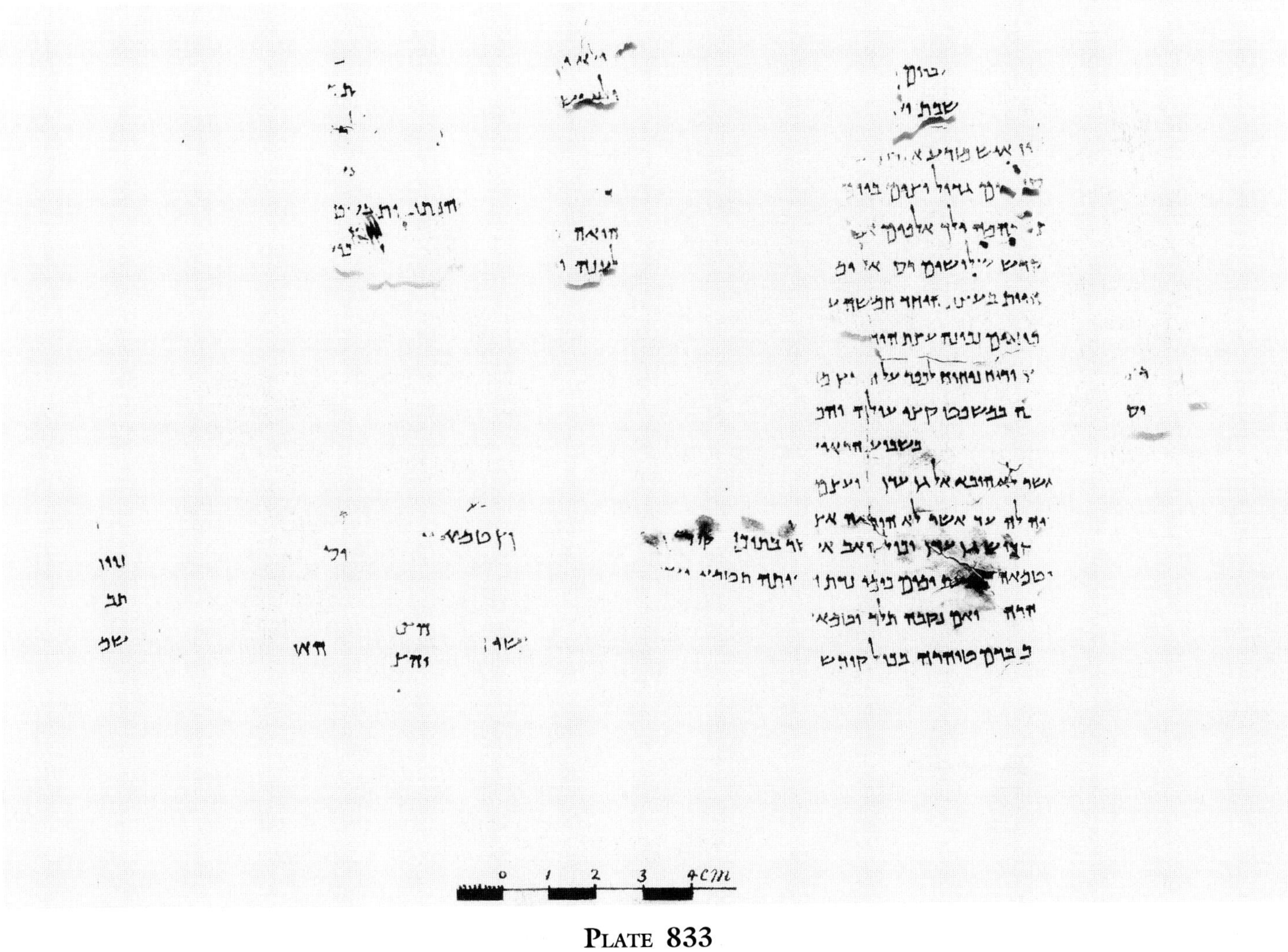

PLATE 833

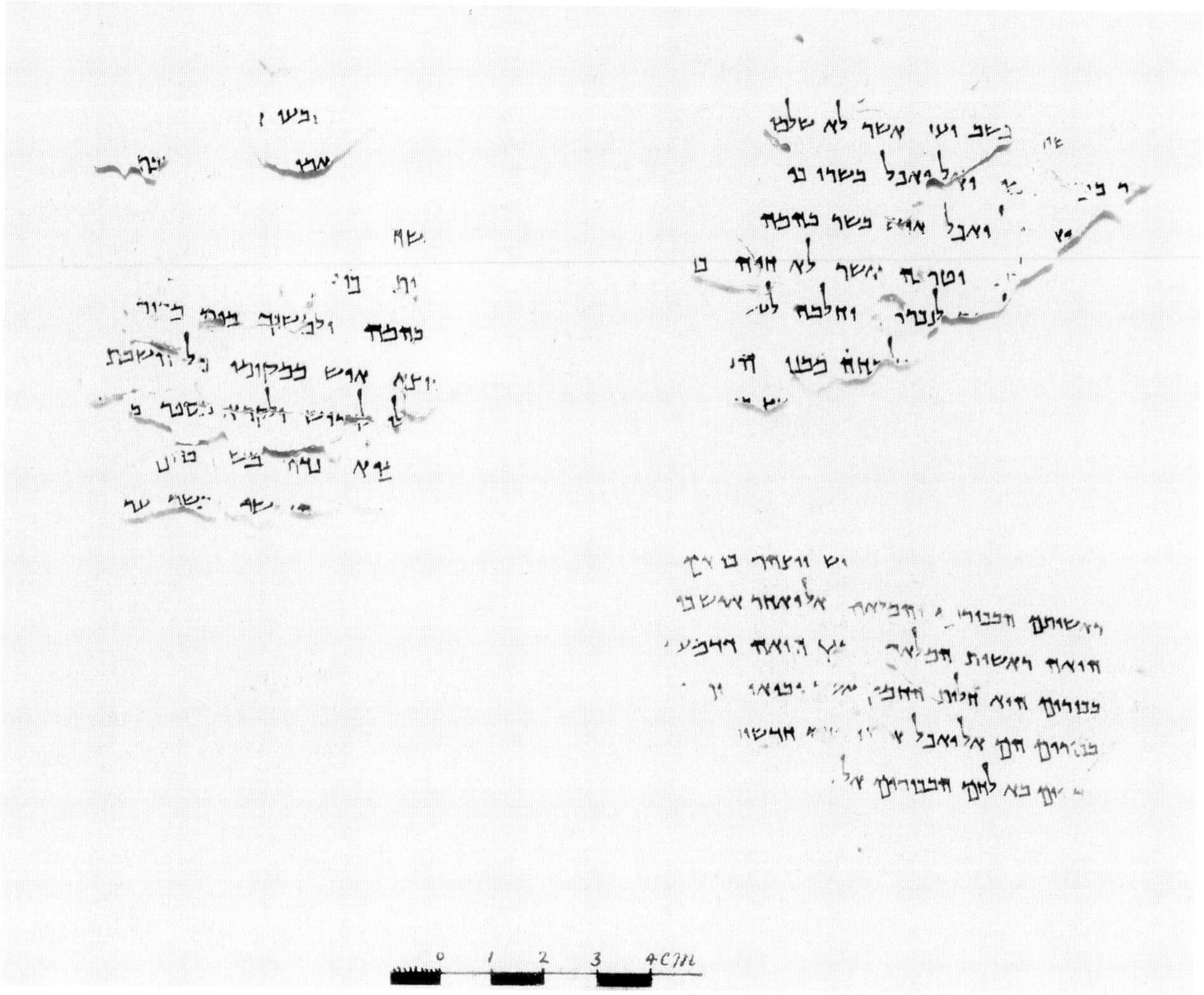

PLATE 834

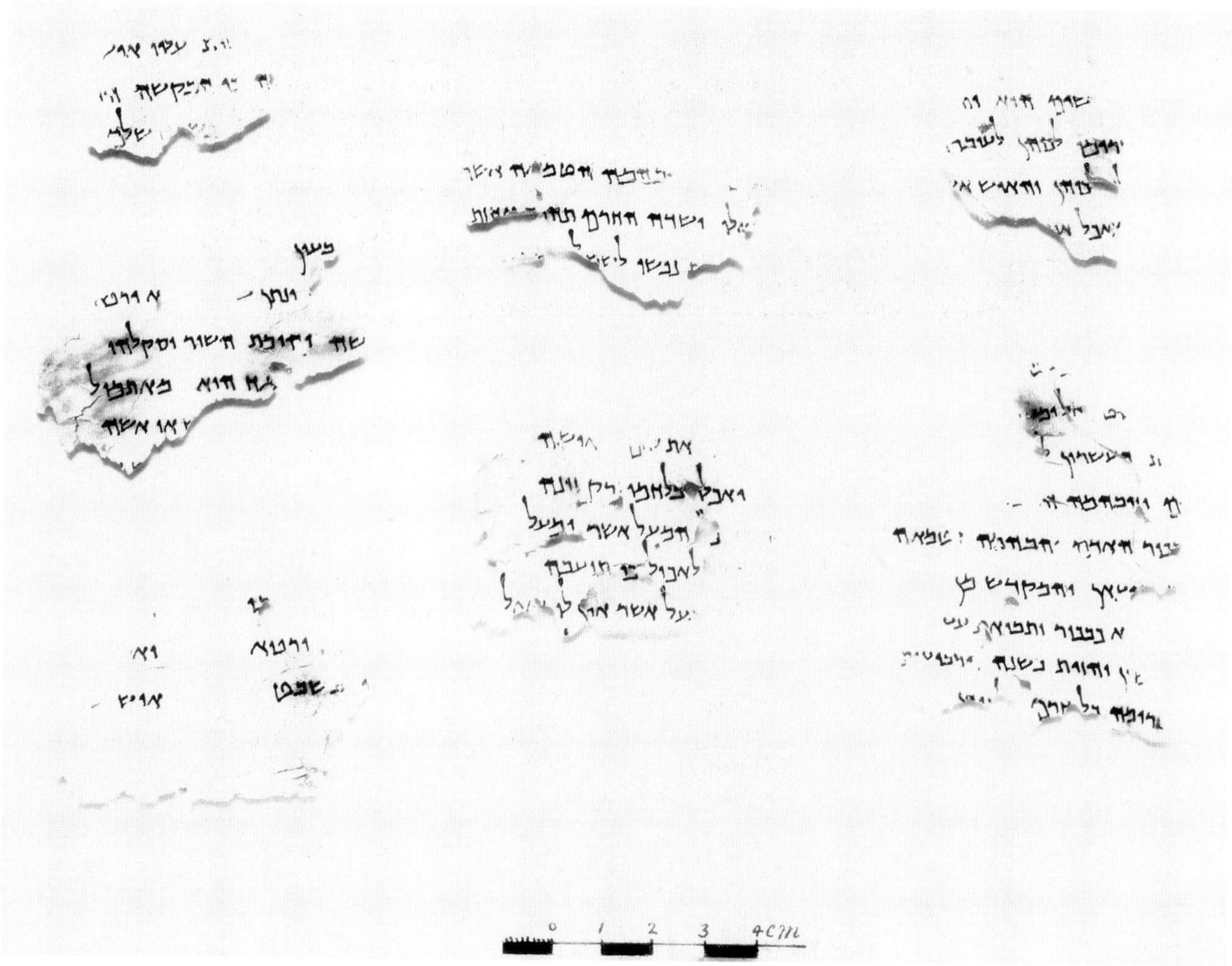

PLATE 835

PLATE 844

PLATE 845

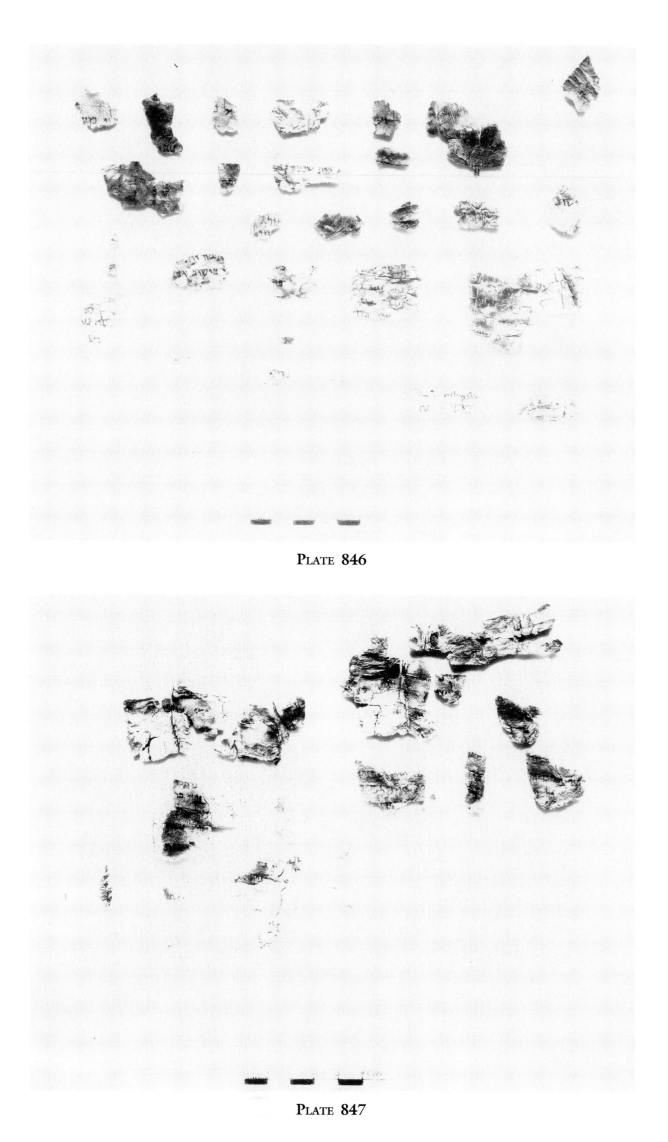

PLATE 846

PLATE 847

PLATE 848

PLATE 849

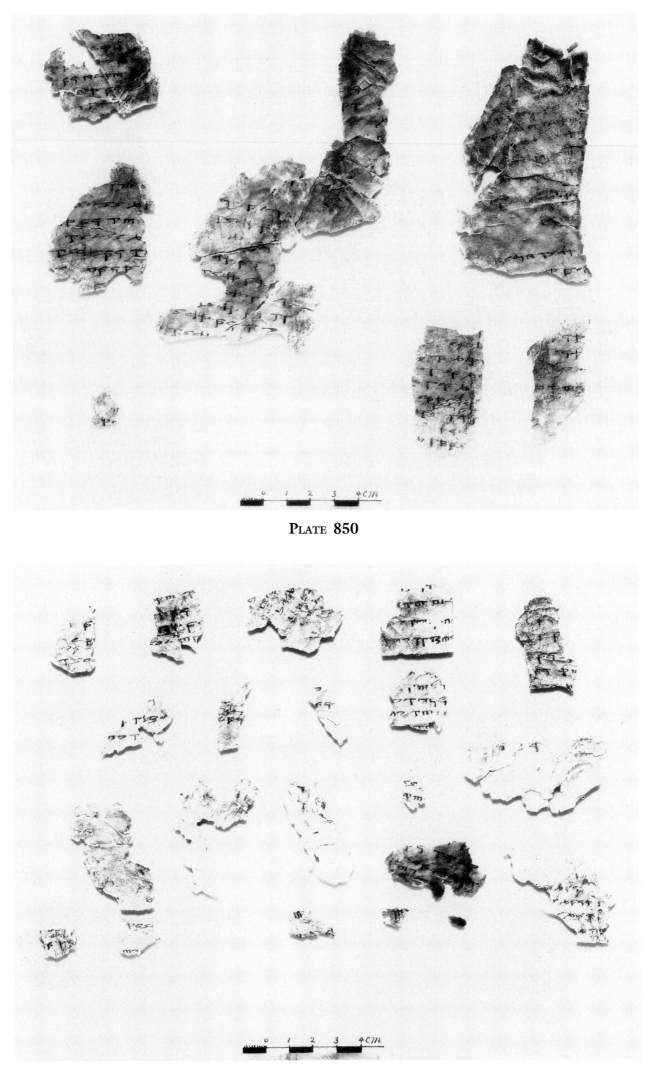

PLATE 850

PLATE 851

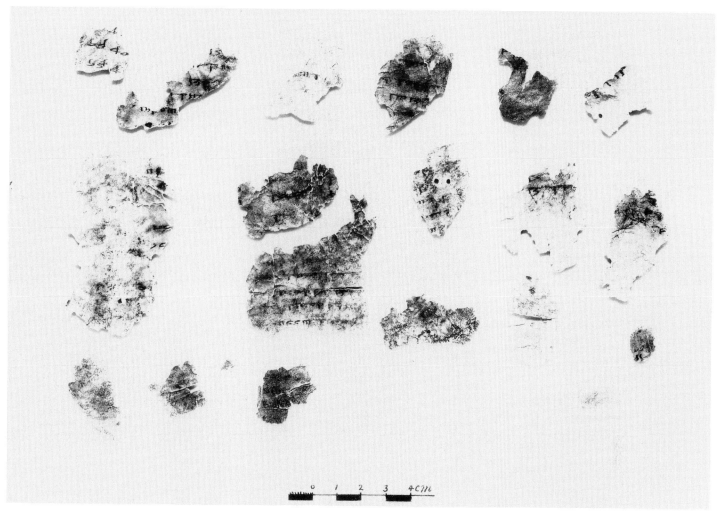

PLATE 852

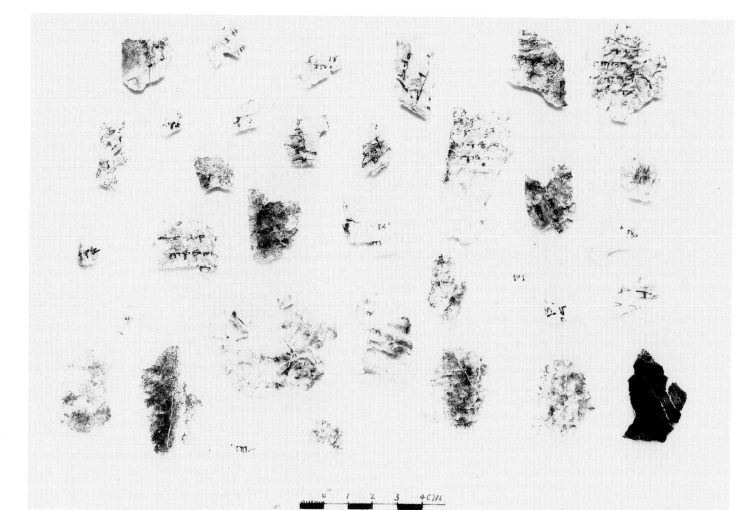

PLATE 853

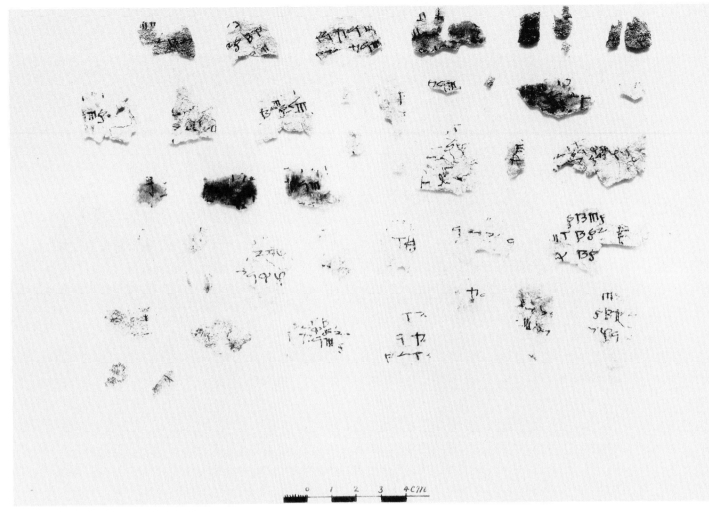

PLATE 854

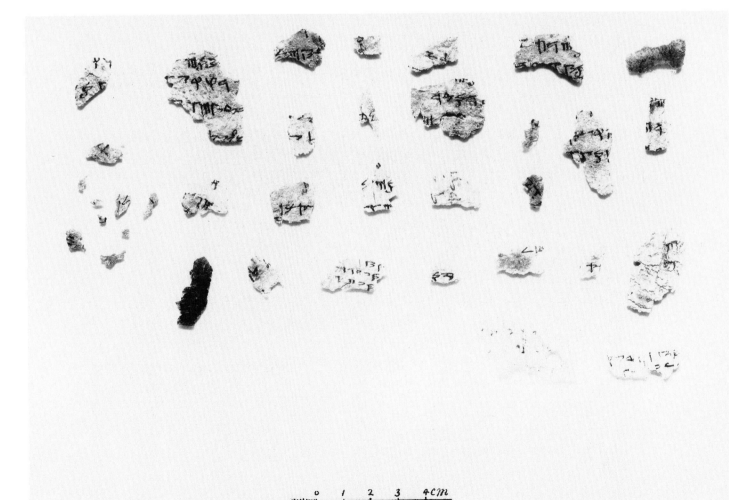

PLATE 855

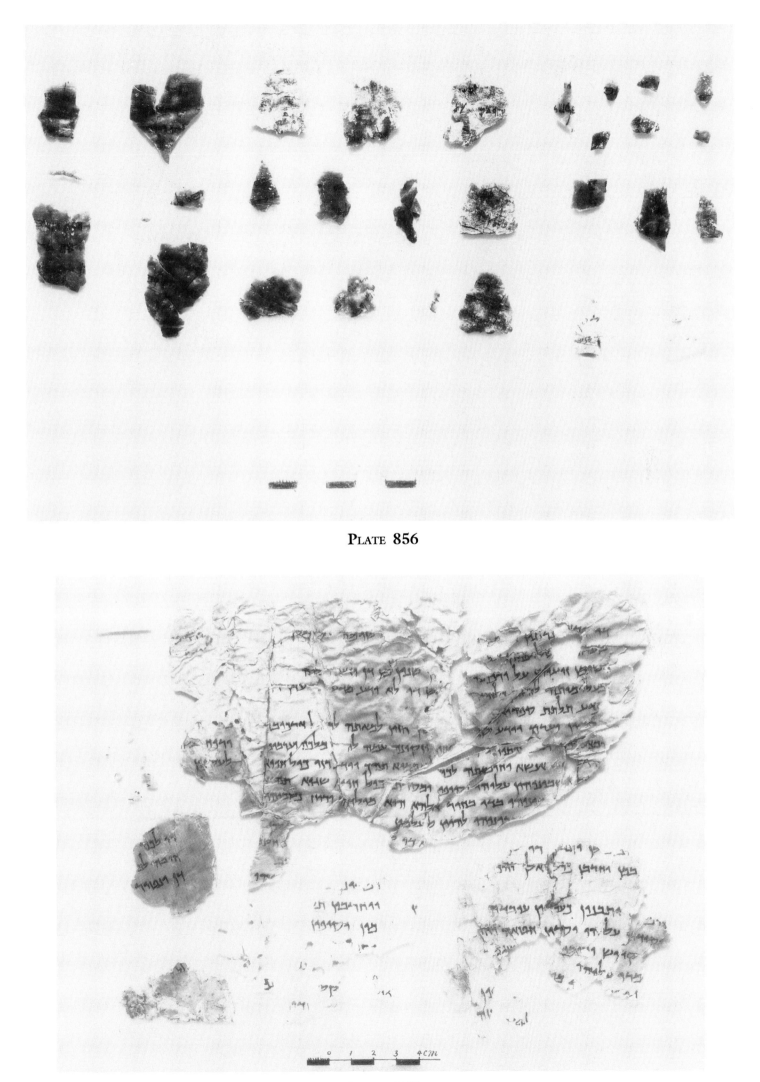

PLATE 856

PLATE 857

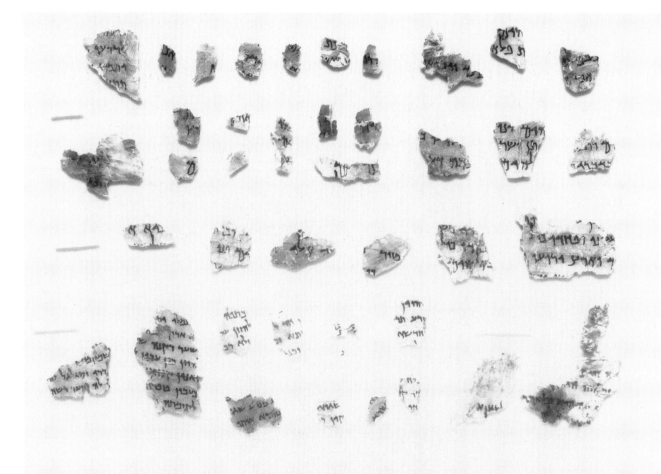

PLATE 858

PLATE 859

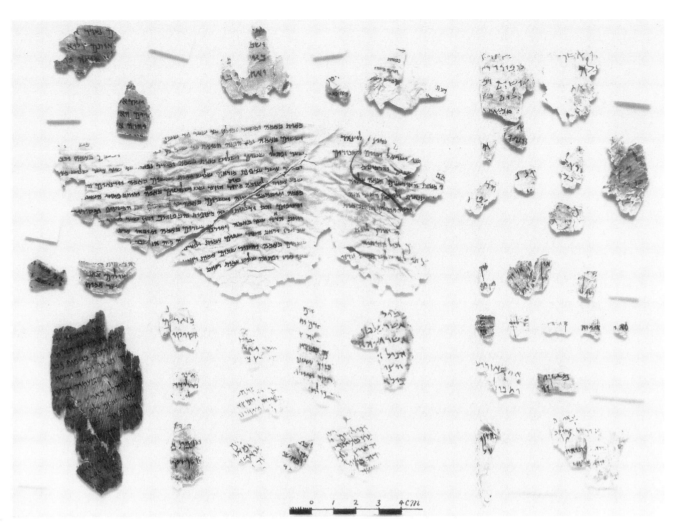

PLATE 860

PLATE 861

PLATE 862

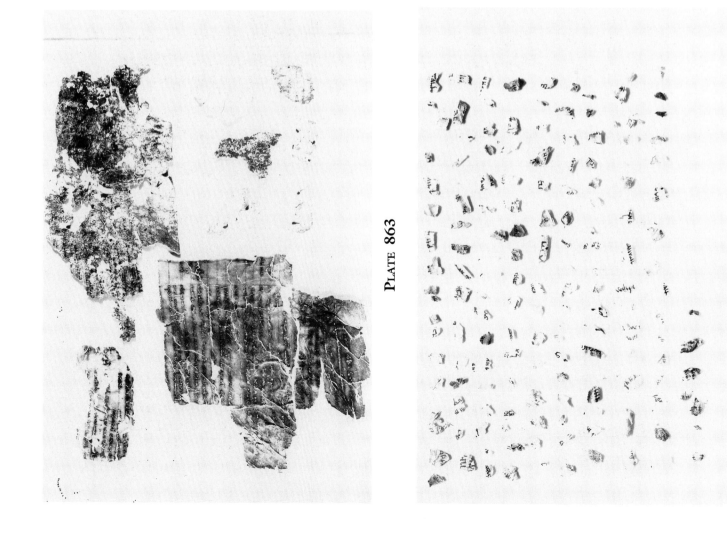

PLATE 863

PLATE 864

PLATE 865

PLATE 866

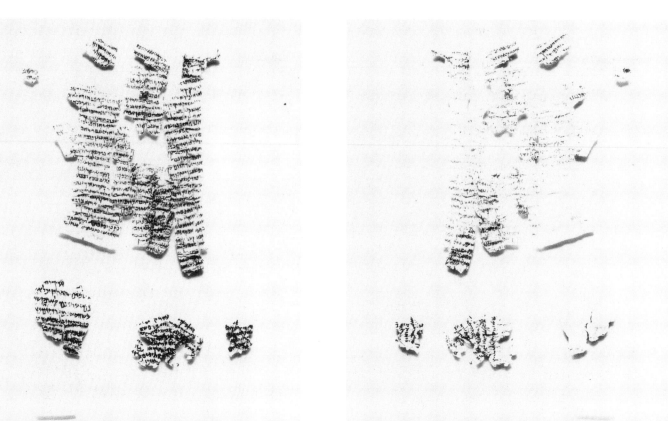

PLATE 867A

PLATE 867B

PLATE 868

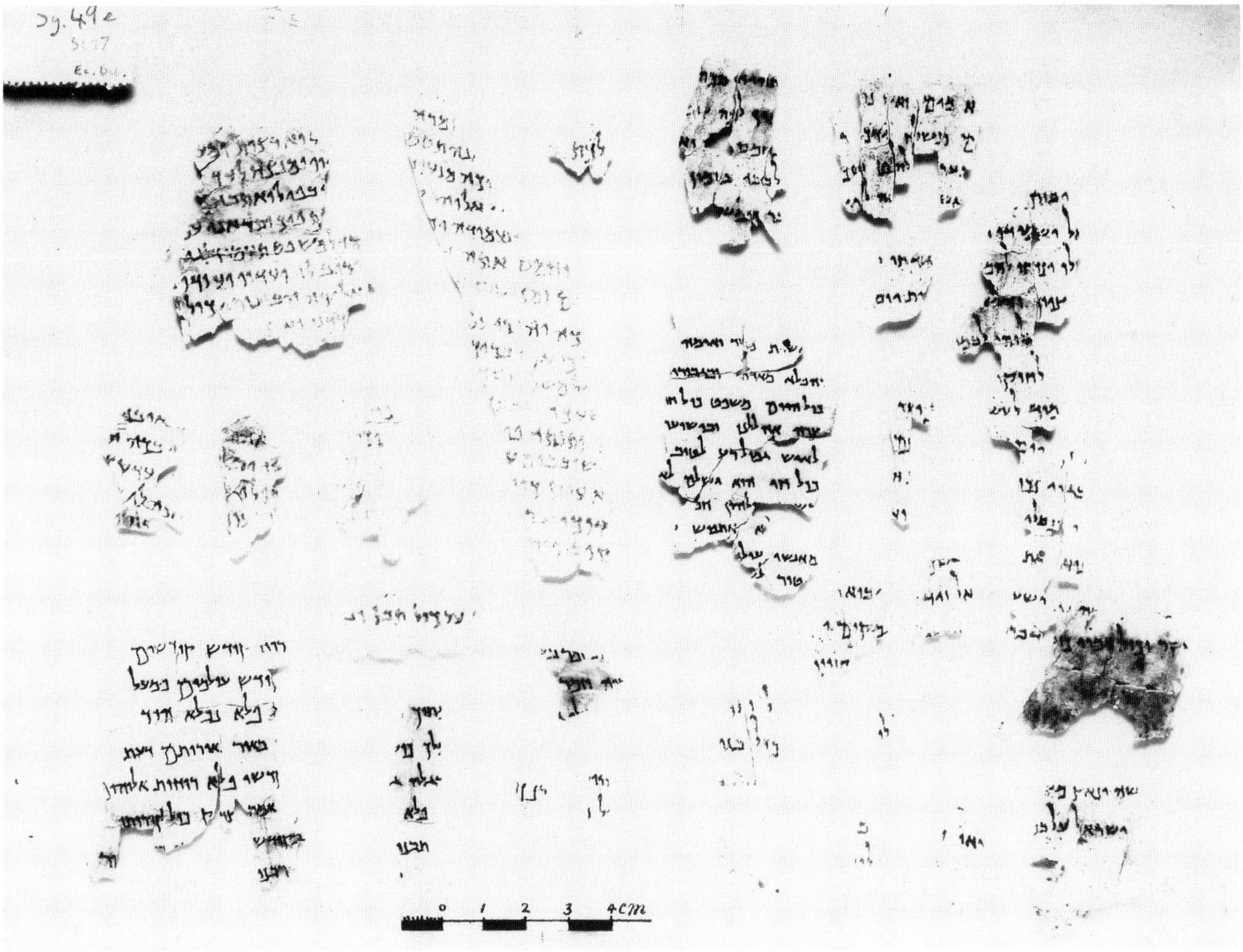

Plate 869

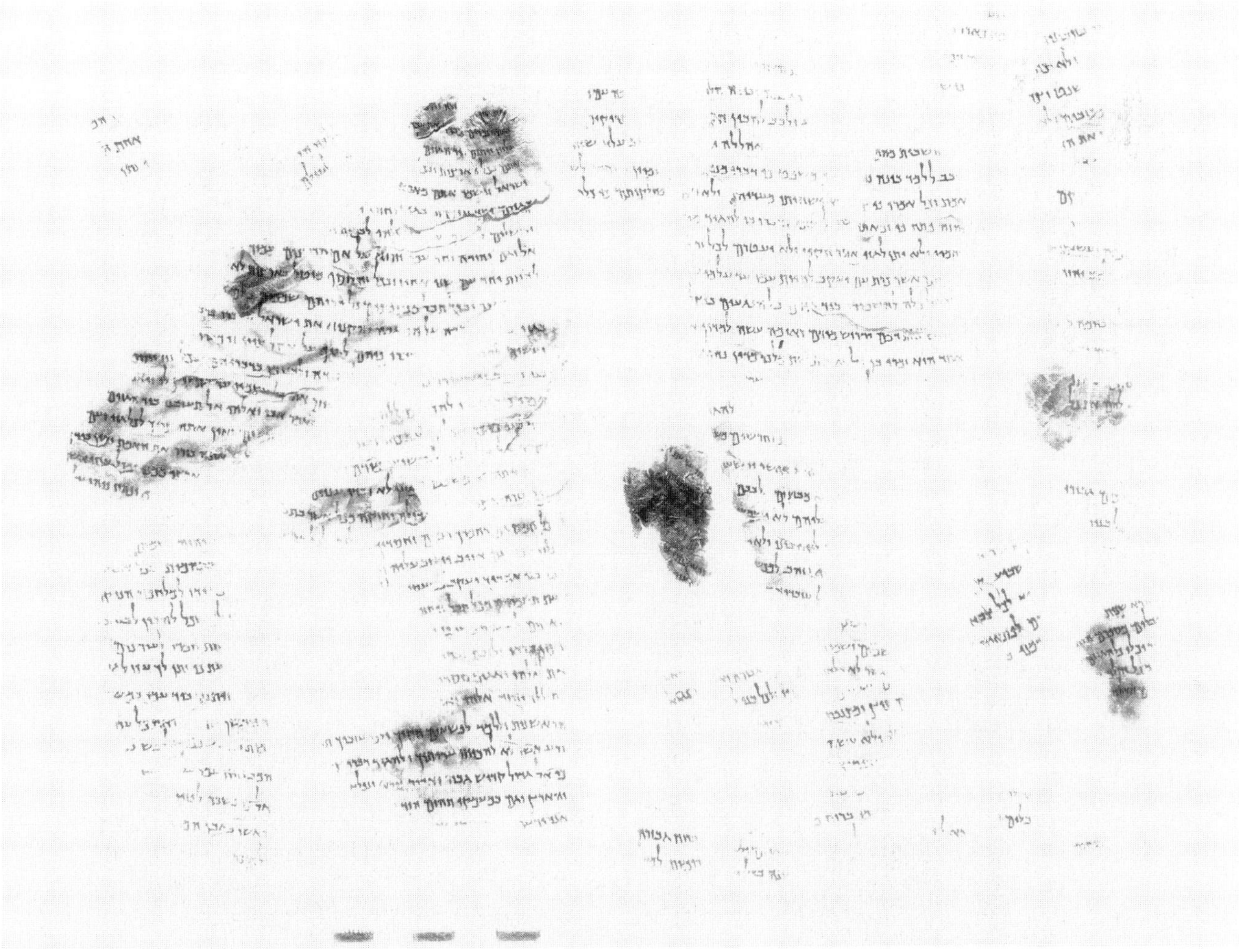

Plate 870

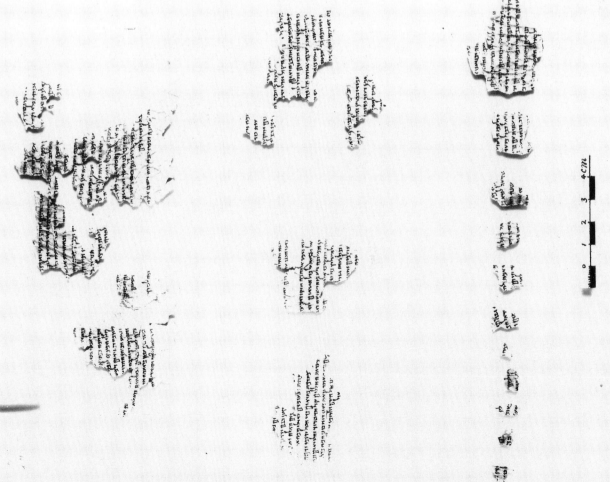

PLATE 871

PLATE 872

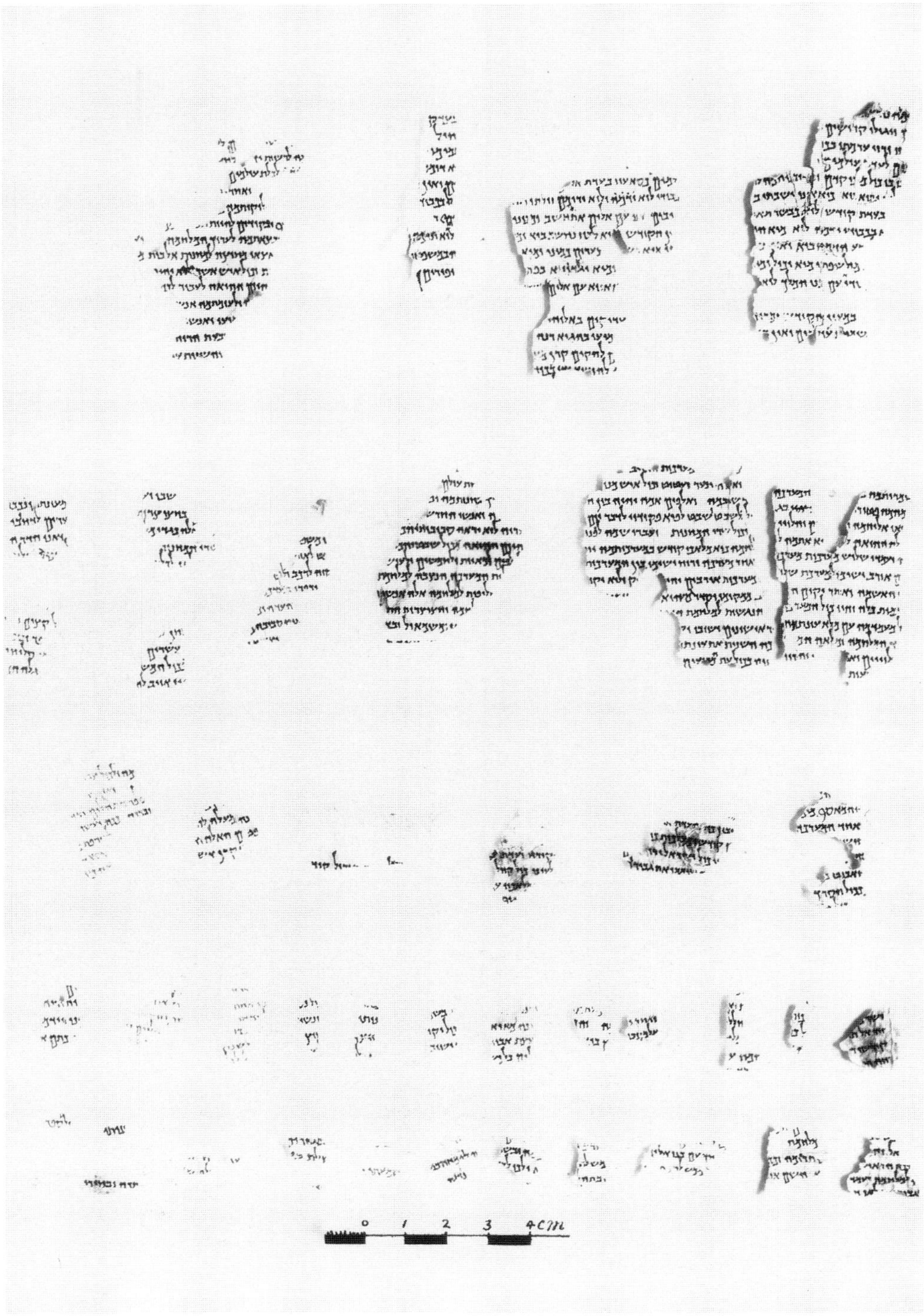

PLATE 874

PLATE 873

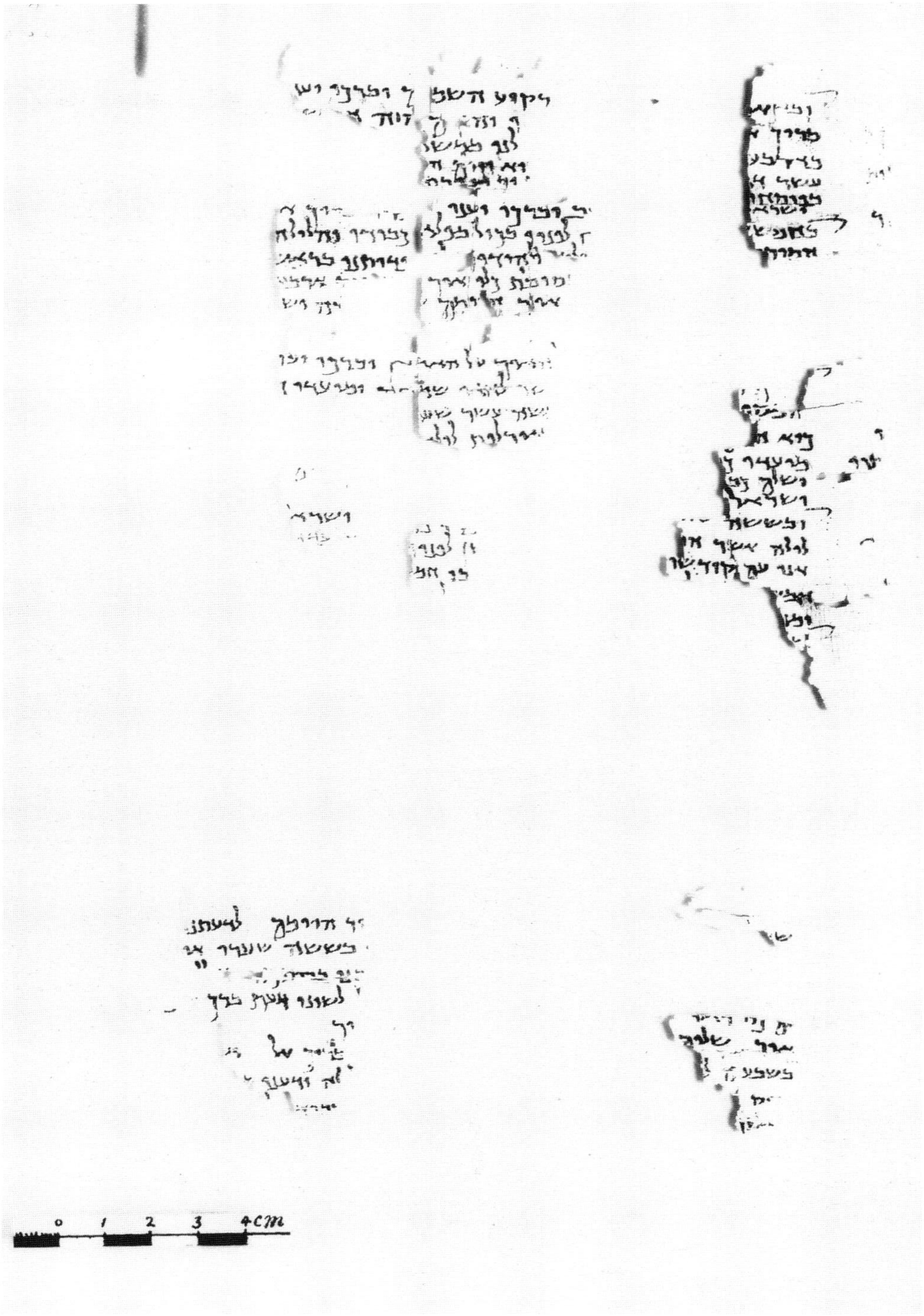

Plate 875

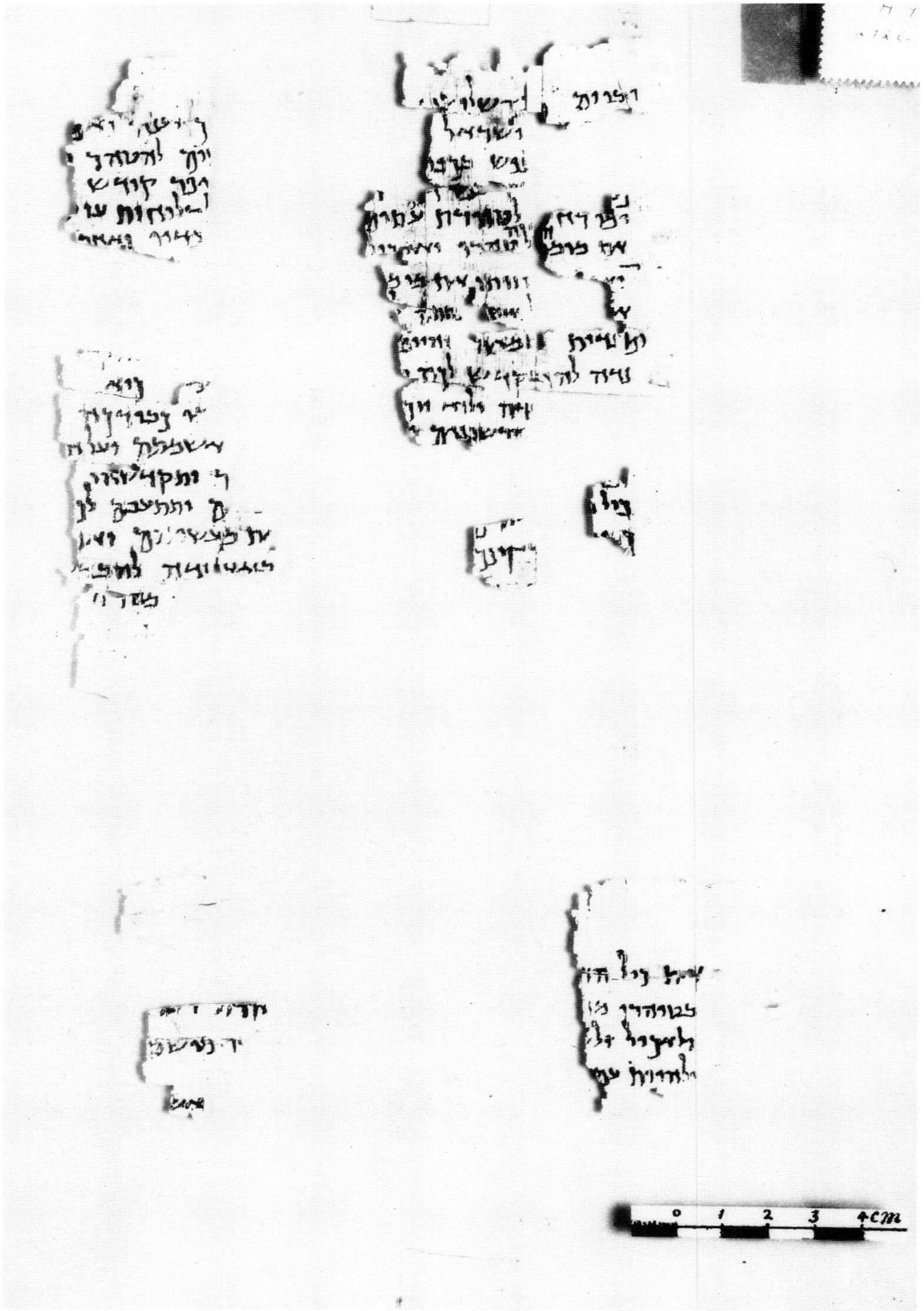

Plate 876

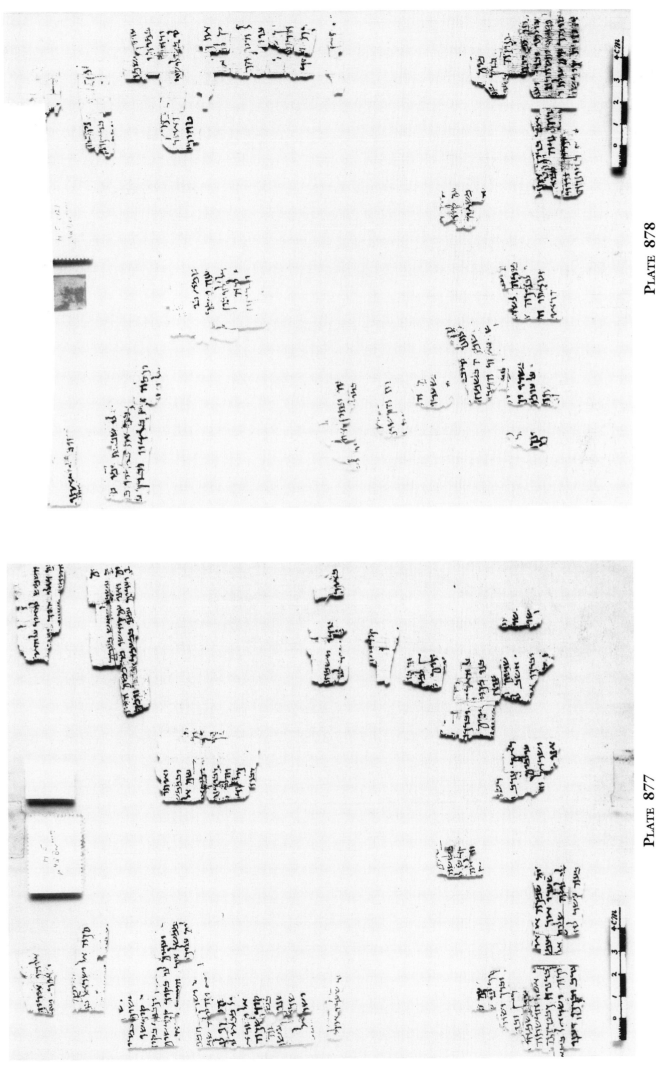

PLATE 878

PLATE 877

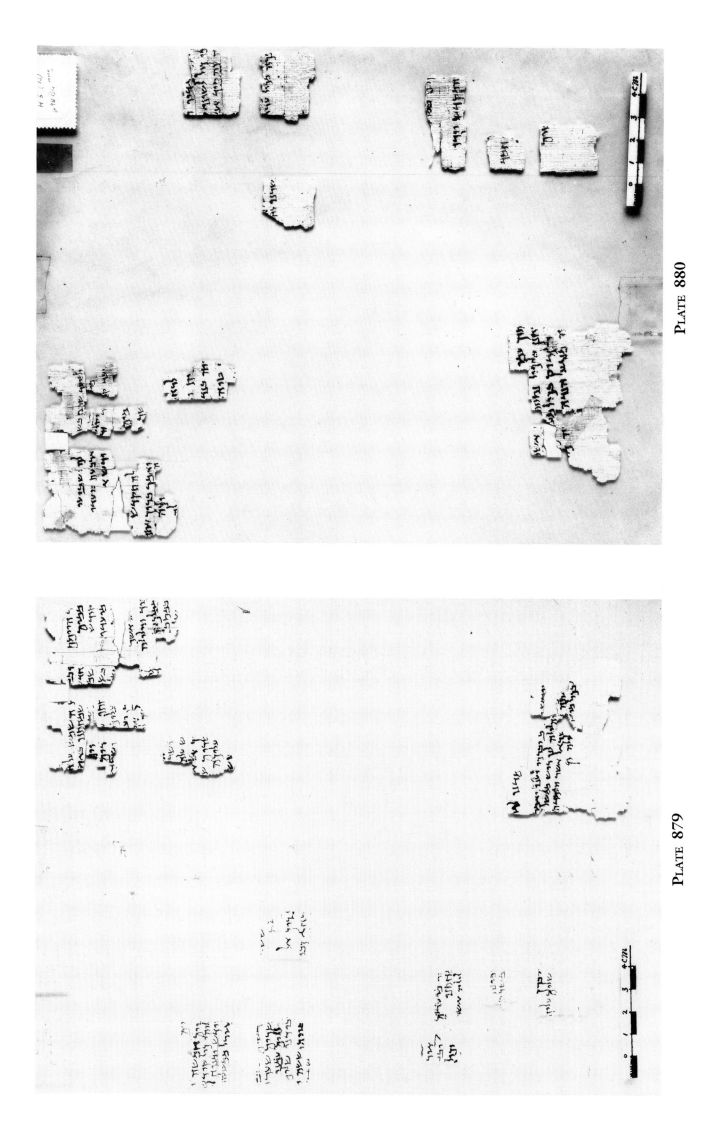

PLATE 880

PLATE 879

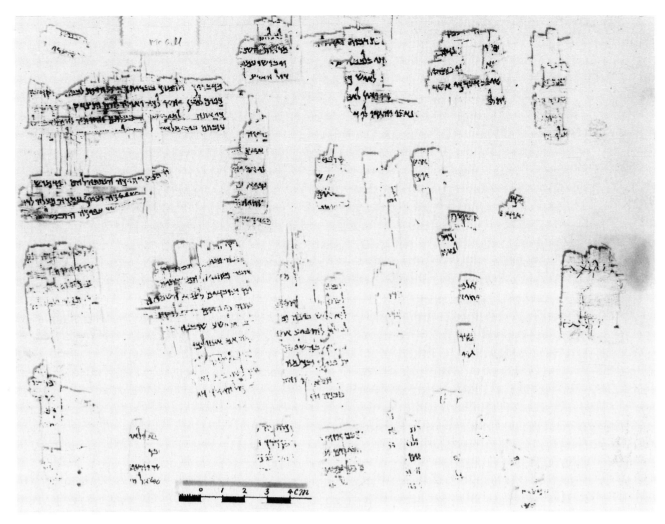

PLATE 890

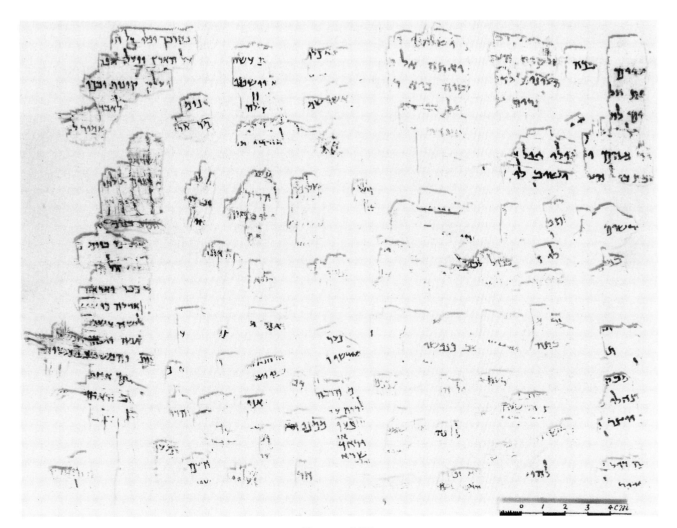

PLATE 891

PLATE 892

PLATE 893

Plate 894

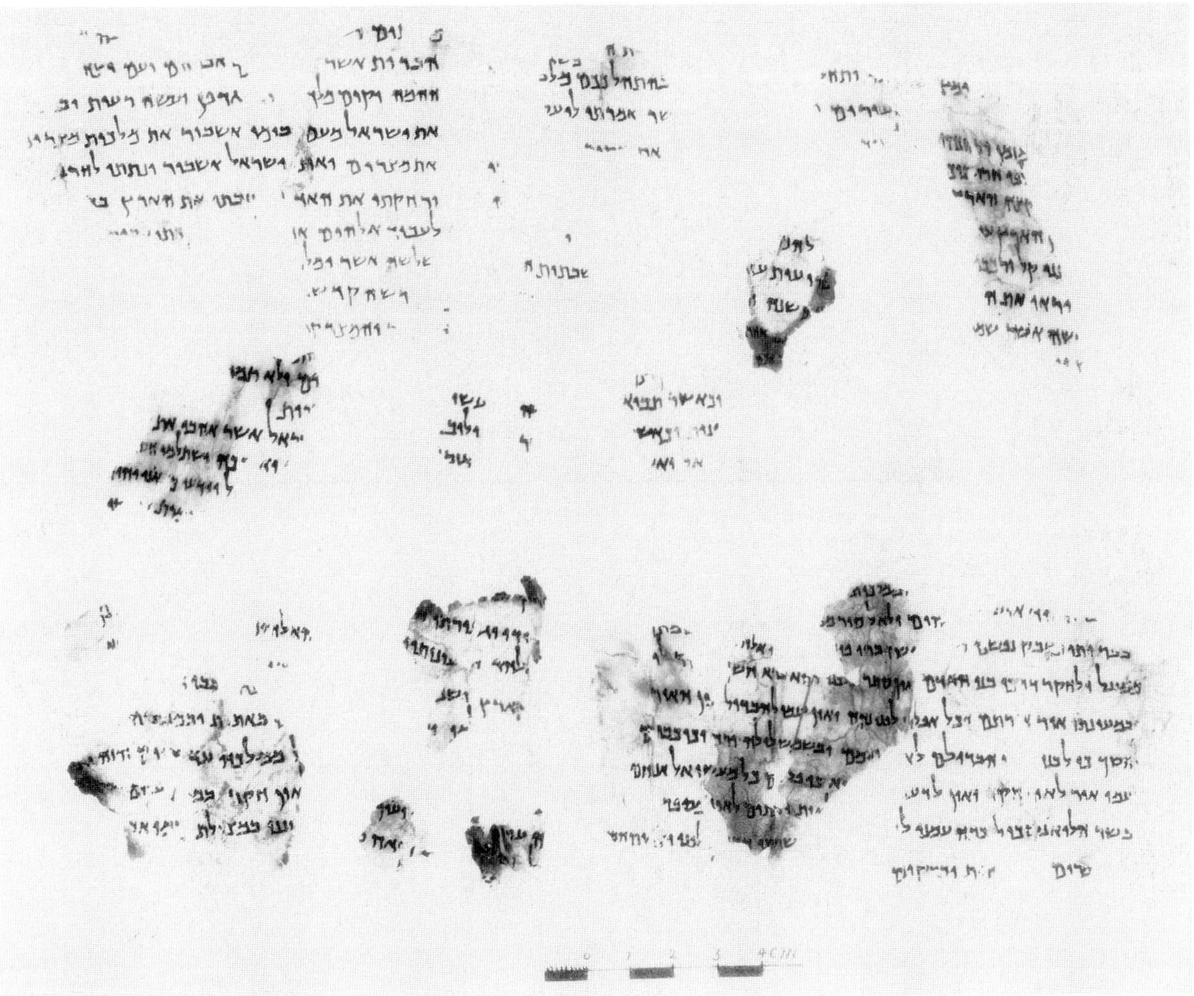

Plate 895

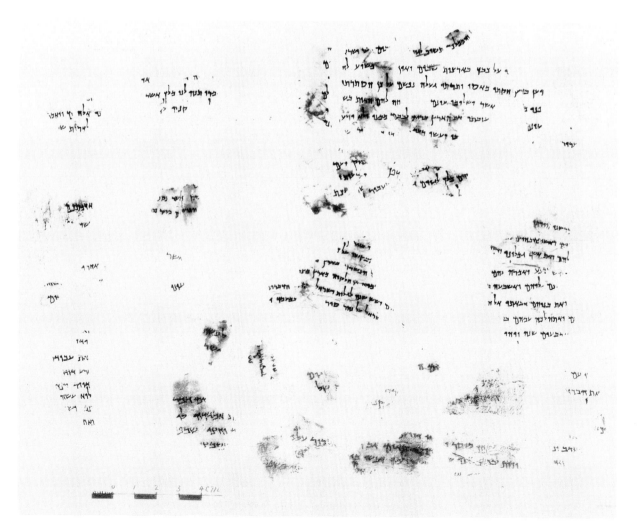

PLATE 896

PLATE 897

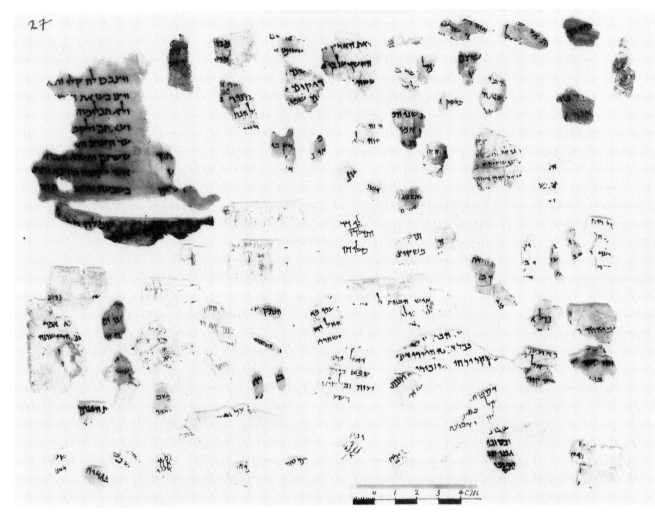

PLATE 898

PLATE 899

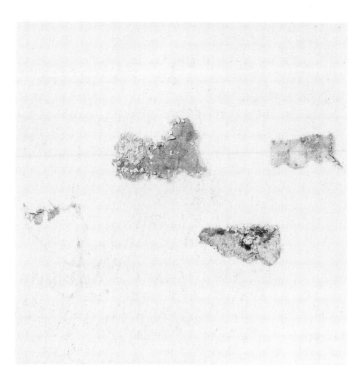

PLATE 900

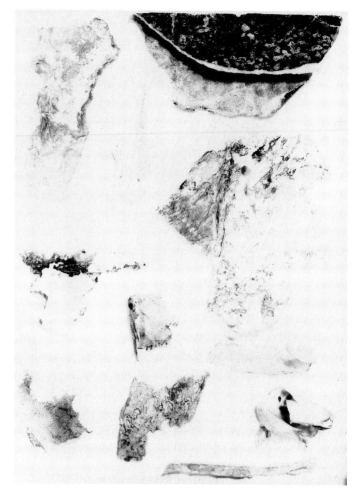

PLATE 901

PLATE 902

PLATE 903